International Social Policy

Also by Pete Alcock

SOCIAL POLICY IN BRITAIN*

UNDERSTANDING POVERTY, 2nd edn*

POVERTY AND STATE SUPPORT

WELFARE, LAW AND ORDER

THE STUDENT'S COMPANION TO SOCIAL POLICY (*editor, with
A. Erskine and M. May*)

DEVELOPMENTS IN EUROPEAN SOCIAL POLICY (*editor, with R. Sykes*)

Also by Gary Craig

COMMUNITY EMPOWERMENT (*with M. Mayo*)

COMMUNITY WORK AND THE STATE (*with N. Derricourt and M. Loney*)

JOBS AND COMMUNITY ACTION (*with M. Mayo and N. Sharman*)

* *Also published by Palgrave*

International Social Policy

Welfare Regimes in the Developed World

edited by

Pete Alcock and Gary Craig

Consultant Editor

Jo Campling

First published 2001 by
PALGRAVE MACMILLAN
Houndmills, Basingstoke, Hampshire RG21 6XS and
175 Fifth Avenue, New York, N.Y. 10010
Companies and representatives throughout the world

PALGRAVE MACMILLAN is the new global academic imprint of
St. Martin's Press LLC Scholarly and Reference Division and
Palgrave Publishers Ltd (formerly Macmillan Press Ltd).

ISBN–13: 978–0–333–74865–7   hardback
ISBN–10: 0–333–74865–4   hardback
ISBN–13: 978–0–333–74866–4   paperback
ISBN–10: 0–333–74866–2   paperback

This book is printed on paper suitable for recycling and
made from fully managed and sustained forest sources.

A catalogue record for this book is available
from the British Library.

Library of Congress Cataloging-in-publication Data

International social policy: welfare regimes in the developed world / edited by
Pete Alcock and Gary Craig; consultant editor, Jo Campling.
        p. cm.
    Includes bibliographical references and index.
    ISBN 0–333–74865–4 (cloth)—ISBN 0–333–74866–2 (pbk.)
    1. Public welfare—Cross-cultural studies. 2. Welfare state—Cross-cultural
studies. 3. Social policy—Cross-cultural studies. I. Alcock, Peter, 1951–
II. Craig, Gary.

HV37 .I58 2001
361.9172′2—dc21   2001027364

10 9 8 7 6 5 4
11 10 09 08 07 06 05

Printed and bound in China

Contents

List of Figures and Tables

Figures

Tables

Acknowledgements

Producing a book such as this, drawing on the expertise of colleagues (both authors within this collection and other friends and colleagues) around the world, has been a particularly complex and consuming exercise. It therefore took some time to compile and to edit the final text; and we would like to thank all those involved in producing and advising on the individual chapters for their commitment and forbearance. The chapter authors – most of whom have already had very many other demands on their time – have been generous with that time, punctual (in one case, where the original commissioned author mysteriously disappeared from view, heroically so), and stoic in their patience with our requests and revisions. None of this was helped by the fact that, by happenstance, each of us moved both jobs and homes during the course of the compilation of the book – but still we have remained friends throughout. The authors have each engaged carefully with the original template which we provided to produce what we hope is a book with broad appeal but one which, as we note in the Introduction, can stimulate further lively debate about comparisons and contrasts between differing welfare regimes. We hope that the outcome of their individual and joint work and the further insights it may offer into the expanding field of comparative social policy will be further – if still scant – reward for all these collective labours.

Pete Alcock would like to thank colleagues and friends for advice and help and, of course, Sandra Cooke for her continued support at home. Gary Craig thanks Pete for taking the strain at difficult moments in the life of this book, and for a continuing warm and supportive relationship in both public and private spheres. He acknowledges with warm and comradely thanks the work of all those others who have supported him, academically and through friendship, to be able to engage in a project such as this without feeling totally overawed by it. Catherine Gray at Palgrave, and Jo Campling, the editorial adviser, have been as always thoughtful, supportive and encouraging in admixture.

The editors and publishers are grateful to the following for permission to reproduce copyright material: Joseph Rowntree Foundation for Figure 7.1; Cambridge University Press for Figure 4.1 (Saunders, *Welfare and Equality*, 1994) and 9.3 (Leisering, Leibfried and Dahrendorf, *Time and Poverty in Western Welfare States: United Germany in Perspective*, 1997; International Labour Organisation for Figure 6.3. Every effort has been made to contact all the copyright-holders, but if any have been inadvertently omitted the publishers will be pleased to make the necessary arrangement at the earliest opportunity.

PETE ALCOCK
GARY CRAIG

Notes on the Contributors

Pete Alcock is Professor of Social Policy and Administration at the University of Birmingham. His research interests include poverty and social security, evaluation of local policy interventions and the role of the voluntary sector in social policy. He is the author of *Social Policy in Britain* and *Understanding Poverty*, 2nd edn (both Macmillan) and the co-editor of *The Student's Companion to Social Policy* (Blackwell). He is currently co-editing *The Encyclopedia of Social Policy*, for Blackwell. He is also the author of a number of other books, papers and academic articles. He is on the Editorial Boards of *Journal of Social Policy, Benefits* and *Public Management*, and is the past chair of the Social Policy Association.

Lois Bryson is Emeritus Professor of Sociology at the University of Newcastle, Australia and Adjunct Professor in the Department of Social Science and Planning at RMIT, Melbourne. Her publications include (with Faith Thompson) *An Australian Newtown*, Australia's first sociological study and restudy (with Ian Winter) of the suburb, *Social Change, Suburban Lives, Welfare and the State, Who Benefits?*; and *Women and Survival*, an edited collection of women's stories of surviving violence. She has also published over one hundred book chapters and papers on the welfare state, public policy and inequality.

John Clarke is Professor of Social Policy at the Open University. Drawing on a background in cultural studies, his interests have centred on the political, ideological and organisational conflicts around social welfare. Much of his recent work has addressed the impact of managerialism on the remaking of welfare systems (*The Managerial State*, co-authored with Newman; and *New Managerialism, New Welfare?*, co-edited with Gewirtz and McLaughlin). He has also researched and written on US culture and politics (including *New Times and Old Enemies: Essays on Cultural Studies and America*.

Gary Craig is Professor of Social Justice at the University of Hull. He returned to academic work from 1988 at the Universities of Bradford, York and Lincolnshire and Humberside. Prior to 1988, he worked in a succession of community development projects, within local government and the voluntary sector. His research interests and writing lie in community development and empowerment, race and ethnicity, local government and the voluntary sector, poverty and community care. His last book was (with Mayo) on *Community Empowerment* and he is currently working with Peter Alcock on a study of local action on poverty. He is President of the International Association for Community Development and a member of the UK Social Policy Association Executive, of which he was formerly secretary.

Judith A. Davey graduated from London University in Geography, followed by a PhD at Durham and post-doctoral research at Cambridge. After moving to New Zealand in 1970, she worked in central government and as a research consultant, eventually becoming Deputy Director of the New Zealand Planning Council. Since 1991 she has been Senior Lecturer in Social Policy at Victoria University of Wellington. Her research focus is the inter-relationship of social trends and social policy, especially the implications of population ageing. Among her publications, Judith Davey is known for the *From Birth to Death* series of social monitoring reports, which analyse social change in New Zealand.

Nadia Davidova is Research Fellow, Russian Independent Institute for Social and National Problems, Moscow (formerly the Institute of Marxism–Leninism). She has worked on regional differentiation in Russia during the 1990s, and social problems and policies of young people. She was a key member of the team working on a 1995–98 research project on employment and household survival in Russia (St Petersburg, Moscow and Voronezh – her home town), and is engaged on a new 1999–2002 research project on poverty, ethnicity and political protest in Russia's poorest region, Northern Ossetia (Moscow, Voronezh and Vladikavkaz).

Valeria Fargion is Associate Professor in the Political Science and Sociology Department, University of Florence. In 1998–99 she was European Forum Fellow at the EUI in Florence and is currently engaged in two international projects jointly sponsored by the International Social Security Association, Geneva, and the School of Social Welfare, University of California, Berkeley. She is also the Italian representative in the Management Committee for the European Union COST A13 action 'Changing Labour Markets, Welfare Policies and Citizenship'. She is author of *Geografia della cittadinanza sociale in Italia* and of numerous articles on the Italian welfare state and on social care services in Europe.

Lutz Leisering is Professor of Social Policy at the Department of Sociology, Bielefeld University, Germany. He has a PhD (Econ.) from the London School of Economics and an MA in sociology and mathematics). His research fields include social policy and the welfare state, poverty, life-course research, intergenerational relations, historical sociology and, more recently, social policy in East Asia and China. His recent publications include *Time and Poverty in Western Welfare States: United Germany in Perspective*, with S. Leibfried; and *The Dynamics of Modern Society. Poverty, Policy and Welfare*, edited with R. Walker. He is a policy consultant to German federal and local governments.

Ernie S. Lightman received his BA in economics and political science from the University of Toronto and his MA and PhD in economics from the University of California, Berkeley. A former Lecturer in Economics at the London School of Economics, he is currently Professor of Social Policy at the University of Toronto. He has published widely in both popular and academic venues with a particular interest in the interplay of economics and social policy. He has recently completed a study on the equity for families in Canada's tax system and co-authored an article on social advocacy for vulnerable adults.

Francie Lund is Associate Professor in the School of Development Studies at the University of Natal in Durban. She trained as a social worker, and specialised in community development. Her research interests in social policy developed through working with community organisations in urban and rural areas. Her study of the impact of the state social pensions and grants reflects an abiding concern with the outcomes of public–private patterns of resource allocation. In 1996 she chaired the National Lund Committee of Inquiry into Child and Family Support. More recently she has been engaged in research on the conditions of work for (women) workers in the informal economy, and their access to social protection.

Nick Manning is Professor of Social Policy and Sociology at the University of Nottingham. He has worked on Russian social policy for 20 years. Recently, with others, he completed studies of environmental and housing movements in Russia, Estonia and Hungary, employment and household survival in Russia, women and social policy in Central and Eastern Europe, and is working with Davidova and others on the project on poverty, ethnicity and political protest in Northern Ossetia. He is also interested in radical and democratic approaches to mental health, and recently completed a project on the effectiveness of therapeutic communities (1997–99). He is currently conducting a national study of therapeutic communities (1999–2002).

Ka-ho Mok is Assistant Professor in the Department of Public and Social Administration, City University of Hong Kong. His major research interests are in social and political development in China and East Asia, particularly in education policy on which he has published widely in academic journals. He is the author of *Intellectuals and the State in Post-Mao China* and *Social and Political Development in Post-reform China*. He is currently editing (with Welch), *Socio-Structural Change and Educational Development in the Asia Pacific Region*.

Frances Fox Piven is on the faculty of the Graduate Center of the City University of New York, where she teaches political science and sociology. Her books include *Regulating the Poor*, *The Politics of Turmoil*, *Poor People's Movements*, *The New Class War*, *Why Americans don't Vote*, and *The Breaking of the American Social Contract*.

Graham Riches is Professor and Director of the School of Social Work and Family Studies at the University of British Columbia, Vancouver. He has held previous academic appointments in Australia, Hong Kong and Canada where for a number of years he was Director of the Social Administration Research

Unit at the University of Regina. His research has focused on poverty and welfare systems, unemployment and social security and food security and human rights. His books include *Food Banks and the Welfare Crisis* and *First World Hunger: Food Security and Welfare Politics* (*ed*).

Tapio Salonen has been a Research Associate at the School of Social Work, Lund University since 1984. He has conducted a range of studies focusing on social assistance systems, modern provision problems, social planning and professional social work. In 1993 he completed a PhD dissertation about the modern functions of the social assistance scheme in Sweden. He was appointed as Assistant Professor 1994 and was accepted as 'docent' (Associate Professor) 1998. On-going research comprises studies in the field of poverty, social exclusion, urban renewal and social work interventions. He has been appointed expert in several Swedish official inquiries and has published widely in journals and book editions.

Takafumi Ken Uzuhashi is Professor of Social Policy in the Department of Economics at Osaka Sangyo University, Japan. He was an Overseas Editorial Adviser of the *Journal of Social Policy* from 1995 to 1999, and was also a Visiting Fellow at the University of York from 1993 to 1994, being involved in comparative projects as a National Informants. He is currently one of the editors of the *Overseas Social Security Journal* (National Institute of Population and Social Security Research, Japan). His current research interests span comparative study of Welfare States, income maintenance for vulnerable groups and welfare-to-work schemes. His recent publications include a comparative study of Contemporary Welfare States (*Gendai Fukushi Kokka no Kokusai-hikaku*), a research study on Divorced Single Mother Families in Six Countries (One Parent Family, *Ni Kansuru Ka-Koku Chosa*).

Paul Wilding is Emeritus Professor of Social Policy at the University of Manchester and Adjunct Professor in the Department of Public and Social Administration, City University of Hong Kong. He has written widely on many aspects of social policy. His most recent books are *Social Policy in Hong Kong*, edited with Tao and Huque and *British Society and Social Welfare* with Vic George.

List of Abbreviations

Country chapters where the terms appear have been indicated except where these are apparent from the title or are in general use throughout the book. English forms have been used throughout.

AAP	Australia Assistance Plan
ACC	Accident Compensation Scheme (New Zealand)
ADC	Aid to Dependent Children (USA)
AFDC	Aid to Families with Dependent Children (USA)
ALP	Australian Labour Party
AMS	National Labour Market Board (Sweden)
ANC	African National Congress (South Africa)
AWO	Workers' Welfare Association (Germany)
CAP	Canada Assistance Plan
CCTC	Canada Child Tax Credit (Canada)
CHE	Crown Health Enterprise
CHST	Canada Health and Social Transfer (Canada)
CIG	Wage Compensation Fund (Italy)
CPP	Canada Pension Plan
CPSU	Communist Party of the Soviet Union
CSSA	Comprehensive Social Security Assistance Scheme (Hong Kong)
DPB	Domestic Purposes Benefit (New Zealand)
EHI	Employees' Health Insurance (Japan)
EI	Employment Insurance (Canada)
EPF	Established Programs Financing (Canada)
EPI	Employees' Pension Insurance (Japan)
EU	European Union (formerly EEC: European Economic Community)
FA	Family Allowance (Canada)
FRG	Federal Republic of Germany ('West' Germany)
GDP	Gross Domestic Product
GDR	German Democratic Republic ('East' Germany)
GEAR	Growth, Employment and Redistribution (South Africa)
GIS	Guaranteed Income Supplement (Canada)
GNP	Gross National Product
GST	Goods and Services Tax (New Zealand)
HCNZ	Housing Corporation of New Zealand
HDI	Human Development Index

HECS	Higher Education Charge Scheme (Australia)
HMO	Health Maintenance Organisation (USA)
HPI	Human Poverty Index
IMF	International Monetary Fund
INAIL	Italian National Work Accident Programme
INPS	Italian National Pension Scheme
LIS	Luxembourg Income Study
LO	(Blue Collar) Trade Union Confederation (Sweden)
MAA	Mutual Aid Association (Japan)
MHW	Ministry of Health and Welfare (Japan)
MMP	Mixed Member Proportional Representation (New Zealand)
NAFTA	North American Free Trade Agreement
NHI	National Health Insurance (Japan)
NHS	National Health Service (UK)
NI	National Insurance (UK)
NPI	National Pension Insurance (Japan)
NSPCC	National Society for Prevention of Cruelty to Children (UK)
OAS	Old Age Security (Canada)
OECD	Organisation for Economic Co-operation and Development
OEO	Office of Economic Opportunity (USA)
PRA	Personal Responsibility Act (USA)
PWORA	Personal Responsibility and Work Opportunity Reconciliation Act (USA)
SSI	Supplementary Security Income (SSI)
QUANGO	Quasi-Autonomous Non-Governmental Organisations (UK)
RCTC	Refundable Child Tax Credit (Canada)
RDP	Reconstruction and Development Programme (South Africa)
RHA	Regional Health Authority
SADC	Southern African Development Community
SAF	Swedish Employers' Federation
SAR	Special Administrative Region (Hong Kong)
SSD	Social Services Department (UK)
TANF	Temporary Assistance to Needy Families (USA)
UI	Unemployment Insurance (Canada)
UK	United Kingdom
UNDP	United Nations Development Programme
UNICEF	United Nations Children's Education Fund
US/USA	United States of America
USL	Local Health Units (Italy)
VAT	Value Added Tax (in Japan: Consumption Tax)

Introduction

PETE ALCOCK AND GARY CRAIG

This book is intended to contribute to our understanding of the comparative study of welfare provision within the 'developed' world – as suggested in the title. It has been edited in the UK; but it has been produced by experts from within 12 different nations across the developed world, all writing with authority and yet with reflective criticism about the historical development and distribution of welfare provision in their respective countries – and the prospects for these in the new century. The chapter authors were presented with a challenging task – to summarise the structure, development and future prospects of national social policy in around 8000 words. It is a challenge to which all have risen.

The book is therefore intended to provide an important and extensive resource for the comparative study of social policy. It is not itself, however, a comparative text. As we discuss in Chapter 1, comparative analysis of social policy can take a number of forms. Different comparisons can be made in different ways across different countries, and all have their strengths and weaknesses. However, the substantive chapters dealing with the different countries covered in this book do not attempt to draw comparisons between the different national contexts and structures which they describe. Each chapter is a review of the development and organisation of policy within that country. Each has been constructed separately and must be read separately. However, readers can themselves draw comparisons between the different stories which each has to tell.

Nevertheless, Chapter 1 does seek to set these different stories within an analysis of the broader international context in which they have developed, as well as providing a guide to the different dimensions of comparative study. The chapter also discusses the most dominant framework for comparative analysis, the welfare regime theory developed by Esping Andersen (1990); and the authors of each of the country chapters discuss briefly the applicability of regime theory to the analysis of policy development in their countries. Not surprisingly this has led to some criticism of the scope and durability of the Esping-Andersen model, drawing as it does on a largely European and Western analysis of welfare regimes. As Chapter 1 briefly discusses therefore there are limitations within even the most well-established of comparative frameworks in explaining the diversity and complexity of welfare development across these 12 countries within the developed world. But this should not be a deterrent to comparative study – far from it. And it is to be hoped that the descriptions provided here provide an enlarged base for future attempts to refine and adapt this framework, and others.

With this in mind the countries were consciously chosen for inclusion in the book because they were representative to some extent of the different kinds of welfare regime to be found throughout the developed world. The United States and Canada are different examples of the North American liberal approach; Australia and New Zealand reveal similar trends in drawing on, and departing from the UK legacy; Japan is an example of welfare provision in the leading 'Asian Tiger' economy; Germany, Sweden, Italy and the UK provide evidence of the different traditions in European politics and policy development; and Russia (part of both Europe and Asia) explores the problems faced by the leading former communist regime. Hong Kong and South Africa are included as two 'special cases' of particular interest to English-speaking audiences; both have experienced substantial recent political upheaval, in part as a legacy of the move away from former colonial control, and yet both are working hard to develop welfare provision in comparable ways to other developed nations – made more difficult in South Africa's case by the legacy of fragmentation from its apartheid past.

The chapters focus on political developments and welfare provision and this focus inevitably dominates both analysis and description. The authors have therefore had little space to discuss the social diversity and differences within their own countries, and the consequences of this for the development and delivery of policy. There has thus not been scope to explore the gendered dimension of welfare in the different countries, nor much exploration of ethnic diversity and the consequences of racism. In a number of countries, however, the legacy of past colonial government on indigenous populations has remained a continued issue for the development of social policy, and one which in some cases is now being directly addressed in politics and policy planning. The position of 'first nation' populations is therefore given prominence in some chapters, and of course it accounts in large part for the selection of South Africa for detailed study. It must be recognised that there are nevertheless significant *lacunae* within the coverage provided in the country chapters; and, in countries such as Russia and South Africa, the gradual emergence of more data will hopefully extend further future analysis and understanding. Clearly no book of this length could hope to cover everything – perhaps these dimensions could be the basis for a further collection in the future – however, we hope that what is provided here will become an important contribution to the widening debates on comparative social policy.

Reference

Esping-Andersen, G. (1990) *The Three Worlds of Welfare Capitalism*, Polity Press.

CHAPTER 1

The Comparative Context

PETE ALCOCK

Welfare State or Welfare Mix

The focus of this book is on the provision of welfare in a selected number of 'developed' countries across the world. As explained in the Introduction, its aim is to provide a resource for the comparative study of social policy or welfare. However, this undertaking immediately raises a number of important theoretical and definitional problems. What do we mean by developed countries? What do we mean by social policy or welfare provision? And, more specifically, to what extent are these terms and concepts understood in a common way across all of the countries covered in the book?

Not surprisingly, perhaps, there are no simple answers to these questions, and indeed there are differences of interpretation and understanding across different nations – and even within them. Nevertheless some conceptual clarification is needed to provide a guide to the issues on which the different chapters will focus and to explain the various approaches taken within them. In focusing upon developed nations the book is concerned with countries which have undergone a significant process of industrialisation, primarily within the context of the international capitalist economy – although Russia's industrialisation, for instance, was largely undertaken within a closed state-socialist economic regime. They are all countries which currently compete within the global export market and are significant players in this – although this is only partly true of the 'special cases': Hong Kong, which is not an independent country, and South Africa, which has only recently been re-admitted to the international trading community. Nevertheless, unlike many of the developing countries in Africa, Asia and South America, these two have industrial capitalist economies which determine the life chances and life choices of all of their citizens.

The economic development of all the countries is also linked to their social development; and to a greater or lesser extent all have developed some degree of collective welfare services, provided by or regulated by the state. What is meant by welfare in this context is the provision of services to meet some of the basic social needs of citizens, including needs for food, shelter, health, education for all and additional care for vulnerable adults and children. In fact, of course, there is considerable theoretical debate about those things which do constitute welfare needs and the extent to which these are universal. For instance, Doyal

1

and Gough (1991) have argued that these can be universally established and are based on the two key pillars of individual health and autonomy, although there is no agreement about an exhaustive list of particular welfare needs which might flow from these. Nevertheless, all of the countries discussed here do accept some measure of public responsibility for meeting many of the same welfare needs, and the development of provision to meet these has accompanied the growth of the industrial economies of all the nations.

There is a danger here, however, of suggesting that the development of welfare provision is an inevitable product of the growth of an industrial economy – that social policy always accompanies economic policy. This has sometimes been referred to as the *industrialisation*, or convergence, thesis (see Wilensky, 1975 and 1976), and is distinct from the Marxist tradition which links the development of welfare directly to the class struggle within industrialised nations (see Gough, 1979). Its implication is that all countries are placed upon a similar development track and are converging towards a similar social and economic future. This shared social and economic development has been discussed more recently in a wide-ranging review of public policy development in 21 OECD nations by Castles (1999). Castles concludes that, in the second half of the twentieth century, all have undergone major changes in economic growth and policy planning. He also points out, however, that there has been much variation between countries due to different political circumstances and different degrees of economic and social development. These differences are also revealed in the chapters of this book, and what is clear from this is that a simplistic convergence approach to the growth and development of welfare policy cannot provide a viable explanation of the real diversity in forms and processes of welfare provision which are found in the countries described here – and in many more. There is no sustainable evidence of the growth of welfare as a linear process which is the natural consequence of industrialisation. And even if some similar trends can be identified, sharp differences of scale and direction can also be found.

This throws into relief one of the contested terms which has been used to describe the structure and development of social policy in developed industrial countries over the past fifty years or so. This is the notion of the *welfare state*. Many of the countries which we look at have been described, by supporters and critics alike, as welfare states. And in adopting such a description commentators have been seeking to capture some important common essence of the place of welfare within the very structure of social and political process itself. In this context a welfare state implies the adoption of a particular stage in the social development of industrial economies, from which the public agencies of the state accept formal responsibility for providing for the welfare needs of their citizens. In a welfare state, therefore, Marshall's (1950) notion of social citizenship is attained, through the use of pubic services to guarantee social rights.

However, many commentators now agree that the notion of a welfare state is a more complex one than that implied in the above linear model of progress (see Pierson, 1998; and Pierson and Castles, 2000). In particular the idea of a welfare state is often associated with a specific period and form of welfare development (Jessop, 2001). Linked to the ideas of Marshall (1950) and Beveridge (1942) it is associated with developments in Western European, or more specifically British, social policy in the mid-twentieth century, when public provision of welfare services seemed to be the only viable or desirable means of meeting all welfare needs (Lowe, 1998). Such a predominance of public, or state, provision is no longer ideologically or empirically dominant in the UK or elsewhere in Europe, as the later chapters in this book demonstrate. The welfare state model is also less applicable to, and less widely used within, countries with different trajectories and structures of welfare support. In Germany, as discussed in Chapter 9 for instance, the idea of a welfare state is associated closely with notions of state monopoly and state control over welfare. This is not compatible with individual freedom within a labour market, or with the principle of subsidiarity in Germany, which devolves responsibility for social policy to the local or community level. In this context the welfare state has connotations of socialism, and the term more generally used to refer to the postwar development of welfare within Germany is the *social state*.

In other countries, such as those in Southern Europe with less extensive public welfare provision through the state, the expectation is that welfare provision will come not only from state sources, but also from extended family support and non-government organisations such as the church (see Chapter 10 on Italy). Here the preferred term to describe such a mix of services is the *welfare society*. What both of these examples reveal, however, is that in different countries the mix of welfare provision between the state, the individual, the family and the other sectors of provider agencies varies from country to country. In most the state is not the only, or even the major, provider of welfare services – and in practice this has always been the case even in the UK, the paradigm example of the 'welfare state'. Even in postwar Britain, private service provision played a significant role in welfare planning. Thus commentators now refer to social policy as being concerned with the *welfare mix* rather than the welfare state (Johnson, 1987); and, in comparing the different countries examined in this book, it is clear that there is a mix within each country, the balance of which is different is all cases.

Nevertheless, in all cases the formal institutions and procedures of the state do play an important role in the delivery of welfare services. However, state involvement in social policy may not always be as a provider of services, states are also involved in regulating services and securing minimum standards, or in subsidising or underwriting other providers (Hills, 1997; Glennerster and Hills, 1998). But in all cases some element of state involvement can be found. The welfare mix may have replaced the welfare state as the predominant concept in comparative analysis, therefore; but the state is still very much in the picture.

Comparative Social Policy

A great deal of social policy research and academic study has been based upon theoretical or empirical analysis of the operation or development of welfare provision within specific national contexts. This is certainly the case with much social policy work in the UK, but it has also been a common feature of policy analysis in many other countries. This is understandable. For the large part, welfare provision and social policy debate have been developed within national contexts, dominated by the policies and practices of national governments. However, this is rapidly changing. Comparative studies of the welfare provisions and policy debates of different countries are now a central feature of most social policy studies, and are increasingly the focus of research into social policy issues. And, perhaps more importantly, *international* forces are increasingly shaping the policy agendas of *national* governments, so that welfare provision is less and less the product solely of national policy debates or political considerations, as discussed by Castles (1998). In short, in this respect as in many others, the world is becoming metaphorically a smaller place. The international pressures on national policy-making are in part a direct and indirect consequence of the growing competitiveness of the international capitalist economy and the power of major corporations within this – a process sometimes referred to as globalisation, which we shall return to discuss in a little more detail shortly. However, it is not just international markets which influence national policies, international agencies are now also seeking to control or influence the social policies of individual countries.

This is most obviously true in Western Europe of the role played by the European Union (EU) which, with the full support of its currently 15 member nations, is pursuing a range of measures to harmonise social policies within the EU and to develop cross-cutting supra-national policy initiatives (see Hantrais, 2000; Geyer, 2000). However, there are other supra-national agencies seeking to influence the social policy agendas of individual nations, which extend beyond Western Europe. Of particular importance here are the World Bank and the International Monetary Fund (IMF). These are the financial agencies of international capital and, through their economic relations with nations who may need their support, they can use powerful financial levers to press for social policy changes. This is a strategy which has been employed quite widely by these agencies in recent years, influencing the policy agendas of both well-developed welfare states, such as the UK in the mid-1970s, and newly developing ones, such as the post-communist countries of Eastern Europe (Deacon *et al.*, 1997) and the economies of Third World countries (Craig and Mayo, 1995).

International influences on national policy development are not only enforced, however; they may also be welcomed and even sought out by nations. In the late twentieth century the role of policy transfer has become an important influence on the political agenda of many nations. Policy initiatives developed in one country may well be of interest and relevance to others who wish to address comparable welfare needs within similar social and economic circumstances. And, even if ideas from one country are not directly replicable in another, they may form the basis of a similar initiative inspired by the successes (or mindful of the failures) experienced elsewhere. This has certainly been the case for a long time of the social insurance ideas promoted initially by Bismarck in Germany in the late nineteenth century; a more recent case is that of the tax-credit measures used to supplement low wages in the USA. Jordan (1998) discusses in some detail the recent debates about policy transfer between the USA and UK under Clinton and Blair; and policy transfer is now more generally a significant focus of study in international scholarship on politics and social policy.

These international pressures on the social policy agenda have therefore resulted in a growing body of research and writing on comparative social policy analysis, and there is now a considerable and expanding literature in the field. There are also a range of different approaches and methods within comparative analysis.

- *Theoretical studies* – these attempt to explore, and to explain, the differences between the different welfare systems of different countries and to assess the extent to which they are the result of internal policy-making or external dynamics. Relatively early examples of this are Wilensky's (1975) US study of the development of welfare states and Titmuss's (1974) discussion of three models of welfare provision. More recently there have been broad-based international studies such as Gough (1979), Castles (1982 and 1999), Offe (1984), Mishra (1990 and 1999), Pfaller *et al.* (1991) and Goodin *et al.* (1999), and more specific attempts to develop a classification of welfare systems through comparative analysis, most notably in the seminal work of Esping-Andersen (1990 and 1996). There have also been the studies of international agencies mentioned above, such as the EU (Hantrais, 2000; Geyer, 2000) and the World Bank (Deacon *et al.*, 1997).
- *Sectors and issues* – a number of international or comparative texts have developed international comparison across a number of sectors of welfare provision – for instance, Hill (1996) and Clasen (1999) – or by focusing on one particular sector such as social security (Ploug and Kvist, 1996) or housing (Doling, 1997). Other collections have adopted a more general approach and have sought to explore more specific issues within a range of different national or supra-national contexts, such as Jones (1993a) and Sykes and Alcock (1998).
- *Policy evaluation* – research projects based on international studies have aimed to evaluate the effectiveness of specific policy interventions across a range of countries. Examples of this can be found in the work of Bradshaw *et al.* on child support (1993) and lone parents (1996), and Ditch *et al.* on social assistance (1997).
- *Country comparisons* – a strong tradition within comparative analysis remains the comparative study of welfare provision across a number of

countries through analysis of a number of selected countries on a general basis. Ginsburg (1992), George and Taylor Gooby (1996) and Bonoli *et al.* (2000) all provide examples of this.

Despite this burgeoning literature, however, there are some significant problems involved in the comparative study of social policy. For a start there are inevitable limitations to the scope and explanatory power of grand theoretical accounts of international social policy development or classification. Such theoretical accounts are attempting to explain what are in practice complex and varied social process across a number of different social and political contexts. In this process the danger of over-generalisation is ever-present. For instance, even Esping-Andersen's empirically-based classification of welfare regimes has been criticised for focusing only upon a limited range of types of welfare provision and for ignoring important comparative factors which might lead to very different classifications than those arrived at in his initial analysis, a point to which we shall return below.

In addition to the risk of theoretical over-generalisation there is also the problem of empirical comparability. Much comparative analysis relies upon data about the nature of social issues or the impact of social policies across a number of countries under review. However, there is no guarantee that such data has been gathered and published on a similar basis in each country – and indeed a much greater likelihood that it has not. Thus, whether one is comparing levels of poverty and inequality or levels of expenditure on health services, there is every risk that one is not comparing like with like. This is a potentially serious problem, of course, and it is one which has been recognised by a number of comparative scholars. This has led to some attempts to overcome such incompatibility by the development of international databases which aim to collect information from a range of different countries and then to store this for comparative analysis using a common methodology or statistical base. An important example of this is the Luxembourg Income Study (LIS), which contains data about the income distribution of over seventeen different countries and can be explored and analysed by researchers worldwide using on-line computer access (Smeeding *et al.*, 1990).

Of course there are theoretical limitations and empirical problems in all areas of social policy study. These should certainly not be barriers to the development of comparative work; and the studies mentioned above reveal that in any event this has not been the case. Both sector and issue-based studies and comparisons between countries can reveal important insights into questions of similarity and difference and patterns of convergence or diversity. In the former it is important to bear in mind the national contexts in which different policy initiatives have developed, and in the latter it is necessary to look beyond the detailed case study to examine cross-cutting themes and issues. As Mabbett and Bolderson (1999) suggest in their review of the theories and methods of comparative social policy, however,

Detailed policy studies can, none the less, yield generalisable theoretical insights. [and ...] Perhaps the greatest challenge in comparative work is to understand not only the idiosyncrasies of national conditions but also the conceptual frameworks of actors in each country. (pp. 50, 52)

In this book, therefore, the focus is upon single-country case studies, drawn from a contrasting range of welfare systems throughout the developed world. Each chapter provides an historical review of the development of welfare policy and a description of current provisions. The chapters have been written by experts from the respective countries, and all follow a broadly similar format; they reveal the contrasting trajectories of the different countries reviewed. However, all the countries have been subject to most of the international pressures discussed above and to the social and economic trends which are experienced across most societies in the late twentieth century. Thus in addition to differences there are also some comparable developments and common responses to social needs. These all might be summarised under the two key concepts of convergence and diversity, to which we shall return later.

A Common International Context

We mentioned above that one of the defining characteristics of the developed world was the process of industrialisation which had been experienced by all such societies, a process which has changed the economic and social structure of those societies. It also created the social conditions and political conflicts which could give rise to the development of modern welfare provision. In simple terms, labour market needs and the conflicts which arise from the struggle between labour and capital gave rise to pressure for the introduction of welfare measures (see Gough, 1979). This impact of industrialisation as an example of an international influence on social policy was explored to some extent by Wilensky (1975) in an early comparative study of welfare states; and the example of this industrialisation thesis is one instance of a convergence approach to comparative social policy study.

There are also other examples of the convergence approach. In particular it is common in Marxist and neo-Marxist analysis of the development of welfare. Following the materialist thesis of Marx, such approaches suggest that, whatever their particular politics or policies, all capitalist economies will inevitably come under the influence of conflicting social forces (Ginsburg, 1979). These will create pressures to develop welfare at some times, to respond to working-class demands (Gough, 1979), but at others to reduce the protection provided by the state to support private capital markets (O'Connor, 1973). For Marxists the development of welfare provision is a contradictory one (Offe, 1984); but one within which increasingly powerful international economic forces determine the direction of national policy decisions.

The problem with the Marxist thesis is that although it can to some extent account for the similarities in the development of welfare states – and there is obviously more than an element of truth in the claim that economic forces do influence the scale and scope of welfare services in similar ways – what it cannot do is account for the differences. And of course in the real world differences can indeed be found, reflecting the different political and social contexts within which decisions about social policy are in practice taken. These contexts vary, and thus so do the political decisions taken within them. As critics of the Marxist and other convergence theorists have put it – politics matters (Pierson, 1998; Bonoli *et al.*, 2000). And much comparative study of social policy has revealed in some detail how different political systems at different times have responded in different ways to the international economic pressures which they have faced (see Stephens, 1979; Korpi, 1983; Esping-Andersen, 1985; Castles, 1999; Goodin *et al.*, 1999). However, it is not just politics that matters. There are other differences between societies which may also influence the development of welfare provision.

Economics

The impact of industrialisation on societies certainly has created economic conditions in which the need for public welfare provision takes on a particular form. At the same time, industrialisation also creates a climate in which the political forces wanting to press for welfare support, the organisations of the working class, are likely to become more influential. The development of public welfare provision is therefore to some extent a response to the needs and demands of the working classes. At the same time, however, such welfare provision also helps to support the continued growth of the industrial economy, for instance through improving the health and education of the population. Within an industrial economy, therefore, the development of public welfare provision can be seen as something of a compromise between the needs of both labour and capital (see Gough, 1979).

The expectation that such a compromise could also result in positive economic growth, and in a political consensus over the desirability of public welfare provision, seemed to many to become reality towards the middle of the twentieth century. At this time in a number of Western nations, in particular, the introduction of welfare reform at the same time as state intervention to support economic growth had become a common feature of national economic planning (Castles, 1999). In the UK this was known as the period of Keynesianism, after the economist Keynes (1936) who developed the theory of state intervention. It was also the time when most of the major state welfare institutions were introduced, giving rise to the notion of the creation of a welfare state.

As we can see from the later chapters of this book, this notion of a Keynesian 'golden age' in the development of welfare was a pattern shared by some, particularly Western, nations; but it was certainly not one followed by all. In Asia-Pacific nations, such as Japan for instance, the links between economic growth and welfare support have taken on a rather different form. Even in the West, however, the Keynesian golden age was a short-lived affair. In the last quarter of the twentieth century most of the capitalist economies of the developed world experienced periods of severe economic recession, fuelled in part by the oil price rises enforced by the oil-exporting nations in the 1970s (Bonoli *et al.*, 2000). The impact of this international recession varied significantly from nation to nation; but in countries where it was most severe, as in the UK, it led to significant shifts in social policy away from commitments to ever-increasing public welfare (Glennerster, 2000; Lowe, 1998).

Seen from a longer-term economic perspective, the recessionary experiences of the late twentieth century are probably better characterised as some of the negative consequences of a broader restructuring of economic forces across the industrialised world. In the latter quarter of the century it has become clear that national economies must compete within an ever more competitive international economy, within which some large multinational corporations, such as General Motors or Coca Cola, have greater economic power that do many individual nations. This process has been referred to by many as *globalisation* (see Waters, 1995; Deacon *et al.*, 1997; Mishra, 1999) – the requirement of all governments to take account of global economic forces in their national economic and social policy planning. Of course the impact of globalisation on national policy planning is a complex and much debated phenomenon (see Sykes *et al.*, 2001). In practice not all countries have responded to the pressures of global forces in the same way; but nevertheless, as Mishra (1999) argues, all have had to respond to them.

What is more the process of globalisation has meant that economic changes within some countries have inevitably taken on a broader common international character. In particular, this is true of what the economists have called *post-Fordism* (Gilbert *et al.*, 1992) – the move away from economic production being dominated by large-scale manufacturing industry to a situation in which a wider range of more flexible producers operate to meet more demanding and more rapidly-changing consumer markets. In such a manufacturing climate the production process becomes more automated and employment shifts instead to specialised production and to work in service industries, serving both producers (insurance and banking) and consumers (catering and leisure). In the Western world in particular, this process has been exacerbated by the relocation of the remaining labour-intensive production processes to less-developed countries where individual wage levels are lower and social and welfare costs are also much reduced. The result of these processes is that, in many of the countries examined in this book, levels of unemployment (especially long-term unemployment) have grown and much waged work has become more flexible (temporary, part-time, and often low-paid).

These changes have inevitably created pressures on welfare policy which are perhaps more significant, and more wide-ranging, than the impact of economic recession itself (see Burrows and Loader, 1994 – especially Pierson, ch. 6). The flexible, post-Fordist, international economy has thrown into greater relief the trade-off between equity and efficiency which is at the heart of all social and economic policy planning in advanced economies, as Esping-Andersen discusses in his more recent work (1996, chs 1, 9). The trade-off is that between the provision of extensive and redistributive welfare services (equity) and investment in competitive economic growth (efficiency). At the end of the twentieth century the choice for industrialised nations can be characterised as that between two contrasting models for social and economic planning:

- The first is the pursuit of growth through the reduction of welfare commitments. This implies acceptance of low wages and insecure work as the price for higher levels of employment with greater inequalities as a result, and the reduction of collective welfare costs through low taxation and social insurance payments. As a result, welfare support is targeted only at the poor and welfare services are reduced to a residual role. In such a society protection and participation are provided largely through the labour market, and public welfare is only available to the casualties who cannot fend for themselves.
- The second is the pursuit of growth through the maintenance of public support and the promotion of social integration and solidarity. This requires political commitment to maintaining and developing a high-skill/high-reward labour market through generous social insurance payments and extensive collective provision for education, training and health. In such a society inequalities are reduced, in part through high levels of taxation and insurance contributions, and access to welfare services is generally provided on a universal basis.

As Esping-Andersen points out there might appear to be considerable pressure from global economic forces to push all nations towards the former strategy – a point taken up in more detail by Mishra (1999). Capital investors can now move their resources rapidly from country to country depending upon their judgements about economic prospects, and the major international corporations are likely to seek to operate where both the direct (wage) and indirect (tax and insurance) costs of welfare are lowest. This could lead to what some commentators have called a 'march to the bottom' in terms of public welfare provision, and what is called in the EU 'social dumping' – the concentration of investment in countries where levels of wages and welfare are lowest. Not surprisingly the EU, and especially the high-wage/high-welfare countries which exert most power within it, are concerned about fears of social dumping and are using the supra-national powers of the Union to counteract such pressures, for instance by seeking to impose EU-wide rights and standards.

However, in practice it is far from clear that a uniform march to the bottom is taking place across the international social policy arena. Economic growth and levels of employment have been high in countries such as the United States, where low wages and low welfare costs predominate. But, despite global pressures, the high-wage/high-welfare countries of Europe, such as Germany and Sweden, have also been able both to maintain economic growth and to expand export markets (see Pfaller *et al.*, 1991; Goodin *et al.*, 1999). High growth has also been associated with very different mixes of work, wages and welfare in other countries such as Japan. All countries must respond to global pressures, but as Esping-Andersen (1996, p. 258) argues, the responses to wage competition have not been unidimensional; and the more egalitarian and integrative welfare models of some countries have been able to sustain stable economic growth as well as avoiding some of the worst anti-welfare outcomes of the more residual welfare model – a point explored in more detail in Sykes *et al.* (2001).

In part, of course, the relative success of the high-wage/high-welfare model is a result of the higher levels of social integration and political support which were instrumental in the establishment of such regimes and have thus been sustained within them. High-wage/high-welfare strategies can attract political support within democratic countries, even if they also extract a high price in terms of international competitiveness. Political calculations can influence economic policy-making, and ultimately can influence economic trends. This is an important element in the analysis developed by Esping-Andersen, Mishra and others, and it reminds us that whilst economic pressures may be important they are not overriding.

Politics

It is quite clear from the different chapters in this book that the different political contexts of different countries have led to different responses to the need for welfare services and to the pressure of economic competitiveness. The welfare-state model which we discussed above is particularly associated with the social democratic or liberal democratic politics of Western Europe. Such political frameworks are based upon a compromise between the representatives of capital and labour over the development of public welfare provision within a predominantly market economy – the Bismarck and Beveridge models. Obviously the nature of this compromise will be different in different countries, at different times. This has been taken up in particular in the work of Esping-Andersen (1990) and his identification of three broad welfare regimes which characterise and classify these differences, based on empirical analysis of Western welfare states, which we return to discuss below.

However, social and liberal democracy have not been the only political ideologies to influence social policy and the development of welfare provision. Both socialist or Marxist politics and new-right or neo-liberal politics challenge the notion of class compromise as a viable basis for the development of welfare policy, and both have been influential at times in a number of countries. Socialist politics were obviously of major importance in determining the welfare services provided in Russia and Eastern Europe during the communist era, and much of that legacy still remains in some of these countries. Socialist politics have also been influential within democratic countries, in particular as a form of left-wing pressure upon social democratic governments to abandon the politics of compromise and pursue instead a public monopoly of welfare services and a nationalisation of the market economy (Deacon, 1983), although in general such pressure has remained outside of the political mainstream.

Neo-liberal politics have also exerted pressure upon democratic governments, in particular in the latter decades of the twentieth century. In the UK, for instance, the Thatcher governments of the 1980s were strongly influenced by the neo-liberal politics of some of their new-right members, and this was also the case during the Reagan era in the USA. Pro-market neo-liberalism has also been a powerful political force in the development of Hong Kong, although here it has operated in a very different social and cultural context. It is debatable whether neo-liberal politics have ever supplanted liberal democracy as the predominant political ideology within any advanced industrial country. Despite the moves to the right by the Thatcher and Reagan governments, for instance, popular support for public welfare provision remained strong and most commentators agree that the policy changes introduced amounted to a restructuring, rather than a withdrawal, of state services (see Johnson, 1990, on the UK).

Clearly, however, the influence of different politics ideologies in different places at different times reflects this varying power of political forces. Thus where working-class organisations have been strong, state welfare services have been extensive, for instance in Sweden and the former communist countries; and, where these organisations have been weak, welfare provision has adopted more of a residual model, for instance in the USA (Goodin *et al.*, 1999). However, it is not just the political ideologies associated with class forces which have been influential in shaping welfare. Other social forces have also had political influence, such as those organised around issues of gender, race (or racism), disability or ecology. They are discussed in more detail in Lewis *et al.* (2000) – and are sometimes refered to as the 'new social movements'.

Feminist politics has had a significant influence on welfare policies in a number of countries in the latter quarter of the twentieth century, both in terms of shaping the nature of public provision (for instance, improved child care support in Scandinavian countries and support for carers of adults in the UK) and of leading to the development of alternative forms of service (for instance, women's health self-help groups). Race and disability politics have also taken on a higher profile in many places; and environmental politics has even entered mainstream government with Green Party representatives in Germany securing ministerial status after the 1998 election.

Politics is not just a matter of representation and campaigning, however. Within democracies, in particular, the political process itself has an important influence upon the determination of policy. For instance, within an electoral democracy public support for welfare is likely to be reflected in the votes cast by citizens. This has led some commentators, such as Therborn and Roebroek (1986) to argue that, once established, welfare states are irreversible by political means, because of the democratic support that the services which they provide will inevitably attract. On a more critical note such ballot-box politics has led other critics to argue that such pressures will lead to potentially damaging upward pressure on welfare growth as politicians seek to outbid each other with promises of improved services in order to secure popular support. This is the argument of the 'public choice' theorists in the USA who are concerned that such pressures will unbalance the equity/efficiency trade-off and prevent economic growth (Tullock, 1976).

There is some truth in the claim that both politicians, and public service bureaucrats, are likely to seek to defend the public services with which they are associated. And this is likely to influence the political climate in a pro-welfare direction, despite the pressures of international economic forces. This may explain, for instance, why the Thatcher governments of the 1980s in the UK were unable, or unwilling, to replace the National Health Service in the country, although their new-right advisors had suggested that this should be a major policy aim (Papadakis and Taylor Gooby, 1987, ch. 2). However, popular support in the UK at the same time for the sale to tenants of their state-owned housing (referred to as the 'right-to-buy' policy) suggests that this is not a unidimensional political process, and that individualist politics may also be able to attract electoral backing (Malpass and Murie, 1999, ch. 5).

Overall, therefore, there is considerable evidence to underline the point that political forces and political processes can influence welfare policies, independently of the economic context within which they are operating. Politics is constructed within a social context too, however, and the social structure of advanced industrial societies has also been undergoing significant change in recent decades.

Demography

Welfare services are constructed to meet the needs of populations. They are therefore determined to some extent by the shape and structure of these populations; and inevitably these shapes and structures are subject to demographic change. Demographic change is a complex phenomenon; it is the product of many different factors, of which birth rates, death rates and longevity are only the most obvious features. It is also a phenomenon which impacts gradually over time as different cohorts of individuals move through the life cycle. We cannot explore all of these factors here, but we can identify some of the more significant ones.

According to most commentators, the most pressing contemporary aspect of demographic change from the point of view of welfare policy is the growing proportion of older people within most advanced industrial countries – both at the end of the twentieth century, and going into the twenty-first. This is sometimes referred to pejoratively as the gerontic 'time bomb' (Walker and Maltby, 1996). It is itself a product of a number of factors including greater average longevity and a declining birth rate in the latter decades of the century, resulting in a smaller relative number of people of working age at the beginning of the next. What is more, this pattern varies significantly between countries, as the chapters in this book demonstrate, with the proportion of older people growing much more rapidly in Japan, for instance, than in the UK or more notably South Africa.

Given these variations, and the long-term nature of demographic change, the panic reaction to the 'growing burden' of the elderly, which seems to have gripped policy-makers in some countries, may in practice be somewhat exaggerated. Pension payments and social care services will have to be provided for a larger number of people in the future; but, of course, these demands can be planned for within economic and political calculations made now. A growing proportion of older people within the population is not, therefore, in itself necessarily a problem.

The same is true of a declining birth rate. Reduced fertility has been experienced in a number of developed countries in the last half of the twentieth century, most notably, within the countries covered in this book, in Italy. And at times such reductions have been perceived to be an issue for social policy; for instance, generous child support provision in France has usually been associated with concerns to encourage families to produce more children. Conversely at other times relatively high birth rates may present a problem for policy-makers as large numbers of children give rise to additional demands for care and education. This is the case to some extent with the 'baby booms' which followed the end of the Second World War in countries such as the UK. And continuing concerns over high birth rates in places like China have led to policy measures being introduced to encourage families there to have only one child.

In addition to changes in the balance between the generations there have also been changes in family patterns experienced in many countries. In many Western nations, for instance, divorce levels have been rising and the numbers of lone-parent families have been increasing both relatively and absolutely. The assumption on which some social policies have been based therefore, that children will be cared for by both of their natural parents in a single stable family structure, cannot be sustained. This has led to the need to support families in different ways and to recognise the diversity of patterns of care for children.

Even where significant changes are not taking place in levels of fertility and longevity, however, demographic issues influence the policy-planning agenda. The welfare needs of all citizens change over the course of their lives, which is true at an individual level but is also true of whole cohorts within the population. And different cohorts born at, and growing older at, different points in time will carry with them the expectations, and the welfare support, which they have experienced throughout their lives. Thus, for instance, in many countries the pensioner population of the mid- to late twentieth century did not have the benefit of being able to contribute to generous private or public pensions during their working lives in the early part of the century. Their pension needs and pension rights and expectations are thus very different to those of the cohorts who reach pension age at the end of the century, whose working lives were spent contributing towards their future pension needs.

These are differences to which social policies must, and in different ways do, respond. They are also, of course, to a large extent predictable developments which can be built into political debate and policy planning – although the extent to which different countries have done this effectively varies in practice, as the later chapters in this book demonstrate. This is especially the case because the long-term planning, which is dictated by such demographic issues, inevitably comes into conflict with the short-term calculations characterising economic pressures and political expediencies. This is revealed most sharply by the difficulties experienced by many nations in the 1990s in planning changes in pension policies.

Ideology

We started off this chapter by pointing out that one of the problems to be faced in the comparative study of social policy is the different meaning attached to different terms in different places and at different times. The welfare policies that are developed to meet social needs depend upon how those notions of welfare and need are defined and understood. This is because different definitions are generated by different ideologies of welfare, and ideologies of welfare differ across countries and, perhaps more importantly, within them. All of us operate with ideological perceptions of welfare and need, and indeed all other social phenomena. However, most ideological differences can be located within the major broad ideological frameworks which dominate much theoretical debate about social policy. George and Wilding (1994) provide an accessible guide to these, and their links to political debate and policy activity, and some more recent developments are discussed in O'Brien and Penna (1998) and Mullard and Spicker (1998).

In the context of comparative study, however, it is important to bear in mind that ideological differences in what might be understood as welfare issues or social needs do lead to differences in the development and operation of welfare provision across different countries. For instance, provision of employment rights and regulation of family patterns are more commonly included within conceptualisation of social policy goals in continental Europe than they are in the UK and other English-speaking countries. Ideological perspectives not only influence how welfare needs are defined, they also influence how they are met. For instance, in Scandinavian countries the common expectation is that the needs of all will be met on a universal basis through the state, whereas in other countries, such as the USA, the predominant expectation is that public welfare should only be available to the poor and needy. Such differences between universal and selective approaches to the principles underlying welfare policy also influence the policy debate within most developed nations, as do ideological differences about the roles which should be accorded to public and private welfare provision. These differences are also represented in the ideological frameworks which underpin different the political traditions of neo-liberals, social democrats and others (George and Wilding, 1994).

Ideological expectations do not just differ across countries, however, they also change over time. The understanding and measurement of welfare needs, such as poverty levels, have altered considerably throughout the twentieth century for instance, with broader and more relative definitions replacing narrower and more subsistence-based measures (Alcock, 1997). It is also argued by some that pressures on welfare services increased in the latter decades of the century as result of higher expectations amongst citizens of needs which should be met by public services. For instance, many more people now continue into higher education than used to be the case in most developed countries, and more people expect health care provisions such as minor operations to be available on demand. Such ideological pressures can create counter-tendencies to the economic pressures to reduce welfare services, which must be resolved within the political processes discussed above.

Culture

The cultural heritages of different countries are in part a product of ideological perspectives and political debates; but they go beyond these, and themselves can shape or change the political climate within which social policy decisions are taken. There are a number of examples of the importance of cultural influences contained within the countries examined in the later chapters of this book.

- The entrepreneuralism and longstanding multiculturalism of the USA has militated against the development of a strong, central, state welfare politics.
- The work-based, male-breadwinner family model of German social structure has mitigated against the development of broad universal welfare provision.
- The Confucian culture of Japan has supported a strong individual and family role in the provision of welfare.
- The colonial traditions of Hong Kong have prevented the development of a democratically-based welfare settlement with a strong commitment to state welfare support.

Cultural differences do not just exist between countries, however. They also exist within them. Most nations now contain within them a range of different cultural traditions, resulting in large part from the patterns of immigration and emigration between countries. The USA, the UK and Australia, for example, all contain a wide range of diverse ethnic cultures, with very different expectations about the structure and extent of welfare provision which is appropriate within these. For instance, Muslim groups have particular views about the importance of family structure and gender roles; some Catholic groups have strong views about family planning; and Afro-Caribbean groups in the UK and the USA carry with them experiences of their subjection to slavery and the lower status which this has accorded them in the eyes of some members of the white majority population. In all of these cases, but particularly in the latter, a culture of racism has influenced the way welfare policies are developed and experienced within societies. Not all cultural heritages have positive welfare manifestations, therefore.

Convergence or Diversity

Welfare states, or welfare systems, have experienced common external pressures, yet they also have varying internal dynamics and social structures. These contrasting influences lead on the one hand to a convergence amongst countries towards similar patterns of welfare provision, and on the other hand to diversity reflecting differing local circumstances. These contrasting pressures have been recognised by comparative social policy analysts, such as Esping-Andersen (1996); and most attempts to compare and contrast welfare systems have attempted to develop analytical tools to explain and account for both similarities and differences – and to predict the ways in which future pressures will be responded to within different countries. This has commonly taken the form of attempts to categorise or classify welfare systems according to identifiable similarities and differences.

An early example of this was Titmuss's (1974) modelling of welfare states. He divided those he examined into three broad categories:

- Residual welfare systems – where provision was available on a 'casualty' basis only to those who could not be expected to provide for themselves.
- Individual achievement systems – where needs were met through involvement in the labour market and through work-related welfare measures.
- Institutional redistributive systems – where universal services were provided for all.

A similar kind of classification was produced much later in one of the seminal studies of comparative social policy by Esping-Andersen in 1990. Esping-Andersen engaged in a major empirical study of most of the major welfare systems of the developed Western world, using national data on public expenditure and the structure of welfare services and examining the social development and political history of welfare provision. From this he extracted evidence about two key features of welfare states: the extent of *decommodification* (that is, the extent to which welfare protection was available independently of market forces), and the levels of *stratification* (the extent to which access to welfare was structured by social class). The countries which he had analysed were thus classified according to these two criteria and, according to Esping-Andersen, they fell into three broad groups (see Table 1.1).

Esping-Andersen argued that these three groups in fact represented three different *welfare regimes*. Within each cluster the countries all exhibited similar features in terms of welfare provision and social and political circumstances, and yet between the clusters there were significant key differences. He also identified three countries which provided near-ideal types of the three different regimes – Sweden, Germany and the United States (see Table 1.2). Esping-Andersen's analysis was based upon *post hoc* examination of the history and structure of these different welfare states. But he argued in the later chapters of the book that the classification could also be used to predict how the different regimes would respond to new economic and political challenges – an approach which he took further in his later work (Esping-Andersen, 1996). According to him, therefore, all welfare systems within developed countries

Table 1.1   The rank-order of welfare states in terms of combined decommodification, 1980

	Decommodification score
Australia	13.0
United States	13.8
New Zealand	17.1
Canada	22.0
Ireland	23.3
United Kingdom	23.4
Italy	24.1
Japan	27.1
France	27.5
Germany	27.7
Finland	29.2
Switzerland	29.8
Austria	31.1
Belgium	32.4
Netherlands	32.4
Denmark	38.1
Norway	38.3
Sweden	39.1
Mean	27.2
S.D.	7.7

Source: Esping-Andersen, *The Three Worlds of Welfare Capitalism*, 1990, Blackwell Publishers, p. 52.

Table 1.2 Characteristics of welfare regime ideal types

	Sweden	*Germany*	*USA*
Regime	Social Democratic	Corporatist	Liberal
Political base	Broad-based compromise	Employer/worker coalition	Free market
Service type	Universal	Occupational	Residual
Public expenditure	High-level	High-level	Low-level
Labour market	High-employment, high-wage	Low-employment, high-wage	High-employment, low-wage

could be subsumed within these three broad regimes, a similar point to that made by Titmuss.

However, more recent analysts have questioned the comprehensiveness and representative basis of Esping-Andersen's three regime types. Castles and Mitchell (1991) argued that from within the countries that he studied a distinct fourth regime type could be found, exemplified by Australia and New Zealand, where a different role for means-tested welfare provision could be found. Leibfried (1993) and Ferrara (1996) also argued for a fourth type, this time based upon the 'Latin Rim' nations of Southern Europe which Esping-Andersen did not look at. And since then others have gone further in expanding the range of welfare regimes to include other models of welfare provision, such as the former communist countries of Eastern Europe (Deacon *et al.*, 1992), or the new welfare systems of the 'tiger economies' of the Pacific Rim (Jones, 1993b).

Of course in some ways these attempts to identify new regime types are forms of expansion or development of Esping-Andersen's analysis rather than criticisms of it. However, there have also been critics who have argued that his empirical material and theoretical analysis were oversimplistic and ignored other features of welfare provision which, if taken into account, would lead to rather different classifications of welfare regimes. For instance, Lewis (1992) argued that he had largely ignored gender dynamics in constructing his regimes, and that attention to gender would alter the way in which the countries he had looked at would be classified.

Both the extensions and the criticisms of Esping-Andersen's regime theory are really only to be anticipated. Inevitably, comparative analysis at such a grand level is bound to lead to elements of oversimplification and lack of attention to some important variables. Nevertheless it has proved to be a groundbreaking development within comparative social policy analysis. By drawing on aggregate data it meant that some attention could be paid to real evidence of welfare provision at a sufficiently broad level to permit international comparison to be made; and by also examining social structure and history it ensured that such differences could be situated within the political context in which they had developed – and would continue to operate. The classification of countries into welfare regimes also meant that analysis could take account of both similarities and differences between welfare systems within a broad overall comparative schema.

Regime theory thus permits us to take account of both convergence and diversity, and because of this it has become a dominant theoretical approach within comparative social policy. This book is not based upon regime theory analysis, although the countries that have been chosen for analysis do include the major examples of regime ideal types identified by Esping-Andersen and his critics. The different countries do all have rather different stories to tell, and it is this diversity of experience that is the strongest message coming out of this book.

Nevertheless, we have sought to draw together some very general evidence about the changing scale of welfare provision in a number of countries, drawn from information about social spending provided by the chapter authors. Table 1.3 shows the trends in welfare spending expressed as a percentage of GDP in the countries covered in this book. Of course, a number of substantial *caveats* must be born in mind when looking at any table such as this. For a start, it is also based upon official, quantitative measurement of welfare provision, which is only one, rather limited way of looking at social policy. What is included in social spending figures in different countries also varies significantly; for instance, many exclude housing and education expenditure – although not all do. Also, of course, the calculation of GDP can vary, especially in different economic contexts such as Russia and Hong Kong. Furthermore data were not available for all countries over exactly the same periods.

Table 1.3   Social spending as a proportion of GDP in selected countries

Country	1950	1970	1990
Hong Kong	1.4	5.3	7–8
New Zealand[1]	7.6	4.9	8.3
Japan[2]	3.5	5.8	13.7
Russia[3]	20.5[4]	23.2	13.4
USA	8.2	14.3	18.5
Australia	11	c11	18
United Kingdom	11.2	17.3	22.6
Canada	8	18.8	24.7
Italy	13.4[5]	21.3	27[6]
Germany	19.2	26	29
Sweden	8	20	36
South Africa[7]			30.6

Notes: [1] benefits and pension expenditure only;
[2] based on national income not GDP;
[3] net material product for 1960 and 1970, probably overstates expenditure;
[4] 1960, 1950 figure not available;
[5] 1954;
[6] 1980, 1990 not calculated;
[7] 1997/8, no accurate figures available before this.

Nevertheless the data in the table is interesting. It does clearly indicate diversity, for instance between the low levels of spending in Hong Kong and Japan, and the high levels in Germany and Sweden. However, those countries falling between these extremes do seem to adopt patterns which would support the broad conclusions drawn from Esping-Andersen's (1990) regime analysis. The historical dimension in the table is also important because it confirms another general trend that we might expect – a significant growth in the commitment to welfare spending in the latter part of the twentieth century. There are, however, a few significant exceptions here, most obviously Russia, but also to some extent Australia and New Zealand. The table is some evidence of the extent to which changes across the different countries discussed in the book can be compared and contrasted, in particular in terms of the longer-term trends within which all can, to some extent, be located.

Responding to Welfare Challenges

In this chapter we have discussed how welfare systems have been subject to similar social and economic pressures and yet have developed divergent responses to these. In all cases, however, they have had to respond to pressures on the equity/efficiency trade-off – the extent to which they are able to maintain welfare provision in the light of global economic competitiveness. In an analysis of the impact of such a trade-off on a number of European welfare states in the 1990s, Taylor Gooby (1996) identified three broad responses to the challenges to welfare – retreat, redirection and investment. This provides a broad framework within which the reader can compare and contrast the different routes taken by the different countries discussed in the case studies presented in this book.

Retreat

Retreat from welfare provision has been championed by new-right and neo-liberal protagonists, who have argued for a reduction in public expenditure and welfare commitment in order to encourage the growth of private markets. There are a number of mechanisms by which this can be achieved including:

- Sale of public assets;
- Introduction of charges for services;
- Privatisation of public provision;
- Subsidisation of private market protection;
- Restrictions on entitlement to public support;
- Dilution in the quality of public services;
- Reduction of wage levels amongst public sector welfare workers.

Redirection

Redirection of welfare provision has been promoted by those who have argued that welfare services can be maintained only by changing the nature of service delivery and shifting the burden to a range of other providers. Such redirection leads to a range of different prescriptions for change from differing ideological perspectives:

- New public management techniques to make existing welfare more efficient;
- Shift of welfare provision to family or community providers;
- Involvement of community and non-profit organisations in partnership planning for welfare services.

Investment

New investment in public welfare is a bold reassertion of the value of the dual role of welfare in meeting the needs of both labour and capital within developed economies. It is supported in particular by social democratic theorists who see high-wage/high-welfare strategies as a viable means of ensuring future economic growth. Such investment strategies include:

- The promotion of high levels of education and training throughout the workforce;
- The implementation of social activation measures to engage all citizens in economic activity;
- The use of public resources to promote economic and social regeneration in deprived locations;
- The continued redistribution of resources, through taxes and benefits, to promote social integration.

Of course these different measures and broad responses are not mutually-exclusive. Indeed the most interesting finding of detailed comparative study of the structure and development of different welfare systems is the extent to which a range of different responses can be found within individual countries in different areas of provision at different times, as we shall see in the countries covered in the other chapters of this book.

References

Alcock, P. (1997) *Understanding Poverty*, 2nd edn, Macmillan.
Beveridge, Sir W. (1942) *Report on Social Insurance and Allied Services*, Cmd 6404, HMSO.

Bonoli, G., George, V. and Taylor-Gooby, P. (2000) *European Welfare Futures: Towards a Theory of Retrenchment*, Polity Press.

Bradshaw, J., Ditch, J., Holmes, H. and Whiteford, P. (1993) *Support for Children: A Comparison of Arrangements in Fifteen Countries*, DSS Research Report 21, HMSO.

Bradshaw, J., Kennedy, S., Kilkey, M., Hutton, S., Corden, A., Eardley, T., Holmes, H. and Neale, J. (1996) *Policy and the Employment of Lone Parents in 20 Countries*, Social Policy Research Unit, University of York.

Burrows, R. and Loader, B. (eds) (1994) *Towards a Post-Fordist Welfare State?*, Routledge.

Castles, F. (ed.) (1982) *The Impact of Parties, Politics and Policies in Democratic Capitalist States*, Sage.

Castles, F. (1999) *Comparative Public Policy: Patterns of Post-war Transformation*, Edward Elgar.

Castles, F. and Mitchell, D. (1991) *Three Worlds of Welfare Capitalism or Four?*, Discussion Paper 21, Australian National University.

Clasen, J. (ed.) (1999) *Comparative Social Policy: Concepts, Theories and Methods*, Blackwell.

Craig, G. and Mayo, M. (1995) *Community Empowerment*, Zed Books.

Deacon, B. (1983) *Social Policy and Socialism: The Struggle for Socialist Relations of Welfare*, Pluto.

Deacon, B., Castle-Kanerova, M., Manning, N., Millard, F., Orosz, E. and Szalai, J. (1992) *The New Eastern Europe: Social Policy Past, Present and Future*, Sage.

Deacon, B., Hulse, M. and Stubbs, P. (1997) *Global Social Policy: International Organisations and the Future of Welfare*, Sage.

Ditch, J., Bradshaw, J., Clasen, J., Huby, M. and Moodie, M. (1997) *Comparative Social Assistance: Localisation and Discretion*, Avebury.

Doling, J. (1997) *Comparative Housing Policy: Government and Housing in Advanced Industrialised Countries*, Macmillan.

Doyal, L. and Gough, I. (1991) *A Theory of Human Need*, Macmillan.

Esping-Andersen, G. (1985) *Politics Against Markets: The Social Democratic Road to Power*, University of Harvard Press.

Esping-Andersen, G. (1990) *The Three Worlds of Welfare Capitalism*, Polity Press.

Esping-Andersen, G. (ed.) (1996) *Welfare States in Transition: National Adaptations in Global Economies*, Sage.

Ferrara, M. (1996) 'The "Southern Model" of Welfare in Social Europe', *Journal of European Social Policy*, 6(1).

George, V. and Taylor-Gooby, P. (eds) (1996) *European Welfare Policy: Squaring the Circle*, Macmillan.

George, V. and Wilding, P. (1994) *Welfare and Ideology*, Harvester Wheatsheaf.

Geyer, R. (2000) *Exploring European Social Policy*, Polity Press

Gilbert, N., Burrows, R. and Pollert, A. (eds) (1992) *Fordism and Flexibility: Divisions and Change*, Macmillan.

Ginsburg, N. (1979) *Class, Capital and Social Policy*, Macmillan.

Ginsburg, N. (1992) *Divisions of Welfare: A Critical Introduction to Comparative Social Policy*, Sage.

Glennerster, H. (2000) *British Social Policy since 1945*, 2nd edn, Blackwell.

Glennerster, H. and Hills, J. (eds) (1998) *The State of Welfare: The Economics of Social Spending*, 2nd edn, Oxford University Press.

Goodin, R., Headey, B., Muffels, R. and Dirven, H.J. (1999) *The Real Worlds of Welfare Capitalism*, Cambridge University Press.

Gough, I. (1979) *The Political Economy of the Welfare State*, Macmillan.

Hantrais, L. (2000) *Social Policy in the European Community*, 2nd edn, Macmillan.

Hill, M. (1996) *Social Policy: A Comparative Analysis*, Prentice-Hall.

Hills, J. (1997) *The Future of Welfare: A Guide to the Debate*, Joseph Rowntree Foundation.

Jessop, B. (2001) *The Future of the Welfare State*, Polity Press (forthcoming).

Johnson, N. (1987) *The Welfare State in Transition: The Theory and Practice of Welfare Pluralism*, Wheatsheaf.

Johnson, N. (1990) *Reconstructing the Welfare State: a Decade of Change 1980–1990*, Harvester Wheatsheaf.

Jones, C. (ed.) (1993a) *New Perspectives on the Welfare State in Europe*, Routledge.

Jones, C. (1993b) 'The Pacific Challenge: Confucian Welfare States', in C. Jones, (1993a) *op. cit.*

Jordan, B. (1998) *The New Politics of Welfare: Social Justice in a Global Context*, Sage.

Keynes, J. M. (1936) *The General Theory of Employment, Interest and Money*, Macmillan.

Korpi, W. (1983) *The Democratic Class Struggle*, Routledge.

Leibfried, S. (1993) 'Towards a European Welfare State?', in C. Jones (1993a) *op. cit.*

Lewis, G., Gewirtz, S. and Clarke, J. (eds) (2000) *Rethinking Social Policy*, Sage.

Lewis, J. (1992) 'Gender and the Development of Welfare Regimes', *Journal of European Social Policy*, 2(3).

Lowe, R. (1998) *The Welfare State in Britain since 1945*, 2nd edn, Macmillan.

Mabbett, D. and Bolderson, H. (1999) 'Theories and Methods in Comparative Social Policy' in J. Clasen (ed.), *Comparative Social Policy: Concepts, Theories and Methods*, Blackwell.

Malpass, P. and Murie, A. (1999) *Housing Policy and Practice*, 5th edn, Macmillan.

Marshall, T. H. (1950) *Citizenship and Social Class*, Cambridge University Press.

Mishra, R. (1990) *The Welfare State in Capitalist Society*, Harvester Wheatsheaf.

Mishra, R. (1999) *Globalisation and the Welfare State*, Edward Elgar.

Mullard, M. and Spicker, P. (1998) *Social Policy in a Changing Society*, Routledge.

O'Brien, M. and Penna, S. (1998) *Theorising Welfare: Enlightenment and Modern Society*, Sage.

O'Connor, J. (1973) *The Fiscal Crisis of the State*, St Martins Press.

Offe, C. (1984) *The Contradictions of the Welfare State*, Hutchinson.

Papadakis, E. and Taylor-Gooby, P. (1987) *The Private Provision of Public Welfare: State, Market and Community*, Wheatsheaf.

Pfaller, A., Gough, I. and Therborn, G. (1991) *Can the Welfare State Compete? A Comparative Study of Advanced Capitalist Countries*, Macmillan.

Pierson, C. (1998) *Beyond the Welfare State*, 2nd edn, Polity Press.

Pierson, C. and Castles, F. (eds) (2000) *The Welfare State Reader*, Polity Press.

Ploug, N. and Kvist, J. (1996) *Social Security in Europe*, Kluwer Law International.

Smeeding, T., O'Higgins, M. and Rainwater, L. (1990) *Poverty, Inequality and Income Distribution in Comparative Perspective: The Luxembourg Income Study (LIS)* Harvester Wheatsheaf.

Stephens, J. (1979) *The Transition from Capitalism to Socialism*, Macmillan.

Sykes, R. and Alcock, P. (eds) (1998) *Development in European Social Policy: Convergence and Diversity*, Policy Press.

Sykes, R., Palier, B. and Prior, P. (2001) *Globalization and European Welfare States: Challenges and Change*, Macmillan.

Taylor-Gooby, P. (1996) 'The Response of Government: Fragile Convergence', in V. George and P. Taylor-Gooby (eds) *European Welfare Policy: Squaring the Circle*, Macmillan.

Therborn, G. and Roebroek, J. (1986) 'The Irreversible Welfare State', *International Journal of the Health Sciences*, 16(3).

Titmuss, R. (1974) *Social Policy*, Allen and Unwin.

Tullock, G. (1976) *The Vote Motive: An Essay in the Economics of Politics, with Applications to the British economy*, Princeton University Press.

Walker, A. and Maltby, T. (1996) *Ageing Europe*, Open University Press.

Waters, A. (1995) *Globalisation*, Routledge.

Wilensky, H. (1975) *The Welfare State and Equality:Structural and Ideological Roots of Public Expenditure*, University of California Press.

Wilensky, H. (1976) *The 'New Corporatism', Centralization and the Welfare State*, Sage.

CHAPTER 2

United States: An American Welfare State?

JOHN CLARKE AND FRANCES FOX PIVEN

Varieties of Liberalism: The American Welfare State

The organisation of USA social welfare poses a distinctive problem for comparative studies of social policy. The absence of a strong, centralised welfare state providing a wide range of more or less universal benefits and services has led commentators to question whether the term 'welfare state' could meaningfully be used in this context. A European view of welfare states has been contrasted with the American experience of complex relationships between federal and state governments, involving a mixture of corporate, philanthropic and public sources of welfare provision exemplified in the organisation of US health care developed without a national universal health insurance system.

Various explanations have been offered for the different development of US welfare (Pierson, 1990), and one recurrent theme in comparative analysis is the relationship between the development of welfare and the role of political parties. In the US case, this argument links the underdevelopment of state welfare with the underdevelopment of an organised labour movement and absence of socialist or social-democratic political parties, associated elsewhere with the development of state welfare (Castles, 1989; Esping-Andersen, 1990).

From New Deal to Great Society: The Elements of US Welfare

This chapter focuses on three periods of major welfare reform, beginning with the 1930s and the 1960s, periods which feature in most accounts of US welfare as formative, where major structural changes in welfare organisation and provision took place. These periods acquired a politicised significance in later controversies about US welfare, the distinction between 'New Deal' and 'Great Society' welfare programmes emerging as a central feature of the politics of welfare in the 1980s. The chapter then examines the last two decades of the twentieth century, a period in which neo-liberal economic programmes and neo-conservative social ideologies dominated and distinctions between 'left' and 'right' in US politics were increasingly blurred.

The 'New Deal' and Social Reconstruction

Prior to the 1930s, social welfare was organised and delivered through states and cities and through voluntary and philanthropic agencies, with the exception of Civil War Veterans' pensions (Amenta and Skocpol, 1989; Skocpol, 1992). The 1930s economic depression exposed the limitations of this highly differentiated welfare patchwork; the scale of unemployment and resulting poverty rapidly outran the capacity of philanthropy and local state arrangements to cope. This failure provoked substantial social movements amongst the poor and unemployed, demanding public intervention to remedy unemployment and relieve poverty.

Roosevelt's New Deal combined measures to remedy unemployment through public works schemes supported by federal funds with longer-term programmes establishing more systematic and rigorously-administered welfare benefits. Amenta (1998) described this as the creation of a 'work and relief state' rather than a 'welfare state', as a way of emphasising the central role of employment-creation measures. The creation of the Public Works Administration in 1933 was followed by the Social Security Act of 1935. This provided the foundation for the subsequent structure of welfare benefits by creating a social insurance system providing benefits for old age and federal encouragement for state schemes for unemployment insurance (instituting a federal tax where states failed to institute their own). It was later extended to widows and their dependants, and for sickness and disability. The scheme's central principle was the accumulation of insurance contributions records through employment. Many occupations, including many in which black people and female workers were concentrated, such as agriculture and domestic work, were excluded. Others involved pay too low to qualify for insurance payments and benefits, again disproportionately affecting both white women and black workers (Quadagno, 1994).

Socialised, rather than individual, insurance had been established earlier as a core principle of welfare provision in Europe. Its introduction into the USA was consistently resisted by politicians and employers' organisations as undermining both market mechanisms and the incentives to individuals to make provision for their own needs (Skocpol and Ikenberry, 1983). The scale of social dislocation created by the Depression led to wider acceptance of the need to supplement local public and philanthropic assistance with a more integrated social insurance system (Piven and Cloward, 1993). The insurance model adopted sought to maintain proper incentives to work, embodying three core principles:

1 Social insurance should not be directed at the elimination of all hardship, but only be concerned with a limited range of specified risks (unemployment, ill-health, old age and widowhood) which were involuntary conditions.
2 Workers should see connections between their income, insurance payments and benefits which they received, avoiding expectations of high benefit levels, and maintaining work incentives.

3 The scheme should be clearly distinguished from public assistance. Benefits should be 'earned' as a right through contributions rather than being stigmatising and means-tested relief from the public purse or private charity (Katz, 1986, pp. 236–7).

The Committee on Economic Security, which oversaw the development of social security, was concerned that the development of new welfare measures should not blur the line between insurance-based provision and 'public assistance' (locally-provided, means-tested support for the poor). Only two New Deal initiatives threatened this principle. The first was the decision to pay old-age pensions immediately to those who had no contribution record – this was a temporary arrangement, to last only until the scheme was fully established. Subsequently, a means-test for those not insured was reintroduced.

The second was the creation of ADC (Aid to Dependent Children) in the 1935 Act, allowing federal government to contribute to the costs of states' programmes for benefits to be paid to families in poverty for the maintenance of children. ADC itself was based on the 'mothers' pensions' programmes which a number of states had developed in the 1920s to provide assistance to widowed or deserted mothers with young children. ADC's federal funding moved public assistance part-way to being a national scheme, although the schemes' administration remained at local level (Koven and Michel, 1993; Gordon, 1994; Bussiere, 1997).

ADC provides a paradigm of the interrelationship between welfare, 'race', class and gender in the USA. Where social insurance was earnings-related, ADC was available if the candidate family passed a series of 'tests', the means test being one. Legislation also provided for 'suitable home' provision at state level, which allowed benefits to be withheld if investigation showed that children were being brought up in an unsuitable environment. This provision effectively became a 'morals test' applied to mothers seeking assistance, drawing on assumptions about 'moral fitness' developed in mothers' pensions schemes.

The New Deal was a small and limited revolution – creating what Katz (1986) called a 'semi-welfare state'. Although it maintained the formal separation between federal and state or city administration of different aspects of welfare, it nevertheless changed the balance between national and local through the creation of some national schemes and greater use of federal funding to support delivery of locally-based welfare. It laid the foundation for a nationally coordinated system of social insurance, with benefits and entitlements for limited categories of the population. The creation of an insurance system aligned the USA with other Western societies in the provision of limited welfare rights relating to unemployment, old age, disability and ill-health; provision restricted to those with contributions' records earned through employment. For those inside the insurance system, the New Deal represented a considerable step forward. But the combination of social insurance with the preservation of local public assistance created a 'two-tier' welfare state in which those outside the system had to prove both need and moral worth to receive assistance, thus perpetuating gender and race distinctions amongst citizens which reflected wider structures of inequality (Mink, 1991, p. 113).

These reforms established the pattern of US welfare till the 1960s, creating the conditions from which the subsequent wave of welfare reform developed. In particular, they established the distinction between insurance-based benefits and public assistance which overshadowed the later politics of US welfare.

The Great Society: A War against Poverty?

The 'Great Society' programmes of welfare reform associated with the 1960s Kennedy and Johnson presidencies need to be understood in the context of the social movements generating the impetus for reform, and as a response to black voter instability and riots. Katz (1986) summarises the pressures to reform, indicating how traditional concerns about welfare intersected with changing social and political conditions:

> Racial conflict, urban riots, militant welfare clients and increased out-of-wedlock births among black women impelled a search for new ways to preserve social order and discipline. Unemployment induced by technology, functional illiteracy, or inadequate education; fear of Soviet competition; new manpower theories; and the realisation that welfare regulations discouraged work, all encouraged the use of welfare policy to shape and regulate labor markets...(pp. 251–2)

Of particular significance were Civil Rights challenges to existing patterns of welfare (Piven and Cloward, 1993). Activists combined with anti-poverty workers in attacking the 'suitable home' provisions of the ADC scheme, used by many states as a racially-exclusionary mechanism (Bell, 1965). Such alliances were significant in focusing political attention on the urgency of reform and in shaping policies which increased the resources of the poorest through food stamp, nutritional and health programmes (West, 1981).

Poverty was primarily understood as the inadvertent effect of historically-created barriers 'blocking' people from taking advantage of the opportunities which the USA presented. Theories of cultural deficit or cultural deprivation among the poor therefore played a leading role in shaping policy responses (Katz, 1989). Conceptions of poverty as the effect of structural economic inequality were marginalised and initiatives such as the Office of Economic Opportunity (OEO) (employment) and Operation Headstart (education) were designed to overcome barriers to participation in opportunity structures by enhancing the poor's skills and capacities.

Specific programmes targeted particular aspects of social life in poor communities, such as juvenile delinquency, civil rights, job training and education. For a brief period, one salient feature of these initiatives was the role given to community action, stressing the need for the 'maximum feasible participation' of the residents (Title II of the Economic Opportunity Act). This stress on programmes being carried out *by* the community rather than *for* the community identified state and city politicians and welfare agencies as part of the problem to be overcome (Marris and Rein, 1967). In reality, the attempt to bypass existing power structures was quickly curtailed, with political resistance leading to restrictions on the OEO's ability to directly fund community groups. The programme ended in 1974 when the Nixon Administration closed the OEO, transferring its responsibilities to other government departments.

Such projects were part of a wider 'war on poverty', conceived in the Kennedy administration, carried through by Johnson and continued in the Republican Nixon administration. From the Public Welfare Amendments of 1962 to the Social Security Amendments of 1974, a major restructuring and expansion of US welfare occurred. Between 1965 and 1972, federal welfare spending rose from US$75 billion to US$185 billion, from 7.7 per cent of America's 1960 gross national product to 16 per cent by 1974. This expansion had three main features:

1   increasing numbers of those eligible for welfare services and benefits;
2   a changing balance between services and benefits; and
3   a new relationship between social security and public assistance.

The reforms expanded the numbers of people eligible for welfare services and benefits in two main respects. The most visible was the reduction in racially-discriminatory welfare programmes, particularly in the shift from ADC to AFDC (Aid to Families with Dependent Children). The less visible, but numerically more significant, change involved the bringing of legal constraints into the administration of means-testing across a range of welfare services (for example, abolishing 'suitable homes' provision and state residence requirements), turning them from conditional entitlements into unconditional rights. This change in access criteria had some effect in destigmatising public services, moving them from a focus on assessing, investigating and supervising the poor towards seeing services as means of promoting greater social integration. Secondly, the reforms placed a greater emphasis on the provision of services (for example health care, housing and access to legal services) rather than on direct cash payments. Between 1964 and 1974, federal spending on 'in-kind' programmes increased from 3 per cent to 20 per cent of social welfare costs (Katz, 1986). The most significant of these developments related to public housing, nutritional programmes (particularly food stamps) and health services.

Health care became a particular focus of attention. The costs of obtaining health care (either directly for services or indirectly through private insurance) had effectively excluded many Americans. At the same time, however, proposals to socialise health care were forcefully resisted by health and insurance industry lobbies. What emerged instead was a package of measures to

subsidise health costs among those in need. Medicare and Medicaid programmes provided public funding for health costs among eligible groups, but
the two schemes reproduced, through their funding arrangements, the different logics of social security and public assistance:

> Though adopted together, Medicare and Medicaid reflected sharply different tradi-
> tions. Medicare was buoyed by popular approval and the acknowledged dignity of
> Social Security; Medicaid was burdened by the stigma of public assistance. While
> Medicare had uniform national standards for eligibility and benefits, Medicaid left
> states to decide how extensive their programs would be. Medicare allowed the
> physician to charge above what the programme would pay; Medicaid did not and
> participation among physicians was far more limited. (Starr, 1982, p. 370)

The two programmes remained the core of US welfare policy and spending and played a major role in its expansion during the 1960s and early
1970s. In relation to public assistance, AFDC played the leading role with
the numbers covered by the scheme increasing from 3.1 million in 1960,
4.3 million in 1965 and 6.1 million in 1969 to 10.8 million in 1974 (Patterson,
1981, p. 171). Popular challenges to entitlement restrictions underpinned
federal and state relaxations of conditions that increased both numbers of
eligible families and take-up rates.

Despite the dramatic increase in AFDC assistance, it was social security
which grew most in the period, partly through demographic trends affecting the numbers eligible, especially the elderly, for insured benefits. Katz
argues that its demography was less significant than its social and political
composition:

> Social security cut across class lines. Like public education, it offered at least as
> much to the middle classes as to the poor. Its constituency, therefore, was broad,
> articulate, effective and, above all, respectable. In 1970, social security payments to
> the elderly, $30.3 billion, were about ten times higher than federal payments
> for AFDC, $2.5 billion. By 1975, the gap had widened: social security cost
> $64.7 billion and AFDC, $5.1 billion. Through-out the late 1970s and early 1980s
> the disparities increased even more ... (1986, p. 267)

Social security emerged as the dominant feature of US welfare, combining
income benefits for the elderly, disabled people and the unemployed, with
insurance of health costs for eligible groups. The value of social security benefits was enhanced by changes throughout the late 1960s and 1970s which
increased benefits beyond the cost of inflation and extended welfare to the
'non-poor'. Attempts by Presidents Nixon and Carter to reform welfare further towards a closer integration of insurance- and assistance-based schemes
(through proposals for a guaranteed family income) failed because, Katz
argues, they threatened the underlying distinction between the deserving and
undeserving poor, embodied in the split between insurance and assistance

(*ibid*.; see also Quadagno, 1994). This distinction between the programmes emerged as the central focus for the politics of welfare in the 1980s.

The Welfare Backlash: The New Right in the 1980s

> The Soviet Union is the immediate danger perceived by Americans. Yet it is not the real threat to our national security. The real threat is the welfare state ... (Friedman and Friedman, 1984, p. 73)

Welfare played a central role in the New Right's agenda for the reconstruction of the USA in the 1980s, reflecting its ability to incorporate a variety of themes about the economy, the state, the family, 'race' and gender that were essential to its diagnosis of America's fall from grace and its prescriptions for a return to greatness. Just as the period of welfare expansion is one which the USA shared with other Western societies, so, too, the period of welfare backlash and retrenchment is one which links the USA to other societies, Britain being an obvious example. Where the long postwar boom underpinned welfare expansion, so the onset of world recession from the mid-1970s provided a starting point for challenges to the costs of welfare. In part, this appeared as a simple question of economics: 'can we afford welfare?' But it was also caught up in how economic and political crises are represented, and the ideological practices through which their causes are explained and remedies defined. The simple question about the cost of welfare was itself part of the changing ideological framework, which now defined welfare as an 'unproductive' cost to national economies, making them less competitive. In the 1960s, at least in part, welfare had been construed as expenditure necessary to modernise society and make it more competitive, as well as more harmonious and socially just.

While the USA shared social and economic changes in common with other societies, the particular response to them was the product of domestic political forces and alliances. The reshaping of the Amercian political right proved to be decisive. A new alliance, comprising different social and ideological groupings, including neo-liberals, neo-conservatives and the radical right, came to dominate the Republican Party, supporting the Reagan presidencies (Saloma, 1984). Neo-liberalism provided an economic rationale for change, identifying an overregulatory, overinterfering and overtaxing state as a major cause of America's declining competitiveness. Individual and corporate 'enterprise' needed to be liberated from the state. Neo-conservatism provided a political rationale for change, arguing that the 'elite liberalism' of the 1960s and 1970s had gone too far, producing an overextended state and a collapse of national leadership. The radical right (itself an uneasy confederation of moral majoritarians, anti-communists and white supremacist groupings) provided a moral rationale for change, arguing that 1960s liberalism had undermined fundamental American values, denied bedrock American freedoms (for example, through enforced desegregation of schooling) and created a moral vacuum (Clarke, 1991).

The Problem of Dependency

For the New Right, the major mistake of welfare expansion in the 1960s and 1970s was clear in its effects on the poor. Where social security programmes, for the main part, could be seen as promoting independence by virtue of earning benefits one received, public assistance (Aid to Families with Dependent Children, in particular) undermined independence, creating a culture of 'demoralisation'. The basic components of this view stretch back to nineteenth-century beliefs embodied in the Poor Law and public relief programmes. Giving people welfare stops them trying to help themselves, makes them dependent on the benefits they receive, and undermines the will to self-improvement. The more particular version of this theme in relation to AFDC pointed to the growth of lone-parent families; these encouraged men to father children without financial responsibility, and freed women from the responsibility of keeping men in the household and in employment. The existence of the benefit, it was argued, created 'perverse incentives' and rewarded inappropriate behaviour.

This critique was exemplified in Charles Murray's *Losing Ground* (1984), a huge and apparently well-documented survey of the impact of welfare on employment, family life and achievement amongst US black people. It was influential far beyond America in its critique of welfare and in the way it linked welfare to the emergence of an underclass. Murray used four key indicators to demonstrate the demoralising effects of poverty programmes:

1   labour force participation (very low for young black males);
2   illegitimate births (very high for young black females);
3   the number of lone-parent families (very high among black people); and
4   the number of homicide victims (very high among young black males).

Together, these indices mapped a section of the population which, he suggested, had become demoralised and dependent. Murray used statistical comparison about the fortunes of black and white people in the USA as the basis for arguments about poverty, despite the fact that twice as many white people as black were in poverty. Claiming that there was no usable data about the poor, he insisted that black people provide a satisfactory proxy for poor people. The effect of this device was to construct an elision between the categories of 'poor' and 'black', and to tell the story of black America solely from the standpoint of welfare. Such constructions were endemic to the New Right's attack on welfare to the extent that many commentators argued that 'welfare' became simply a synonym for 'race' in US politics during the 1980s. The culmination of this connection was to be found in the idea of the 'underclass'.

The complex mixture of the metaphors of a dependency culture and the underclass in the New Right's demonology of welfare underpinned the 1980s retreat from welfare spending, which toughened up welfare eligibility and conditions and increasingly used welfare as a means of controlling the poor. Welfare came under attack at all levels, federal, state and city, through budget-trimming practices and changing regulations (Gans, 1995), an attack concentrated on public assistance and social service programmes rather than social security – reflecting their different political constituencies:

> by 1983, under complex, new regulations, 408,000 people had lost their eligibility for AFDC and 299,000 had lost their benefits...Through these reductions federal and state governments saved $1.1 billion in fiscal 1983. Other regulations restricted eligibility for food stamps and sliced $2 billion out of the program's $12 billion budget...Spending on Medicaid dropped 3 per cent in fiscal year 1982... The social services block grant to the states was chopped by 20 per cent in 1981... (Katz, 1986, p. 287)

The exception was benefits paid to disabled people under the Social Security Act. Congress amended the Act in 1980 to require a periodic review of all cases, which the Reagan administration accelerated. Katz notes that between March 1981 and April 1982, 400,000 cases were reviewed from which 190,948 cases were ruled ineligible; many were later, however, restored to the rolls by the courts.

The cumulative effect of these and other changes are shown in reductions in spending as a result of government action on a number of programmes between 1982 and 1985:

AFDC:	12.7 per cent
Food stamps:	12.6 per cent
Child nutrition:	27.7 per cent
Housing assistance:	4.4 per cent
Low income energy assistance:	8.3 per cent

(*Source: ibid.*)

These changes set the tone for welfare policy and politics in the 1980s. Although the Reagan administrations did not 'abolish the welfare state', as some New Right ideologists would have wished, programmes, staffing and resourcing were significantly diminished – albeit selectively – by 1990. The brunt of the 'war on welfare' was borne by the poorest – those dependent on public assistance programmes rather than social insurance.

The Failure of Health-Care Reform

The election of President Clinton in 1992 reopened a public discussion about the organisation, coverage and cost of US health-care provision.

A complex and costly system had historically excluded many Americans or, at best, provided them with minimal coverage and services. Economic uncertainty in the 1980s and 1990s led to many more American citizens becoming anxious about the security of their health-care arrangements. Many of these citizens were covered by health insurance schemes arranged by employers, and widespread job losses (particularly in white-collar and middle-class occupations) threatened both insurance arrangements and workers' sense of health security.

The other key issue on health-care was the problem of rising costs, a challenge shared by other Western health-care systems. What distinguished the USA was the organisational setting of these problems, with direct public provision forming a negligible part of health-care. Most provision had been arranged through private (for-profit and not-for-profit) organisations, with payment for services financed through a variety of routes. The balance of funding had shifted from the 1930s pattern of direct payments by users, supplemented by public assistance for the poor through non-profit mutual insurance schemes organised by hospitals, such as Blue Shield, to one dominated by employment-based health insurance plans. By 1983, 58 per cent of Americans were covered by employment-based schemes, 12 per cent were covered by Medicare and 8 per cent were covered by Medicaid; 15 per cent of Americans had no health coverage (Staples, 1989). Health insurance followed familiar patterns of employment stratification, reproducing labour market disadvantages in terms of 'race', gender and class.

The 1980s welfare cuts affected both Medicare and Medicaid coverage. Tighter limits were introduced on insurance-based Medicare payments (usually involving transfer of costs from the insurance scheme to the patients themselves). In parallel with restrictions on other aspects of public assistance, Medicaid payments became even more restricted, discouraging health providers from taking on Medicaid patients. At the same time, changed eligibility criteria and increased administrative complexities meant that around 60 per cent of the poor were either ineligible for or not receiving Medicaid (Ginsburg, 1991).

Two particular changes affected the mix of provision. One was the growth of Health Maintenance Organisations (HMOs), which offered health-care packages on the basis of an annual fee (which employers might pay or contribute towards). The HMOs then either provided direct services themselves or contracted with other service providers. By the late 1980s, HMOs covered about 12 per cent of the population. The second major development was the growth of 'for-profit' hospitals and health provision. Wohl (1984) coined the phrase 'the medical–industrial complex' to describe this trend towards the corporate domination of health-care provision. It was a trend seemingly likely to create a tripartite division of health-care, with the corporate sector 'creaming off' the most profitable patients, a second layer of not-for-profit or smaller for-profit hospitals taking all but the uninsured, and the bulk of

Medicaid patients remaining in an increasingly residualised public hospital system.

This system posed major problems for those worried about cost containment. For the most part it was driven by the power of the medical profession, which had resisted attempts to socialise the costs of health-care through national health insurance from the 1940s onwards. One result of the system's complexity was that no alternative concentrations of power existed to check the power of the medical profession, given that payment for health-care was distributed between state and federal governments, insurance schemes, employers (paying workers' health insurance) and private individuals. The 1980s saw changes challenging the institutional dominance of the medical profession, including federal attempts to impose bureaucratic means of limiting medical costs (Bjorkman, 1989). These moves were paralleled by pressure from insurance companies and employers for greater cost control. The growth of corporate health-care provision suggests a third source of financial pressure: the corporations' desire to rationalise costs and increase profits. Wohl (1984) and Starr (1982) both argued that this corporate pressure, and the ability of the corporations to exercise greater control over doctors who are employees and not independent professionals, may be the most significant long-term development in cost containment.

Clinton took up the issue of health-care reform in 1993, establishing a task force headed by his wife. The task force proposed a 'middle way' between a nationalised (or state-provided) health-care system and an extension of individually-arranged (or free-market) health insurance. The aim was to produce a system that would ensure health-care insurance for all American citizens, preserve a degree of individual choice, and use the power of the state to drive down costs. Although health-care reform was a popular issue, the task force's proposals were abandoned in 1994. Many reasons have been advanced for their failure, including problematic political tactics, a widespread public mistrust of government, and the powerful and effective lobbying campaigns of medical, insurance and employer interest groups likely to be adversely affected by the reforms. Skocpol's (1997) analysis highlighted other political issues, arguing that the reform proposals were vilified by the Republican Right as an extension of 'big government', creating more bureaucracy and government interference, but as significant was the collapse (triggered by the withdrawal of some of the insurance companies) of the provider coalition, which the Clinton proposals had aimed to appease.

The political and ideological paradoxes surrounding the role of government in promoting forms of social welfare created an impact that went beyond the failure of the health-care reform proposals. Other areas of social welfare became the ground on which the new Democratic conservatism of the Clinton presidency encountered the revival of the Republican Right: an encounter that resulted in a competition between a Democratic President and a Republican Congress to bring about 'the end of welfare' (Piven, 1998).

Ending 'Welfare As We Know It'

The distinction between entitlements (social security) and welfare (AFDC) continued to play a central role in conflicts over social policy in the 1990s (Gordon, 1994), and welfare remained a primary target for neo-conservative and neo-liberal attacks (for example Tanner, 1996). The most dramatic policy change, however, was Clinton's commitment in 1992, showing his credentials as a 'new Democrat', to 'end welfare as we know it' by bringing about reforms that would 'time-limit' welfare and get people 'off welfare and off to work' (quoted in Piven, 1998, p. 21). This commitment was fulfilled in 1996 when the President signed a bill effectively terminating AFDC, changing federal funding, instituting a two-year maximum for welfare benefits, and enabling states to operate tighter time limits as well as 'behavioural conditions' in respect of mothers and their children.

The Personal Responsibility Act (PRA) of 1996 dramatically transformed the character of welfare and the status of welfare recipients, redefining the purposes of welfare to:

- provide assistance to needy families so that children may be cared for in their own homes or in the homes of relatives;
- end the dependence of needy parents on government benefits by promoting job preparation, work and marriage;
- prevent and reduce the incidence of out-of-wedlock pregnancies and establish annual numerical goals for preventing and reducing the incidence of these pregnancies; and
- encourage the formation and maintenance of two-parent families.

(Quoted in Mink, 1998, p. 66)

The Personal Responsibility Act (PRA) had three significant features. First, it emphasised work rather than welfare as the basis of personal and familial independence. Neither federal government nor individual states were obliged to find or provide employment for claimants. 'Personal responsibility' had a strict interpretation in the Act: a maximum of two years' welfare benefit could be claimed before the state withdrew any support.

Policy analysts have argued that 'welfare mothers' have been subjected to oscillating interpretations of their role and responsibilities (Gordon, 1994; Handler, 1995; Mink, 1998). In the early twentieth century, 'maternalist' policies, such as mothers' pensions and ADC (Aid to Dependent Children), had been introduced to support poor women in the task of raising children. Other policies subsequently emphasised the mothers' responsibility to go out to work to provide for their children. The PRA announced that the primary obligation of poor mothers was to find employment (a requirement distinguishing them from non-poor mothers).

The second significant feature of the PRA was its explicit commitment to the 'formation and maintenance' of two-parent families. Marriage was put forward as the only legitimate alternative to employment for poor mothers, and the patriarchal norms of conventional family formation were to be encouraged and enforced by the states through welfare conditions (Mink, 1998). For example, under the Act, states can refuse additional benefit for any child born to a mother already receiving welfare. The Act marked a significant moment in the conflict over 'family values' in the USA, embodying the backlash against household diversity in general, lone parents specifically and against aspects of greater female economic independence. The triumph of family values meant that one form of household formation (the 'conventional' family) became the only valued family through its embodiment as a governmental objective in legislation (Stacey, 1998). The PRA thus created a combination of incentives, demands and powers to engage the states in policing the morality of their poorest citizens. There was also a third significant element of the end of welfare. The PRA redefined relationships between the federal government, states and citizens, breaking the link between the federal government and citizens in need of welfare by shifting funding for AFDC to block grants to the states, thus undoing the welfare relationship established in the New Deal. The cash-limited central subsidy to the states provided them with an incentive to cut benefit levels and numbers of recipients – which most took advantage of. At the same time, the Act gave states greater 'flexibility' in the implementation of welfare reform.

The Clinton administration continued the practice inaugurated under Presidents Reagan and Bush of granting waivers of the Social Security Act (to 43 states in all) to permit the states to 'experiment' by imposing time limits on the receipt of AFDC benefits and various sanctions against disapproved benefit-recipient behaviours. Disgruntled at the Democratic effort to capture 'their' issue, the new Republican Congressional majority elected in 1994 replaced AFDC entirely by Temporary Assistance to Needy Families (TANF), a programme imposing strict federal time limits and work requirements on lone mothers receiving cash assistance and giving the administration of the scheme to the states.

The effect of these changes was to create substantial geographical unevenness in the conditions for, and administration of, welfare across the United States. The PRA did indeed mark 'the end of welfare as we know it', representing the culmination of neo-conservative and neo-liberal attacks on 'welfare' that had been developing since the late 1970s. The ideological segregation and demonisation of 'welfare mothers' as a cause of America's social and economic problems thus resulted in their disentitlement, stigmatisation and subjection to new forms of moral surveillance and economic discipline. Even this outcome, however, failed to satisfy the reforming zeal of neo-conservatives and neo-liberals. For some neo-liberals, the fact that government remained in the business of welfare at all was a problem. They would rather have seen the 'needy' and the 'philanthropists' settle matters within civil society without government interference (Tanner, 1996).

The labour market consequences of these welfare changes were predictable. As hundreds of thousands of women lost welfare benefits, whether because of time limits or sanctions or of the bureaucratic obstacles inevitable when conditions for eligibility become complex and discretionary, they streamed into the labour market to compete with other women, and men, for less-skilled and low-paying jobs. Many of them actually failed to find steady work, even in a booming economy with low overall unemployment levels (although not necessarily low unemployment levels among the less skilled, especially in the older central city ghettos). State estimates varied, but between 40 and 70 per cent of those dropped from the welfare rolls appear to have been unemployed in the past few years, and few of those who were employed were earning wages sufficient to bring them above the poverty line. Whether they found work or not, wages in these sectors of the labour market where they were competing for jobs were likely to be driven down, by about 12 per cent according to early estimates – and falling more in states where proportionally more people had been on welfare. One estimate suggested a wage reduction of 26 per cent in the exposed sectors of the labour market in New York City or the displacement of 58,000 workers, or some combination of the two.

Welfare cutbacks were only the most publicised of the changes in decommodifying programmes. Under the Reagan administration, the federal formula measuring state unemployment levels, which triggered the availability of long-term unemployment benefits in a state, was revised to reduce their availability, with the little-noticed but nevertheless dramatic consequence of reducing the proportion of the unemployed who received these benefits, from 75 per cent in the 1970s to a mere one-third in the 1980s (Meerpool, 1997). Other obscure changes were made in social security, the main old-age pension programme, where the age of eligibility was raised, although so gradually as to attract little comment, from 65 to 67 years, while adjustments to the cost of living formula cut pension benefit levels and new rules encouraged the pensioned to continue to work. This was an opening shot in a continuing campaign to undermine public confidence in social security and build support for the privatisation and retrenchment of old-age pensions.

New restrictions on social supports for immigrants were also incorporated in the Personal Responsibility and Work Opportunity Reconciliation Act (PRWORA). With some exceptions, legal immigrants were no longer entitled to Medicaid, food stamps or cash assistance, moves which appeared to pander to public opinion. In reality, the idea that benefit cut-offs would deter immigration has hardly been confirmed by data or experience (Massey, 1998), and the exclusions simply ensured that immigrants who did enter the USA remained without any public protection to tide them over periods of unemployment or low wages. This may indeed be just what was intended, since the congressional bloc that led the fight to cut benefits for immigrants simultaneously opposed tighter controls on immigration (Stern, 1998). During 1996, when cutbacks on aid to legal immigrants were made law, almost a million legal immigrants were admitted to the USA, the largest number since 1914 (Schuck, 1998).

Cutback or Commodification?

However, these much-publicised cutbacks did not tell the whole story. The pattern of change in the income maintenance programmes was uneven, and complicated. Whilst families on welfare fared badly, some of the much-heralded cuts of the early 1980s were rather quickly reversed and spending on some programmes actually increased. Overall, federal expenditures on major means-tested programmes steadily increased, from US$88 billion in 1980 to US$205 billion in 1995 (OMB, 1996). The widely-held view that the USA has simply retrenched its spending on the poor does not entirely fit with these facts (Melnick, 1998).

   First, not all the attempted cuts succeeded. An early Reagan proposal to do away with a legal minimum payment in social security pensions was quickly defeated by an overwhelming vote of the congress. Then, after the initial successes of 1981/2, Reagan administration attempts to make additional cuts in means-tested programmes were blocked by a Democratic Congress, and some cuts were even reversed. The huge reductions in the disability rolls of the early 1980s were largely restored by the courts by the end of Reagan's first term. Expenditures on the Supplemental Security Income (SSI) programme, which included payments to the impoverished aged and disabled, then slowly rose during the remainder of the 1980s, and accelerated upward by 20 per cent per year in the 1990s, largely as a result of the expansion of the disabled rolls. Federal spending on health care for the poor under Medicaid also rose rapidly, from US$26.3 billion in 1980, to US$89.1 billion in 1995 (measured in 1995 dollars) (ERP, 1996). The food and nutrition programmes had been sharply cut in the early 1980s, but subsequent steady increases pushed spending – and the number of beneficiaries – up to levels higher than prior to the cuts. In 1996, under the aegis of a Republican Congress intent on welfare reform, the food stamp programme was targeted for further cuts, but a number of these cuts were rescinded the following year. Meanwhile, and despite vigorous political argument discrediting public housing programmes, federal expenditures on housing assistance for low-income people increased steadily throughout the period (Jencks, 1998).

   These twists and turns require a complex explanation. One possibility is simply that industrial-era theories which posited the durability of the welfare state because of the economic, social and political functions it served in a democratic and capitalist society should not be so quickly dismissed. Another possibility is suggested by the fact that different programmes fared quite differently, which suggests that the influence of provider groups with an interest in some of the programmes might account for their durability; the continued expansion of the health-care programmes is a case in point. A further possibility is suggested by the fact that, in 1999, the Department of Agriculture began legal action against states and localities that denied food assistance to the poor, perhaps representative of the interests of the Department's farmbelt constituency, than suffering from a surfeit of agricultural commodities.

However, there is no doubt that a major shift occurred, away from spending on less-work-conditioned, or less-commodified programmes, to spending on programmes that shore up labour market participation, or commodify labour. Spending has continued to rise essentially because even commodified programmes cost money. Indeed, this is just what relief reformers discovered in the past when they succeeded in replacing direct relief with 'houses of industry'. The most dramatic commodification occurred in TANF, where federal requirements stipulated that states should show that a rising proportion, year-on-year, of the mothers receiving aid are working. Official data revealed that, nationwide, 28 per cent of the adults on welfare were working, and in some states virtually all recipients were working. The arrangements varied: in many states, recipients were assigned to private employers who paid them the minimum wage and receive the welfare cheque (and handsome tax write-offs) as subsidies. Alternatively, recipients might simply work for their welfare cheque, either for private employers or for local government. The most important of the new labour market-related programmes is the Earned Income Tax Credit which operates like a negative income tax with earnings below US$24,000 per year, but only if the family head was working. The programme originated as a little-noticed tax provision in 1975, and with the support of Presidents Reagan and Bush, and later Clinton, was expanded from the late 1980s. By 1996, the programme provided US$25 billion to some 20 million families, outpacing even peak-year spending on AFDC, except that the monies spent operated to shore up the incentives of low-waged work instead of creating alternatives to it.

Changes in the food stamp and Medicaid programmes have also tilted spending towards work enforcement. For most of the thirty or so years in which these programmes have existed, the main route to eligibility has been through AFDC. Now, however, the application process for cash benefits (and hence access to health and food in-kind benefits) for the non-working poor has been littered with new procedural obstacles. At the same time, every recent legislated expansion of the Medicaid programme is for working families whose earnings make them ineligible for cash assistance (Melnick, 1998). Clinton's 1999 budget proposed expanding health-care benefits to allow tens of thousands of the disabled to return to work, and the 1998 housing legislation introduced 'welfare-to-work' provisions into the low-income rental assistance and public housing programmes.

The impact of changing social policies on labour markets is, however, not only the result of the interplay between the material incentives of wage work and income-maintenance programmes, characteristic of the policy shifts in many Western countries. The process of commodification of welfare in the USA has also been effected by cultural sanctions. The programmes and the discourse surrounding them also help to define the identities of both those participating and not participating in the labour market. The campaign to reform welfare was itself a powerful intervention in American culture which argued the worthlessness of poor women raising children on the dole. And the new punitive practices ushered in by the legislation – sometimes called 'tough love' – reinforced those derogatory meanings at the same time as reinforcing the importance of work regardless of declining real wages and increasing hours. Indeed, at first glance, these welfare reforms seemed to be entirely about questions of the personal morality of the women who subsist on the dole and not about labour markets. The problem was, the argument went, that a too-generous welfare system was leading women to spurn wage work for lives of idleness and 'dependency' (Fraser and Gordon, 1994), thereby undermining sexual and family morality among the poor.

The chorus of criticism focused relentlessly on personal morality, tapping into the deep antipathies in American culture towards the poor, towards black and Latin minorities who were widely understood to be the main beneficiaries of welfare, and drawing on the energy and excitement evoked by public debate about women, sex and sin. In reality, though, it had a good deal to do with labour markets, for it created a national drama which heaped insult on women who were poor if they were presumed not to work (Harris, 1993). The politics of the 1960s had reduced the stigma of being on the dole, and as a consequence more people in need applied for welfare and the welfare rolls rose; the politics of the 1990s increased stigma and contributed to the rapid fall in the rolls. This aspect of the reconstruction of American programmes also inevitably reverberated upwards, underlining for the working poor and less-than-poor the imperative of wage work and the degradation of falling out of work.

Over the past 25 years, income inequalities in the United States have risen spectacularly, and wages have stagnated or declined. The economic expansion of the late 1990s, together with the historically low levels of unemployment it produced, should in principle have led to a wage recovery through which workers would share in the boom. But the boost in wages and income has been slight, barely to the level of 1989, and poverty levels have remained high, with childhood poverty rates unchanged. Testifying before the Congress in the summer of 1997, Alan Greenspan, head of the Federal Reserve, explained this unusual combination of wage stagnation and a buoyant American economy. His message was to the point. The economy's performance in the past year was, he said, 'extraordinary' and 'exceptional', and a major contributing factor to this performance was 'a heightened sense of job insecurity and, as a consequence, subdued wage gains' (Pollin, 1998). The reconfigured American welfare state played a part in this development, not by rolling back programmes or slashing costs as is commonly thought, but by winding back history in another sense, redesigning programmes to reinforce the sanctions and incentives of the labour market.

References

Amenta, E. (1998) *Bold Relief: Institutional Politics and the Origins of Modern American Social Policy*, Princeton University Press.

Amenta, E. and Skocpol, T. (1989) 'Taking Exception: Explaining the Distinctiveness of American Public Policies in the Last Century', in F. G. Castles (ed.), *op. cit.*

Bell, W. (1965) *Aid to Dependent Children*, Columbia University Press.

Bjorkman, J. W. (1989) 'Politicizing Medicine and Medicalizing Politics: Physician Power in the US', in G. Freddi and J. W. Bjorkman (eds), *Controlling Medical Professionals*, Sage.

Brinkley, A. (1994) 'Reagan's Revenge: As Invented by Howard Jarvis', *New York Times Magazine*, 19 June, pp. 36–7.

Bussiere, E. (1997) *(Dis)Entitling the Poor: The Warren Court, Welfare Rights and the American Political Tradition*, Pennsylvania University Press.

Castles, F. G. (ed.) (1989) *The Comparative History of Public Policy*, Polity Press.

Clarke, J. (1991) *New Times and Old Enemies: Essays on Cultural Studies and America*, HarperCollins.

Esping-Andersen, G. (1990) *The Three Worlds of Welfare Capitalism*, Polity Press.

Fraser, N. and Gordon, L. (1994) 'A Genealogy of Dependency: Tracing a Keyword of the Welfare State', in P. Jones (ed.), *Critical Politics: From the Personal to the Global*, Arena Publications.

Friedman, M. and Friedman, R. (1984) *The Tyranny of the Status Quo*, Harcourt Brace Jovanovich.

Gans, H. J. (1995) *The War against the Poor*, Basic Books.

Ginsburg, N. (1991) *Divisions of Welfare*, Sage.

Gordon, L. (1994) *Pitied but Not Entitled: Single Mothers and the History of Welfare, 1890–1935*, The Free Press.

Handler, J. (1995) *The Poverty of Welfare Reform*, Yale University Press.

Harris, K. M. (1993) 'Work and Welfare among Single Mothers in Poverty', *American Journal of Sociology*, 99(2).

Jencks, C. (1998) *The Homeless*, Harvard University Press.

Katz, J. (1986) *In the Shadow of the Poorhouse: A Social History of Welfare in America*, Basic Books.

Katz, J. (1989) *The Undeserving Poor*, Pantheon.

Koven, S. and Michel, S. (eds) (1993) *Mothers of a New World: Maternalist Politics and the Origins of Welfare States*, Routledge.

Marris, P. and Rein, M. (1967) *Dilemmas of Social Reform: Poverty and Community Action in the United States*, Routledge & Kegan Paul.

Massey, D. (1998) 'March of Folly: U.S. Immigration Policy after NAFTA', *The American Prospect*, March/April, pp. 22–3.

Meerpol, M. (1997) 'A Comment on the Wood–Magdoff vs. Cloward–Piven Debate', unpublished manuscript, Western New England College.

Melnick, R. S. (1998) 'The Unexpected Resilience of Means-Tested Programs', Paper prepared for delivery at the 1998 Annual Meeting of the American Political Science Association, 3–6 September.

Mink, G. (1991) 'The Lady and the Tramp: Gender and Race in the Formation of American Welfare', in L. Gordon (ed.), *op. cit.*

Mink, G. (1998) *Welfare's end*, Cornell University Press.

Murray, C. (1984) *Losing Ground: American Social Policy, 1950–80*, Basic Books.

OMB (1996) *Economic Report of the President, Office of Management and Budget*, US Government Office.

Patterson, J. T. (1981) *America's Struggle Against Poverty*, Harvard University Press.

Pierson, C. (1990) 'The Exceptional United States: First New Nation or Last Welfare State?', *Social Policy and Administration*, 24(3), pp. 168–98.

Piven, F. F. (1998) 'Welfare and Electoral Politics', in C. Y. H. Lo and M. Schwartz (eds), *Social Policy and the Conservative Agenda*, Blackwell.

Piven, F. F. and Cloward, R. (1993) *Regulating the Poor: The Functions of Public Welfare*, 2nd edn, Vintage Books.

Pollin, R. (1998) 'Living Wage, Live Action', *The Nation*, 23 November.

Quadagno, J. (1994) *The Color of Welfare: How Racism Undermined the War on Poverty*, Oxford University Press.

Saloma, J. S. (1984) *Ominous Politics: The New Conservative Labyrinth*, Hill & Wang.

Schuck, P. H. (1998) 'The Open Society', *New Republic*, 13 April.

Skocpol, T. (1992) *Protecting Soldiers and Mothers: The Political Origins of Social Security in the United States*, The Belknap Press of Harvard University Press.

Skocpol, T. (1997) *Boomerang: Health Care Reform and the Turn Against Government*, 2nd edn, W.W. Norton & Co.

Skocpol, T. and Ikenberry, J. (1983) 'The Political Formation of the Welfare State. An Historical and Comparative Perspective', in R. F. Tomasson (ed.), *Comparative Social Research*, 6, Jai Press.

Solow, R. (1998) *New Yorker Review*, 5 November.

Stacey, J. (1998) 'The Right Family Values', in C. Y. H. Lo and M. Schwartz (eds), *Social Policy and the Conservative Agenda*, Blackwell.

Staples, C. (1989) 'The Politics of Employment-based Insurance in the United States', *International Journal of Health Services*, 19(3).

Starr, P. (1982) *The Social Transformation of American Medicine*, Basic Books.

Stern, M. (1998) 'A Semi-Tough Policy on Illegal Workers,' *The Washington Post National Weekly Edition*, 13 July.

Tanner, M. (1996) *The End of Welfare: Fighting Poverty in the Civil Society*, The Cato Institute.

West, G. (1981) *The National Welfare Rights Movement: The Social Protest of Poor Women*, Praeger.

Wohl, S. (1984) *The Medical-Industrial Complex*, New York: Harmony Books.

CHAPTER 3

Canada: One Step Forward, Two Steps Back?

ERNIE S LIGHTMAN AND GRAHAM RICHES

Introduction

In the early 1900s, Wilfrid Laurier, the Prime Minister of Canada stated that 'the twentieth century belongs to Canada'. Few would have challenged him, for Canada had seemingly infinite natural resources in great demand in the United States, Europe and (in later years) the countries of the Pacific Rim; there was an endless supply of hard-working, white immigrants mainly from Central and Northern Europe, bringing with them traditions of self-help and social solidarity; railways had been laid to link the vast reaches of the country from one side of the continent to the other; and Canada was at peace with its only land-based neighbour, a relationship certain to grow closer with the passing years.

The century, as it evolved, did not prove Laurier entirely correct. Though the natural resources generated massive wealth for some, at the year 2000, Canada faces dramatically reduced demand for what it produces: world economies have substantially shifted from a resource base to an information and technology base, areas in which Canada has no particular comparative advantage; immigration through the century shifted to include many new arrivals from the Third World, resulting in racial problems previously unanticipated; aboriginal peoples (both First Nations and Inuit) neither assimilated into the mainstream nor died off, but instead remained in poverty and squalor, with average life expectancies of about 35 years, glaring testimonials to the worst excesses of capitalist exploitation; intimacy with the United States proved a mixed blessing, at best, as resources and jobs flowed south and cultural domination came north.

Social solidarity in Canada was increasingly replaced by a Darwinian individualism and belief in the unconstrained market. Since the early 1980s, charitable food banks have become the main response to growing hunger, particularly among children; women's rights have been seriously eroded through cuts to child care and equity programmes; and the winter of 1998–99 witnessed stinging declarations by the local councils in Toronto and several other cities that homelessness had become a 'national disaster'.

The twentieth century produced considerable aggregate economic well-being for Canada, but the equity – the distribution of the spoils of this growth – proved far less acceptable. A recent United Nations Report (UNDP, 1998, p. 186) ranked Canada first among 21 developed countries in terms of its Human Development Index (HDI) for 1995, but only tenth in terms of its Human Poverty Index (HPI). In other words, Canada was a great place to live, but not for the poor or marginalised! And the disparities between the have's and have-nots have clearly been widening in the face of radically neo-conservative governments in several provinces.

The most serious threat to Canada, however, does not emerge from the growing economic disparities between rich and poor. Rather, Canada's very existence as a country has come under fundamental challenge because of the separatist movement in the largely French-speaking province of Quebec. The most recent referendum on separation in Quebec voted against secession from Canada by the narrowest of margins (50.4 per cent to stay; 49.6 per cent to leave: among the French-speaking population there was a clear majority in favour of separation). Though the threat of separation by Quebec has been present at least since the first election of a separatist provincial government in 1976, the broader issue of conflict between the federal government and the provinces has been pervasive throughout Canada's history. To understand Canada, and the past and future of Canadian social welfare in particular, it is essential to plunge into the muddy waters of federalism, of federal–provincial agreements and conflicts, of shared and joint and exclusive responsibility for the delivery of various social programmes and of restricted and unlimited access to the tax base.

Overview

In framing the British North America Act (1867), the Fathers of Confederation in Canada, unlike the architects of the United States constitution a century earlier, opted for a highly centralised federal state. High on their agenda was the economic development of the vast country, and to attain this goal efficiently most powers would lodge at the central level. Thus the federal government was given unlimited powers of taxation, while the provinces were restricted to certain enumerated categories of 'direct' taxes; service-delivery responsibilities of the federal government were substantial (within the context of what a government was expected to do in 1867), while the provinces had much more limited tasks to perform.

Just as the passage of time, reinforced by court interpretations, reversed the original intentions for the American federal system, so too a series of early Canadian Supreme Court decisions headed it in the direction of a highly decentralised federal state. This resulted in provinces having exclusive jurisdiction (formally at least) over the social policy arena which barely existed in the early years of the century and which has shown exponential growth over the years.

However, there are significant differences between the provinces. The oil-rich province of Alberta, heavily influenced by immigration from the United States, manifests residual and market-based approaches to social welfare. Conversely, the neighbouring province of Saskatchewan, settled by European immigrants, has reflected social democratic ideals; Quebec's social policy prior to the 1960s was dominated by the Church whilst today the state is a significant force in health, income security and social services. Today Quebec has a very exciting programme of universal day care at a cost of C$5.00 a day while Ontario is busy shutting down all publicly and non-profit childcare in favour of for-profit services. And, in more recent years, the need to placate the separatist tendencies in Quebec (by showing how national and cultural aspirations of the French-speaking population could be satisfied whilst remaining in Canada) has led to what some today would suggest is the world's most decentralised but still functioning federal state.

Thus, there emerged over time the central, recurring and fundamental dilemma of social policy in Canada: the imbalance between fiscal capacity and responsibility for the delivery of services in a federal state. Today, social policy comprises the largest share of governmental fiscal responsibility in Canada: but the provinces lack the necessary tax base to pay the bills. The result has been a series of creative, often acrimonious, frustrating and seemingly permanent federal–provincial negotiations, leading to tax-sharing arrangements, shared-cost programmes and even constitutional amendments. The most recent of these ritual dances – labelled the 'Social Union' talks – was met with massive public indifference in 1999, as the federal and provincial governments attempted to disentangle their respective areas of in terms of both service delivery and fiscal capacity. While a full historical understanding of Canadian social welfare state would require a review of provincial, municipal and First Nations social programme developments, this chapter focuses principally on federal social policy. As such it is primarily concerned with developments in the field of income security (see Box 3.1) and health care (Box 3.2).

Esping-Andersen has located Canada within the cluster of liberal welfare state regimes, along with the United States and Australia, in contrast to the corporatist cluster comprising Austria, France, Germany and Italy, and the social democratic grouping of the Scandinavian countries (1990). This 'liberal' categorisation of Canada is in many ways correct. Yet, it is important to note that post-Second World War, at least until 1988 when the North American Free Trade Agreement (NAFTA) began to bind Canada and the USA more closely together, Canada's more collectivist social policies (such as family allowances, old-age security, medicare) set it apart from its more individualist and residual neighbour to the south. Indeed Lightman (1991) documents identifiable differences in attitudes to the welfare state between Canada and the USA, though he does express apprehension about whether these differences would be sustainable over time in a context of free trade between the two countries. In retrospect these concerns were well-founded.

Box 3.1   Income Security

(All federal schemes unless noted otherwise)

Early Development

Income maintenance developed with an employer-funded workers' compensation scheme in 1914 covering most of the paid labour force. In the 1940s, following the Beveridge model, insurance-based schemes were introduced, including:

- Unemployment insurance, funded jointly by employers and employees – frequent eligibility changes; replaced by Employment Insurance (see below);
- Family allowances (non-contributory) for all children, funded from general taxation;
- Old-age security pensions, also funded from general taxation.

High Tide (1960s)

Further developments included:

- Canada Pension Plan (1965), contributory premiums for all earners; pay-as-you-go replaced by fuller funding in 1998);
- Canada Assistance Plan (1966), basic public assistance, based on determination of need, funded by taxation jointly from federal and provincial governments;
- Guaranteed Income Supplement (1967), means-tested benefit for poor elderly, funded from general taxation.

A Period of Steady Cuts (1970s onwards)

- Child Tax Credit (1978) and Canada Child Tax Benefit (1998), for children in low-income families, funded from general taxation and delivered through tax system; CCTB for working poor only;
- Registered Retirement Savings Plans, for those with taxable income: pensions for higher earners, highly regressive;
- Employment Insurance, limited scheme, funded 60:40 between employers and employees;
- Canada Health and Social Transfer (1996) provides block funding to provinces.

Box 3.2 Health and Social Services

- These areas are constitutionally the responsibility of the provincial governments, though there is usually a federal role in funding and, at times, in setting Canada-wide standards for service delivery.
- Service delivery is a provincial responsibility though this can be devolved to municipalities, voluntary agencies or NGOs, and/or to the commercial (for-profit) sector.
- Variations across provinces in the sharing among government, voluntary and commercial sectors are substantial and cannot be readily summarised, except to note that the neo-conservative provinces (Alberta and, since 1995, Ontario) tend to rely most on the commercial sector; others use a mix; while in Quebec the state has traditionally assumed an active role, viewed as an agent of nation-building.

Education – a provincial responsibility with major federal financial support for post-secondary education and manpower training. Federal support was cut with the introduction of the Canada Health and Social Transfer (CHST) in 1996.

Health: Hospital Insurance – since 1954, this covers all (non-physician) insured health services in hospitals. Financing varies across provinces, usually based on general taxation revenues with some element of premiums in certain provinces.

Health: Physician Services – since 1966, all insured health services, including doctors, are covered in a universal health care programme for all residents, with no user fees or other charges at the point of use. Coverage is portable (from province to province) and administered by a public non-profit agency in each province. The definition of 'insured services' varies across provinces and there are differences in financing including premiums, payroll taxes and (primarily) general revenues.

Personal Social Services (family services; child care; youth services; home care) – also a provincial responsibility with federal financial support, often on a project or area basis. Substantial devolution to municipalities, NGOs, voluntary agencies and the commercial sector, which varies across provinces depending on factors such as ideology and local fiscal capacity. No summary data are available.

Housing – until the 1990s there was always a major federal role, primarily in the financing area. In the last number of years, Ottawa has vacated this area to the provinces. The result has been a dramatic increase in homelessness, Canada-wide, and in many provinces a complete end to the construction of co-op, non-profit and low-income housing.

(Continued)

(Box 3.2   Continued)

Immigration – this is an area of shared federal–provincial responsibility, though only Quebec has chosen to assume an active role as it seeks to ensure a large French-speaking population in that province.

First Nation Peoples – Inuit and status Indians hold a sovereign status and attempt to negotiate with the federal government as equals, as sovereign peoples with Aboriginal rights and treaties. They formally refuse to deal with provincial governments, though there is some involvement with the delivery of personal social services. Metis peoples also claim Aboriginal rights by virtue of their share in Indian Title.

The Early Years to 1945

In the years after Confederation, there was little role for government except to promote the economic development of the vast frontier. Social needs, when they were acknowledged, would be met by voluntary and charitable, often church-based, local organisations. Customs and excise duties were the main source of government revenue, and it was not until the First World War that the first personal income tax was introduced, a 'temporary, emergency measure', which, of course, was never removed. The first system of workers' compensation was introduced (1914 in Ontario) as an employer-funded and operated programme; employees were denied the common law right to sue for job-related injuries, but instead payments were allocated administratively.

The Great Depression hit Canada hard, as foreign markets for the natural resources (wheat, fish, minerals, wood and paper) largely disappeared. By the end of the 1930s, unemployment was so severe that a national unemployment insurance scheme became necessary. Only the federal government had the capacity (and the interest) to develop such a programme, but employment was deemed to be within provincial jurisdiction: the solution was to enact a formal constitutional amendment (which, at the time, had to be formally passed as a statute by the British Parliament), so that today unemployment insurance remains the only significant social programme exclusively within federal jurisdiction. The first Canadian unemployment insurance programme became law in 1940. This period reflected a limited role for the state and a primary reliance on the church and voluntary sector.

Postwar: The Influence of Keynes and Beveridge

As in the rest of the world, the Great Depression did not simply 'burn out' and end on its own. The onset of the Second World War gave policy-makers everywhere a clear example of how government spending could draw a country (or a world!) out of recession. The ideas of Keynes seemingly worked in practice, as unemployment disappeared almost overnight.

As the war began to wind down and Germany's defeat appeared inevitable, policy-makers in Canada began to fear for the postwar period. There was a concern that with the end of government spending on war-related matters, aggregate demand would decline and the country would slip back into recession. In 1943, the Report on Social Security in Canada (otherwise known as the Marsh Report after its author who had both worked with Beveridge and was a disciple of Keynes) was released and it represented, in modified form, Canada's own version of the Beveridge Report (Canada, 1943). While it was not as comprehensive as its British counterpart, it nevertheless firmly placed Canada in the Keynes–Beveridge tradition.

In part to ensure the adequacy of consumer demand in the postwar period, 1945 saw the introduction of Canada's Family Allowance (FA) programme, a universal non-taxable monthly payment to the mother for every child (to age 16). This was followed in 1952 by Old Age Security (OAS), a universal, non-taxable monthly payment to every senior over the age of 65 who met a residence (but not a citizenship) requirement. These two federal programmes, together with the Unemployment Insurance scheme and the National Housing Act of 1944, formed the foundation of Canada's welfare state.

Family Allowances

The family allowance programme was less important operationally than the OAS, as the monthly payments were small to begin with and were not increased regularly thereafter. The major importance of the programme was perhaps symbolic, in that it spoke to universality, social solidarity and the legitimacy of claims upon the state to assist in the costs of rearing children. In 1984, when Brian Mulroney led the Conservative Party in the federal election, he ran on a mildly anti-welfare platform, making great rhetorical statements about the waste involved when his personal banker received a government cheque each month. Women's groups, in particular, pointed out that the cheque was payable to the banker's wife, rather than the banker, and thus helped, in a modest way, to redress income and power imbalances within families. A later book, entitled *The Wealthy Banker's Wife* (McQuaig, 1993), documented in some detail the extent of financial benefits delivered to upper income groups in Canada through the tax system. It made the simple point that relatively few dollars every month directed to children were trivial alongside the other substantial advantages which a regressive tax system provided to the rich. When the Family Allowance programme was terminated by Mulroney in 1992, replaced by a means-tested child benefit, the maximum monthly payment per child was hardly enough to make a significant impact upon a family's living standard.

Old Age Security

In contrast to FA, OAS was built on the assumption that many seniors had
no personal savings or other sources of income, and that they would be completely financially dependent upon the monthly government cheque. The
amounts were more substantial than the Family Allowances and provided an
income that was almost sufficient to live on. There has always been considerable political support for this programme: though its net benefit was reduced
in later years by making payments taxable, a major government initiative fundamentally to revamp the programme was suddenly abandoned in 1998
when it was clear that public support was not there. The proposals were
badly designed, in that the targeting to the poor came at the expense of the
middle class and the benefits were to be based on family, rather than individual, incomes, thereby reinforcing woman's traditional financial dependence
upon the male earner. But, arguably, the OAS programme was also seen as
important in its own right, with many seniors arguing the case for social
rights and entitlements. The postwar years witnessed an increasing role for
the state, with heavy reliance on the voluntary sector.

1965–73: High Points of Welfare State Development

Canada reached the high point in its welfare state development during the
1960s. Three important pieces of legislation, within a two-year period,
formed the reference point against which all subsequent retrenchments may
be assessed. Except only for an expansion of the unemployment insurance
scheme in 1971, virtually all social policy activity since 1973 has consisted of
cutting benefits, restricting entitlements and narrowing the boundaries of the
public sector.

Canada Pension Plan

The Canada Pension Plan (CPP, 1965), the Canada Assistance Plan (CAP,
1966) and Medicare (1966) were the three landmark programmes of the federal government. CPP, whose introduction was strenuously opposed by private insurance lobbies, was a contributory (employer and employee equally)
earnings-related, occupationally-based pension scheme for those in the paid
workforce. The ceiling for maximum contribution was reached at a relatively
low level of earnings, which meant that the greatest benefit was derived by
the lower middle classes. The programme included a disability pension
(Canada's only system of publicly-administered disability insurance), child
and survivor benefits and a small death benefit.

   Because the government wished the initial benefits to be quickly available,
CPP was largely funded on a pay-as-you-go scheme, in which premiums are

credited to general government revenues and current benefits are paid from the same source. This approach stands in contrast to building a fund, as is done with private insurance: Quebec, which chose to operate its own parallel Quebec Pension Plan, used the funded approach which today has yielded massive revenues, invested for public social purposes.

It should be noted that, in 1967, the Guaranteed Income Supplement (GIS) was introduced as an add-on to OAS for those seniors who had not paid into the CPP scheme and who lacked private resources. The GIS was means-tested and based on family rather than individual income; this typically disadvantaged women as their independent access to financial support was replaced with a dependence on the income of the male wage-earner in the household. Though the importance of the ideological shift in moving from the universal entitlements of the OAS to the Poor Law tradition embedded in the GIS should not be underestimated, the two programmes together have largely served their intended purpose. Today, serious poverty among seniors is relatively rare in Canada, compared to most developed countries.

However, a crisis has now emerged with respect to anticipated future payments out of CPP, resulting from a major demographic bulge as the postwar 'baby boomers' approach retirement. The numbers expected to claim CPP in the early years of the next century would place a massive financial burden on a decreasing labour force, which would have to pay for the benefits out of current taxation. The year 1999 saw a major increase in CPP premiums, and further options now being considered include raising more money (for example through further increases in premiums or raising the ceiling on covered earnings) or decreasing future payouts (by decreasing payments or by delaying the age of retirement, both of which are probably politically unacceptable). Some have even called for the abolition of CPP and its replacement by compulsory, tax-supported private savings schemes in which people would have greater control over the investment possibilities for their 'own' contributions.

Canada Assistance Plan

The second Act, the Canada Assistance Plan (CAP) must surely stand as one of the most progressive pieces of social legislation in Canadian history and a prime example of cooperative federalism. CAP constituted the basic public assistance programme, the final and ultimate safety net, and also provided federal funding to support the development of provincial personal social services, including child welfare. Ottawa, because it wished to act in this area, offered to cost-share with the provinces provided they met certain basic conditions (set by Ottawa). Federal government would pay 50 per cent of all eligible provincial expenditures on public relief, without absolute limit. These national standards (as they became known) included eligibility for assistance based solely upon a determination of need; the right to income in any province without a minimum residence requirement; and the right to appeal. The provinces were given considerable latitude in assessing whether an individual was, in fact, 'in need', but once this condition was satisfied no further barriers could be imposed upon the receipt of benefits. This meant, in practice, that receipt of public assistance could not be conditional upon the performance of any task (such as workfare or enrolment in a training programme). The right to benefit was absolute and unconditional. In practice, however, provinces used their discretion to determine whether an individual was 'in need' as a way of separating the deserving from the undeserving claimants and the adequacy of provincial welfare benefits have remained a contentious issue. They have always fallen well below Statistics Canada's low income cut-offs ('poverty lines').

Almost immediately upon its enactment, CAP became a source of controversy. Critics on the right attacked its allegedly generous eligibility terms, arguing for a tougher and more punitive American-style welfare programme. Far more significant, however, was the opposition to CAP from within the federal bureaucracy. Senior Department of Finance officials did not like the open-ended federal financial obligation: for planning purposes, it was difficult to prepare the annual federal budget without knowing the final total obligation for CAP until after the end of the fiscal year when the provincial bills were submitted for reimbursement. (Federal scrutiny of eligible provincial expenditure was also weak, or perhaps non-existent, from an auditing perspective.) Thus, virtually from the first day, the Finance Department began its quest to eliminate CAP, a task made more difficult by the belief that though CAP was a piece of federal legislation, it could only be altered with the unanimous consent of all provinces. While CAP was under constant scrutiny, it survived relatively unscathed until 1991 when, as part of a federal expenditure control programme and at a time of high unemployment resulting in great demands on CAP, Ottawa unilaterally imposed an absolute ceiling on the dollars it would contribute in the three wealthier provinces of Ontario, British Columbia and Alberta. In these three settings, the federal contribution dropped well below the 50 per cent level specified in CAP – to 31.8 per cent in Ontario in 1991–92 (Graham and Lightman, 1992). Court action determined that the federal government had the unilateral right to alter its own legislation and that there was in fact no legal obligation to secure provincial approval.

In 1996, the Department of Finance finally got its way when CAP was abolished and replaced by per capita, essentially unconditional, grants to the provinces as part of a major restructuring of federal–provincial fiscal relations. The end of the conditions for federal payment to CAP meant the provinces were now free to 'experiment' with American-style welfare reform and new ways to deliver public assistance. While Alberta and Saskatchewan had experimented with workfare – work as a condition of receiving assistance – by the late 1990s, such programmes became established across the country. There is no evidence that workfare actually created jobs or even improved employability on a wide scale, but rather the programme served a largely symbolic purpose, a punitive and inefficient exercise carried out on the backs of the poor (Shragge, 1997).

Medicare

The real jewel in the social policy crown of the 1960s was Medicare, involving a uniquely Canadian approach towards ensuring health care for all. Though many Canadian social programmes were built upon early British experiences, the NHS model was deemed unacceptable for Canada, in part because of the even greater political power of the medical profession and its linkages with the more extreme US medical lobbies. The Canadian story began in 1954 when hospital health care was provided without user charge. Because virtually all hospitals were publicly-owned and operated on a not-for-profit basis, there was little organised opposition to the early moves – particularly as physicians continued to be paid on a fee-for-service basis and their perks were not touched. By the 1960s, however, it was clear that free (at the point of use) health care in hospitals induced people to use that high-cost mode of service provision compared to less costly alternatives in the community (such as visiting a doctor's office).

In 1962, in the face of a doctors' strike, Saskatchewan introduced Canada's, indeed North America's, first medical insurance scheme. The scheme proved successful and the Royal Commission on Health Services Report (Canada, 1964) led to the introduction in 1966 of Medicare across the country. For jurisdictional reasons, Ottawa's role was limited to sharing costs with the provinces, though in this case there were five key principles to be honoured in order to secure federal monies: universal access; public administration; no user fees; portability; and comprehensive coverage. While medicare since its inception has enjoyed considerable public support, there have been continuing pressures favouring privatisation. In 1984 the Canada Health Act was introduced with the intent of safeguarding medicare from the threat of user fees/extra-billing. More recently, since 1995, medicare has again come under serious attack largely because of federal and provincial underfunding. However, Ottawa has consistently used its cost-sharing powers to withhold payments from provinces that were not in compliance with the five principles of medicare. In the end, the provinces inevitably fall into line.

Unemployment Insurance Expansion

By 1970, it was clear that many Canadians still fell through gaps in the income security net, but that substantial expansion of CAP was neither feasible nor desirable. As a result, the Minister responsible for Unemployment Insurance (UI) developed a major expansion of that programme: generous maternity benefits were introduced and, perhaps more importantly, seasonal benefits were introduced: many industries in Canada have very short seasonal work periods through the year. Fishing in the Atlantic region, for example, can occur for as few as 10 or 12 weeks (due to the hostile climate), and there are few alternative sources of regional employment for the rest of the year. Logging in many areas is subject to similar seasonal limitations. The 1971 UI amendments drastically reduced the number of weeks of work required to qualify to as few as 12, depending on the regional unemployment rate. The result was a famous 12/40 scheme, in which some people contributed to UI for 12 weeks and drew benefits for the remaining 40. In effect, whatever actuarial or insurance base UI may originally have had, was replaced with an income redistribution focus in which the wealthier provinces transferred funds (through UI premiums) to poorer provinces (where benefits dramatically exceeded contributions). The 1965–73 period proved to be that of maximum state involvement, with a more limited role for the voluntary and private sectors, especially in health care.

Cutting Back: The Arab Oil Embargo and After

Canada's welfare state was at its most fully developed during that period to 1973. Since then, it has been a story of continuing cutbacks and a slow decline from institutional to residual arrangements. Though Canada was at least self-sufficient in oil, on a net basis, prices were those of the world markets, set by the multinational companies. Thus Canada was fully affected by the huge increases in world oil prices. Many social benefits and other government spending were indexed to the rate of inflation, and thus overall nominal public sector spending rose dramatically in a short period of time. Revenues, however, did not increase commensurately, as this was the era in which Ottawa discovered the beauty of tax expenditure. Exemptions, deductions, credits and other measures to reduce tax liability began to proliferate through personal and corporate tax systems: through them government was able to target tax relief very specifically without the visibility associated with direct government spending. As a result, tax revenues lagged behind spending, and substantial deficits began to accumulate, steadily increasing the total public debt.

A major review of the social services was begun in the early 1970s, a process that involved extensive consultation with stakeholders. However, in 1976, the election of an avowedly separatist government in Quebec threw all the planning into disarray. Prime Minister Trudeau, an implacable foe of the provincial government, was determined to show Quebec that their national aspirations could be met within a decentralised Canadian federal state. As a result, the social service review was aborted and, in 1978, Established Programs Financing (EPF) was put forward as Ottawa's answer to separatism. This Act combined all federal contributions in three areas of hospital care, medicare and post-secondary education into one lump sum block grant to each province, to be given annually with an automatic escalator provision based on factors such as population change. There were few conditions attached to the use of the funds (except continuing adherence to the principles of medicare and a requirement that the funds be spent in the three designated areas). In this way, provinces were given considerable discretion over the allocation of federal (and provincial) monies and were thereby encouraged to determine their own priorities.

There was fear, however, within the social policy community of a possible displacement effect by the provinces, through which the EPF dollars would be spent in the designated areas, but other provincial discretionary money would be reallocated away to other areas (such as building highways): there was no federal requirement that total provincial spending in the three areas would be required to increase, or even remain constant.

Refundable Child Tax Credit

An interesting innovation occurred in 1978 when Ottawa decided to use the personal income tax system to distribute child benefits. The refundable child tax credit (RCTC) involved a selective cash payment steeply tapered so benefits went to the very poor, and the cut-off point was relatively low on the income scale. Eligibility was based on taxable income and those persons who paid no income tax (due to low income) would receive a cash refund from the federal government. Payments were monthly, based on the previous year's income-tax return, and the programme met with general approval: though it was highly selective, the means-testing was through the tax return (and was thus impersonal and non-stigmatising) and the targeting seemed to work in that the desired population group actually appeared to receive the benefits.

The election of 1984 led to Brian Mulroney becoming Prime Minister. His attacks on universality, noted earlier, resonated well with the public, and federal Department of Finance officials began a long march to reduce spending and the deficit, and also to remove Ottawa from any role as a direct provider of social services. Benefits were reduced, in real terms, through complex procedures such as partial deindexation (benefits no longer rising in line with inflation). These approaches, buried in fiscal jargon, were of little interest to the broader public, but did result in significant decreases in the purchasing power of benefits. Mulroney's attempts to reduce the deficit appeared to contain more rhetoric than substance, though whatever strides were made were largely on the backs of the poor, described as 'social policy by stealth' Battle (1996).

A Fuller Assault: The Mid-1990s

Talk of the importance of deficit reduction continued through the Mulroney years, but it was not until the Liberals returned to power 1993 that action began in earnest. Reducing the federal deficit to zero was deemed essential to retain the confidence of the business community, domestically and abroad. This was to be achieved through a fundamental restructuring, downsizing and downloading of federal social policy responsibilities.

In 1996, CAP was terminated; with it went the conditions for federal cost-sharing and national welfare standards. Ottawa's payments to the provinces for CAP were combined with the EPF monies to produce a single lump sum annually, known as the Canada Health and Social Transfer (CHST). There were virtually no federal restrictions on the use of this money, except for continuing adherence to medicare principles. However, in the process of combining the various payments, Ottawa also moved to reduce its total fiscal contributions, so that CHST actually entailed a very substantial decrease of $6 billion in federal transfers to the provinces. In addition, the provinces were now free to cut back on welfare (formerly delivered through CAP and subject to a variety of conditions) and to introduce programmes such as workfare for claimants. Some of the provinces, such as wealthy Ontario, now ruled by a neo-conservative government, used the occasion of federal cuts to social programmes to introduce additional cuts. At the time it was feared that battles for funding among the areas covered by the CHST would advantage the politically powerful (medicare and the doctors' lobbies) at the expense of the weaker and less popular areas (assistance for the poor) (Torjman and Battle, 1995).

The federal government also terminated its extensive involvement in social housing. Ontario followed suit by also withdrawing and downloading all responsibility for social housing to the municipalities which were clearly incapable of responding given their limited tax bases. Major changes also occurred to the unemployment insurance programme in 1997. Now renamed Employment Insurance (EI), benefit levels were cut modestly, and eligibility tightened dramatically. Whereas in the early 1990s over 80 per cent of unemployed persons received benefits from UI, after the reforms less than one-third of the same population qualified for EI. For many years earlier, premiums had increased regularly, and the UI fund built up a surplus far in excess of what might be required in times of serious recession: each year the Finance Minister made a bookkeeping transfer of the UI surplus into general revenues, and so was able to use the money to reduce the deficit. The struggle was ultimately successful, and the last federal budget of the century was the first in many years to produce a budgetary surplus, thanks in part to the appropriation of the UI/EI surpluses over many years.

The Long Road Back: Towards the New Century

Three new federal initiatives emerged in the last years of the twentieth century, all in response to the extreme cuts earlier imposed through the CHST.

Millennium Scholarship Fund

As part of a millennium effort to improve access to higher education in Canada, the Prime Minister announced substantial new funding for a federal scholarship fund. The details were consciously vague, but the scheme was presented in a context of human capital investment for the future. Though the provinces had been informed of the plan in advance, they were not were really consulted at this intrusion into their constitutional domain, and argued that they wanted to control the money, to direct as they saw fit within the realm of higher education. The scholarship fund was never presented as part of a comprehensive strategic government review of Canadian higher education funding, but was widely seen as simply a federal attempt to solve a problem by throwing money at it. The government soon went on to new issues, believing that it had now 'solved' a major problem of inadequate investment in human capital in Canada.

Canada Child Tax Credit (CCTC)

In 1998, a Canada Child Tax Credit (CCTC) was introduced, the first substantial new social programme in over a decade. The federal programme, developed in conjunction with the provinces, was targeted specifically to the working, rather than the welfare poor. It was designed to replace a variety of previous federal child-focused initiatives. As with the previous RCTC, eligibility was to be determined and payments to be delivered through the income tax system. Maximum payments were to go to the very poor, with a tapered reduction as earned income increased. Although payments were to be made to all low-income households, provinces were permitted to reduce welfare payments, dollar for dollar, provided the funds would be reinvested in child-focused programmes such as expanded child care; the working poor, by contrast, would suffer no income reductions and would be better off as a result of the programme. The payment amounts were sufficiently large that within a few years it was anticipated that most poor children in Canada would be supported through the CCTC and would be removed from the welfare rolls. The two major criticisms of the programme were that there was no benefit for families on welfare (who, arguably, needed the most help), and there were no meaningful measures to ensure appropriate provincial reinvestment of the funds clawed back from those on welfare.

Health Care

Federal discussions concerning a national pharmacare plan (Canadian prescription drug prices being among the highest in the world) and a coherent system of home care, in the face of hospital and institutional closures and an aging population, were brought forward. The provinces wanted no part of these schemes, but instead wanted the money back which had been removed with the introduction of the CHST. Ottawa, for its part, was ready to invest in health care out of its newly-discovered surplus, but did not trust the provinces – particularly extreme neo-conservative Alberta and Ontario – to spend the money 'appropriately'. There followed an extremely complex set of negotiations which were under pressure to deliver, as inadequate access to health care was now ranked by polls as Canadians' top concern, and the leading contenders for the succession to the prime ministership all felt the need to carve out social agendas.

First Nations

Crucial to any understanding of the development of the Canadian welfare state must be the consequences of social policy for Aboriginal peoples. Whilst the Royal proclamation by the Crown in 1763 recognised Aboriginal title to land in British North America not ceded to or purchased by the Crown (Vedan and Tester, 1998), Aboriginal peoples in Canada continue to struggle for the right to govern themselves, and to control social programmes and child welfare. The Indian Act of 1876 established a separate authority for services to native peoples based on treaty obligations incurred by the Crown and, subsequently, on the Indian Act itself (Armitage, 1996). In 1951 the Act was amended with the result that provincial laws of general application such as child welfare applied to Indian living on reserves (*ibid.*). This did not lead to common standards and well-provided services but to 'an incredible disparity in the quality of child welfare programs available to Status Indians from one province to another' resulting in unequal treatment of Indian children across Canada (Johnston, quoted in Armitage, 1996, p. 123). As First Nations communities seek control of their own child welfare arrangements, they now have to contend with both federal and provincial jurisdictional issues.

In 1996, the Report of the Royal Commission on Aboriginal Peoples provided a comprehensive analysis of the profound issues confronting Aboriginal peoples. The federal government offered a Statement of Reconciliation in 1998 and a $350 million healing fund to be administered by Aboriginal peoples (Vedan and Tester, 1998). It seems doubtful whether such gestures can atone for past wrongs or hold out much promise for significant change.

Future Prospects: Government as Dilettante

It is difficult to look to the future with much optimism about the prospects for Canadian social policy. Universality is seriously wounded, if not dead, and residual welfarism rules. The rise and institutionalisation of food banks are at once symptoms of the breakdown of the social safety net (in terms of the gaping holes left by the changes made to unemployment insurance and public assistance) and symbols of this new residualism and lack of regard for the citizenship rights of the poor and vulnerable, many of whom are women and children (Riches, 1997). Hunger, homelessness, child poverty, unemployment, and the continuing exclusion of First Nations peoples, crowd the social policy agenda.

There is a deep irony in all of this given the introduction of the Charter of Rights and Freedoms in 1982 and the ratification by Canada over the years of a number of United Nations human rights conventions. These include the International Convenant on Economic, Social and Cultural Rights (1976) and the International Covention on the Rights of the Child (1991) which commits governments, internationally and domestically, to respect, protect and fulfil their obligations to meet basic human needs and assert the rights of their peoples. However, the fact is that over the past two decades the social policy landscape in Canada is littered with cutbacks and denials of entitlements. It has been a case of one step forward, two steps back.

Through the 1990s, the justification for the cuts was based on economic imperatives, the need to reduce the debt and balance the budget; by 1998 the federal budget acknowledged the end of deficits and the arrival of an era of surpluses. This then loosened the gates on the more overtly ideological debates about the future of social policy in Canada, debates that are certain to continue well into the future. Some have argued that surpluses should be directed towards reducing the aggregate debt, a rather pointless exercise given that it is really only the carrying costs on the debt which are relevant for policy purposes (Mendelson, 1998). The more crucial debates are between the desirability of tax reductions, which will inevitably be regressive in impact, and social reinvestment of the surpluses to rebuild the infrastructure – both human and physical capital – which were decimated in the last decades.

But the debate may well be an uneven struggle: Of the five parties currently in the House of Commons, none is prepared unambiguously to argue the case for social investment, and two parties at least are reaching for the far right end of the political continuum. Over a decade of free trade with the United States (since 1988) has not produced clear economic gains to the majority of the population, but the greater intimacy has led to increased cultural domination and hegemony: classic American values of extreme individualism and reliance upon voluntary charities combined with the unpaid labour of women in the home are now promoted as legitimate and appropriate paths to the future in Canada. The British welfare state legacy is fading fast, if it has not already disappeared. Homogeneity in the message of the media is virtually complete with quasi-monopolistic control of the newspaper industry and little to choose among the radio and television options.

The transition in Canada from a modest welfare state to a more market-oriented society occurred quickly and with little debate. The shift has largely been from government and well-funded non-government organisations

directly to the for-profit world, private charity and the exploitation of
women. Canada was in a fortunate position, potentially, and had the opportunity to learn from the mistakes made abroad. Britain's experience with
Thatcher clearly showed that ideological purity is not enough to meet basic
human needs, and that the ideology of the right is perhaps more frightening
than that of the left, given that the right, in power, actually attempts to
implement its ideology. The end of the Thatcher years left a Britain that was
certainly wealthier overall, but it was also a Britain that was deeply unequal in
access to income and wealth, starved of compassion and institutional help for
the vulnerable.

While Mulroney engineered the shift to the right in Canada, it was not
really until Thatcher and indeed Reagan and Bush in the United States had
left office that Canada began its plunge to the abyss of the market. So history
is perhaps doomed to repeat itself, and Canada seems fated to follow the neo-
conservative path, knowing full well the direction in which it leads. The
Americanisation of Canada's welfare state seems increasingly assured confirm-
ing Esping-Andersen's view that Canada is firmly situated within the liberal
welfare-state regime. The prospects for a middle way as typified by Blair,
Jospin and Schroeder, let alone the Scandinavian examples, which perhaps
offer more caring and less punitive models for Canada to follow, seem
unlikely. The highly decentralised nature of the Canadian federation, and by
implication its welfare state, is a complicating factor, as is the continuing
threat of Quebec separation. In other words the recurring crisis of federalism
makes it difficult to predict the future. However, what is clear is that if the
twentieth century did not exactly belong to Canada it seems highly improba-
ble that Canadian social welfare will provide a beacon for its citizens and the
international community in the twenty-first century.

References

Armitage, A. (1996) *Social Welfare in Canada Revisited*, 3rd edn, Oxford University
    Press.
Badgely, R. and Wolfe, S. (1967) *Doctors' Strike*, Atherton Press.
Battle, K. and Torjman, S. (1996) 'Desperately Seeking Substance: A Commentary on
    the Social Security Review', in J. Pulkingham and G. Ternowetsky (eds), *Remaking
    Canadian Social Policy*, Fernwood.
Canada (1943) *House of Commons Advisory Committee on Post-war Reconstruction*,
    (Marsh Report).
Canada (1964) *Royal Commission on the Health Services*, Queen's Printer.
Esping-Andersen, G., (1990) *The Three Worlds of Welfare Capitalism*, Polity Press.
Graham, B. and Lightman, E. (1992) 'The Crunch: Financing Ontario's Social
    Programs', in T. Hunsley (ed.), *Social Policy in the Global Economy*, Queen's
    University, Ontario, School of Policy Studies.
Guest, D. (1997) *The Emergence of Social Security in Canada*, 3rd edn, University of
    British Columbia Press.

Lightman, E. (1991) 'Support for Social Welfare in Canada and the United States', *Canadian Review of Social Policy*, 28, autumn, pp. 9–27.

McQuaig, L. (1993) *The Wealthy Banker's Wife*, Penguin.

Mendelson, M. (1998) *To Pay or Not to Pay: Should the Federal Government 'Pay Down' Its Debt?*, Caledon Institute of Social Policy.

Riches, G. (ed.) (1997) *First World Hunger: Food Security and Welfare Politics*, Macmillan.

Shragge, E. (1997) *Workfare: Ideology for a New Under-Class*, Garamond.

Torjman, S. and Battle, K. (1995) *The Dangers of Block Funding*, Caledon Institute of Social Policy.

United Nations Development Programme (UNDP) (1998) *Human Development Report 1998*, Oxford University Press.

Vedan, R. and Tester, F. (1998) 'Resistance and Renewal: Social Programs and Aboriginal people', in N. Pollack with R. Vedan and F. Tester, *Critical Choices, Turbulent Times*, School of Social Work: University of British Columbia.

CHAPTER 4

Australia: The Transformation of the Wage-Earners' Welfare State

LOIS BRYSON

Overview

The Commonwealth of Australia is a federation dating from 1901, in which power is distributed between a national, six State (formerly colonies) and two Territory governments, and a third tier, local government. Early in the twentieth century, in a climate of optimism and social experimentation, the Commonwealth government laid a promising foundation for the national welfare state. A century later, by conventional criteria, that promise has not been fulfilled. Compared with other OECD countries, Australia devotes a relatively small proportion of national income to social expenditure. Its income security provisions are means-tested and, though relatively widely available, provide an income replacement rate of only around 25 per cent of average weekly earnings.

Australia has been grouped, with the UK, the USA, Canada and New Zealand as a 'liberal welfare state' (Esping-Anderson, 1990). Of these countries, Australia most closely resembles New Zealand, though Australia's welfare state has mostly been less generous and, partly because of the affects of a more complex federal governmental structure, often lagged behind (see Chapter 5). Historically, the two countries have shared a distinctive configuration of occupational and social welfare, which led Castles (1985) to challenge their classification as 'liberal' welfare states. He claims they represent an antipodean variant, a 'wage-earner's welfare state', on the basis of a raft of policies. These include: a progressive taxation system; the regulation of employment, particularly the enforcement of a minimum 'living' family wage (for male workers: women only achieved formal equal pay in the 1970s); the encouragement of home ownership; the protection through tariffs of local industry in the interests of both business and workers; as well as basic income security and other social welfare measures. This policy framework Castles (1994) sees as having promoted relatively equal income distribution, contributed by selective provisions and non-contributory income security schemes.

Whatever its strengths, the 'wage-earners' welfare state' comprehensively failed to promote the interests of Aborigines and Torres Strait Islanders,

64

Australia's dispossessed indigenous peoples making up 2 per cent of the population of 19 million. Until the middle of the twentieth century the vast majority were excluded from both occupational and social welfare provisions and subjected to a separate oppressive 'welfare', or more accurately 'illfare' regime, the effects of which rendered them by far the most disadvantaged Australians (see Table 4.1). If we take account of the groups excluded, as well as the interests served, Castles' aphorism for Australia's welfare regime needs modification, as historically it was a white, male wage-earner's welfare state.

The neo-economic orthodoxy of recent decades (which in Australia tends to be called economic rationalism), challenges the very basis of the wage earners' welfare state, particularly non-market wage setting. Nonetheless, until 1996, with the election of the Howard Coalition (Liberal/National) government, the fundamental structure was not seriously threatened. It had, however, already been modified for economic reasons as well as reasons of social inclusion, by the previous Hawke/Keating-led Labour governments in power from 1983 to 1996. The Howard government, not constrained by traditional Labour concerns, sought radical reform of the economy, industrial relations, taxation and social welfare. Whilst many proposals were reminiscent of the Thatcher government in the United Kingdom, and both Labour and National governments in New Zealand in the 1980s and 1990s, there was not the same immediate policy redirection because of the lack of a majority in the upper house, the Senate. Overall, though, at the end of the twentieth century the 'wage-earners welfare state' was subject to considerable neoliberal pressure.

Table 4.1 Characteristics of Aboriginal and Torres Strait Islanders, 1996

	Aborigines and Torres Strait Islanders	Rest of Australian population
Per cent of total population	2.1	97.9
Median age	20.1	34.0
Life expectancy, female	61.7	81.1
Life expectancy, male	56.9	75.2
Per cent with post-school qualifications	11	31
Per cent Unemployed	23	9
Median weekly female income	$190	$224
Median male weekly income	$189	$145
Per cent Home owned/purchasing	31	71
Per cent of all in improvised housing	33	67
Per cent in dwellings of 10+ residents	7	0.14
Per cent of juvenile justice population	40	60
Per cent of imprisioned adults	19	81
outside urban areas	1 in 4	1 in 7

Source: Based on data from ABS and AIHW (1999), pp. 1–6.

Influences on the Australian Welfare State

As well as the dispossession of the indigenous peoples, the effects of which remain a major issue, British settlement of Australia as a penal colony from 1788 left many legacies. The colonisers' belief that they were creating a brave new egalitarian, but very much European, society was to find expression in racist policies which until the late 1960s prohibited immigrants of colour at the same time as it influenced the labourist policies which created the wage-earners' welfare state. There was considerable cross-class enthusiasm for interventionist government (Pember Reeves, [1902] 1969) and Beilharz, Considine and Watts (1992, p. 73) suggest Australia's administrative state represents the 'historic expression of the middle class interest in servicing and mediating between capital and labour'.

The British heritage of the majority of free settlers infused the nature of the markets, charitable organisations and informal support systems that the settlers brought from Britain, and that came to form the mixed economy of the welfare state. Often with government financial assistance and usually under religious auspices, charitable organisations quickly became important. By the middle of the nineteenth century they dominated social welfare activity, including that focused on Aborigines (Dickey, 1980). Later, local governments were established though they never achieved as extensive a role as in the United Kingdom.

British intellectuals made an influential contribution to Australian political debate and they continue to do so with the 'third way' much discussed in the late 1990s. Important nineteenth-century figures included Bentham and John Stuart Mill, and later the Fabian socialists. Discussions were stimulated by 'a large troupe of visiting social reformers', including the redoubtable Webbs (Kingston, 1988, p. 173). New Zealanders were also involved in Australian debates on government and social policy; they were concerned with similar issues and joining the federation was seriously considered (Pember Reeves, *op.cit.*). Beveridge's social reforms and Keynesian economics were influential from the 1940s, the latter expressed in a full-employment policy based on a national development strategy, including an expansive public housing programme. At the end of the twentieth century, as with other Anglo-American societies, it was neo-liberal economic theories initially from the USA (for example Friedman, 1962; Friedman and Friedman, 1979) which gained the ascendancy. Their influence was very much absorbed through international bodies such as the OECD, the International Monetary Fund, and world trade organisations as well as private organisations including credit rating agencies such as Moody's. By the late 1990s, a revival of interest in Keynesian economics was discernible among intellectuals though not within the senior ranks of government (Smyth and Cass, 1998)

The labour movement became a key influence at a critical stage of Australia's history. In the 1890s, after a series of unsuccessful strikes, labour parties were formed in the colonies, with a national party (to become the

Australian Labour Party – ALP) formed in 1896. The choice of a parliamentary road for labour politics quickly bore fruit. In New South Wales in 1891, labour candidates won 35 of the 141 seats in the colony's legislature and the world's first (brief) labour government was elected in Queensland in 1899 (Buckley and Wheelwright, 1988, p. 198). In the first decade after federation, there were two periods of Labour Party minority government at the national level, and Labour majority governments between 1910–13 and 1914–16. These were world firsts, the next being New Zealand Labour which did not come to power until 1938 and Sweden's Social Democratic Party which followed in 1940 (Castles, 1985, p. 18). Electoral success, itself dependent on the payment of parliamentarians and equal weighting for each vote, allowed a strong labourist influence on welfare state development (Beilharz, 1989). This labourist focus on achieving equality through occupational welfare and progressive taxation was, however, at the expense of support for those universal social measures typical of welfare states classified as 'social democratic' (Castles, 1994).

The Structure of the Welfare State: National and Regional Welfare

Australia was progressively settled as six independent self-governing colonies becoming, at federation in 1901, the States of New South Wales, Queensland, South Australia, Tasmania, Victoria and Western Australia. More recently the States have been joined by the two (Australian Capital and Northern) Territory governments. Though these Territories fall short of statehood, for most governmental purposes, including welfare, they play a similar role to the States.

As with other federations, including those of Canada and the USA, limited powers were originally accorded to the Commonwealth government. With respect to social welfare, the federal Constitution (Section 51: xxiii) granted the capacity to 'make laws ... with respect to ... invalid and old-age pensions', and because defence powers were also granted, veterans' welfare was covered as well. The Commonwealth gained power in cross-border industrial relations and a highly influential decision, the 1907 Harvester Judgement, established male workers' entitlement to a 'living' family wage (McCarthy, 1976). The balance of power changed significantly towards the Commonwealth after it gained power over income taxation during the Second World War, which allowed it to shape policy more effectively. Around the same time, the federal Constitution was amended to include all income security matters, though not until 1967 did it acquire constitutional power to legislate in respect of indigenous people.

At federation the State governments retained all powers not specifically ceded, including responsibility for indigenous peoples, regional industrial relations and all social welfare service delivery, including education, health, housing and community services. Because of their relative independence, history and the distinctive patterns of State and Territory politics, there is regional variation in welfare regimes. The degree to which regional independence can be asserted was illustrated by the Victorian Kennett (Liberal–National Coalition) government in the 1990s. It pursued a radical neo-liberal agenda taking privatisation, marketisation and contracting to a level unparalleled in Australia (Costar and Economou, 1999). Voters responded in 1999 when a Labor minority government came to power. This Victorian example indicates that in some circumstances, for some purposes, national and regional welfare regimes should be distinguished. However, because the Commonwealth influence ensures a considerable level of uniformity, the national welfare regime is the major focus of the discussion here.

A third level of government is formed by about 800 local governments, a number decreasing as amalgamations proceed as part of an economic restructuring agenda. Local government has traditionally provided services to property, with a largely discretionary role in the delivery of community services, such as child care and support services to the ill or frail aged, though where such developments have occurred it has usually been with Commonwealth funding. This was the case with child and community care services which were quite widely established in the 1980s and 1990s under a national Labour government.

A Mixed Economy of Welfare

The economy of Australian welfare is multi-layered, though most of this discussion is focused on governments. However employers, voluntary agencies, markets and community groups, as well as families and individuals, are all crucially implicated in the regime as well.

Employers have been intimately involved in the wage earners' welfare state through having to meet the wage rates and conditions of employment, as regulated by national and state industrial relations systems. Employer responsibility also includes the provision of workers' compensation insurance and, more recently, compulsory superannuation contributions for employees (see below, p. 72ff). Employers also have long had to provide short-term sickness coverage, with a statutory obligation to provide at least five sickness days per year on full pay (Castles, 1994). Discretionary provision of private retirement pensions, in Titmuss's (1974) view, a classic form of occupational welfare for more-highly-paid workers, has attracted taxation relief, and this system remains in place beside the modest compulsory superannuation scheme established in 1992. Private employers may also provide private health insurance and other occupational welfare benefits.

Markets are involved in the welfare regime at many points, from health and education, to housing and community services. The medical profession, for example, continues to largely operate on a fee-for-service basis, with the national health service reimbursing patients a 'standard' fee for different types of consultation. Doctors are free to charge more, except when the patient is a pensioner with full entitlements to health care (established via means-testing). As with the workers' compensation system and the compulsory superannuation scheme, private insurers also provide a system of private medical insurance, alongside the national health scheme, covering for example ancillary services such as dental, optical and physiotherapy, private hospital accommodation, and choice of doctor in public hospitals. In 1998 around 30 per cent of Australians were covered (ABS, 1999). The Coalition government aimed to increase the numbers through the introduction in 1999 of tax concessions for those who join, and a tax penalty for high-income earners who do not (Leeder, 1999, p. 28).

The market has always, also, been the major source of housing, even though home ownership is crucial for making feasible Australia's low-cost welfare state. From the 1950s to the late 1980s, when home-loan interest rates were deregulated, government control of interest rates assisted house purchase through low-interest long-term loans and other schemes, such as for first-home purchasers (Burke, 1998). Unlike in the United Kingdom and many European countries, however, interest on owner-occupied house repayments has never been tax deductible nor has imputed-rent ever been taxable. The private rental market became central to the welfare regime from 1987 as rental assistance for private housing, rather than public housing provision, became the major form of housing assistance (AIHW, 1997, p. 156).

The trend to rely on the market was also evident when eligibility for Childcare Assistance was extended to those using private childcare centres in 1991 (AIHA, 1997, p. 106). At the same time there was increased involvement of for-profit organisations in services and care for the aged, including residential services, where previously services were mostly provided by not-for-profit organisations. Markets have been of increasing importance in a wide range of service areas as direct government activity was progressively curtailed in favour of contracting goods and services.

Voluntary organisations make up what Shaver (1982) has termed the 'non-government state', another layer of Australia's mixed welfare economy. Her term neatly encapsulates the network of not-for-profit organisations, including classic religious organisations and charities collaborating with state organisations, often with government funding. Since soon after white settlement, voluntary organisations have played a central role in service provision. Among other areas, they are involved in health and social services, particularly emergency relief. As the state pulled back from the direct delivery of services in the 1980s and 1990s, government funding was increasingly directed to the more traditional non-government organisations as well as to the market, with government funding dominating the incomes of the major charitable organisations (ABS, 1997, p. 125). In 1994–95, the hours worked by volunteers in the welfare/community services sector constituted about 43 per cent of the total of paid hours worked in the sector (AIHW, 1997, p. 38).

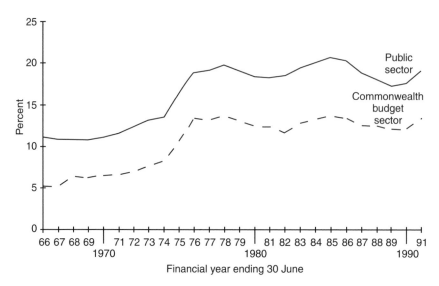

Figure 4.1   Social outlays as a percentage of GDP

Notes: Social outlays include education, health social security and welfare.

Source: Saunders, *Welfare and Equality*, 1994, p. 54. Reproduced with the permission of Cambridge University Press.

A more recent addition to the non-government welfare state structure is a spectrum of representative bodies stemming from Whitlam Labour government (1972–75) reforms. These provided greater formal recognition and financial support for previously muted groups, including Aboriginals and Torres Strait Islanders, women, Australia's many linguistic and cultural groups, as well as functionally-organised 'self-help' consumer groups. After 1996, the Howard Coalition government showed less enthusiasm for such a representative approach but did not entirely abandon such funding.

The final layer of support on which welfare regimes have always rested is informal care, mostly from families and households. It is ironic that this level of welfare provision has received increased recognition over recent years, propelled at least partly by an intention, not highly successful, to reduce the size of government (see Figure 4.1). This focus led to the establishment of support for carers, including carer's pensions and respite care programmes. There is also now routine statistical recognition of the household sector's extensive contribution to welfare services, this being estimated to be of the value of A$16.6 billion in 1995–96, compared with a total monetary expenditure of A$8.9 billion (AIHW, 1997, p. 10).

The Indigenous 'Welfare' Regime

The process of dispossession left Aborigines and Torres Strait Islanders marginalised and subject to a separate, indigenous 'welfare' regime. The colonial government 'veered from policies of protection to the mounting of punitive expeditions and the declaration of martial law' (Reynolds, 1996, p. 128). Early sporadic attempts were made by the churches, with government support, to provide educational opportunities, but Aboriginal people were mostly not attracted to the lifestyle and employment situation offered by the colonisers, though they did show an interest in the more culturally compatible tracking and pastoral work (Markus, 1994). The uniqueness of their situation was first officially recognised in 1838 when Victoria employed 'protectors', charged with the task of watching over Aboriginal interests, protecting their rights and gently leading them towards assimilation (*ibid.* pp. 23–5). The scheme was abandoned within ten years because of costs and unpopularity with local settlers.

Versions of 'protective' policies were to become the way in which State governments dealt with the majority of Aboriginal people, on the understanding that the population would soon die out. These policies involved forced relocation to reserves, with travel requiring a pass signed by administrators who were often brutal and racist. Some defrauded those under their 'protection' of their entitlements (Stevens, 1984). Even if personnel were benign, this apartheid system failed disastrously, and in the 1950s the dominant policy was replaced by one of assimilation. Indigenous Australians became eligible for pensions and benefits in 1959 unless 'nomadic or primitive', a proviso which was removed in 1966 (Markus, 1994, p. 177).

A 'protective' policy of many decades forcibly removed children who had one white parent from their Aboriginal families to be raised in children's homes, usually church-sponsored, or adopted by white families. Thousands of children were swept into this net mostly with devastating consequences for both the children and their families. This was only acknowledged publicly in the 1990s through an inquiry into the 'stolen generations' (Wilson, 1997). Although its conclusions were contested, the report strengthened a movement to achieve formal reconciliation between Aboriginal and non-Aboriginal Australians; Prime Minister Howard, however, refused to make a formal government apology.

In the 1970s, under international pressure and from an increasingly activist Aboriginal population, the assimilation policy too was modified. As a top-level meeting of State, Commonwealth and Territory ministers expressed it: 'the policy of assimilation seeks that all persons of Aboriginal descent will choose to [formerly be 'expected to'] attain a similar manner and standard of living to that of other Australians' (Reynolds, 1996, p. 134). Aborigines became even more publicly involved in their own affairs, though Aboriginal activism has a long history. An Aboriginal Tent Embassy remained outside the Commonwealth Parliament for many months and there were 'freedom rides' around the country. From the 1970s, Aboriginal organisations took a leading welfare role by developing Aboriginal-controlled services, including legal, health and child-care services.

The relationship between the people and the land is a special aspect of indigenous culture and dispossession is a fundamental issue for indigenous welfare. Despite this, and the British government's formal acceptance of Aboriginal prior land-ownership 12,000 miles away, settlers finessed a fiction that the land was not originally owned but empty (*terra nullius*). The 1970s Whitlam Labour government became the first government to tackle the issue of land rights, in the Northern Territory, because the Commonwealth had constitutional power to legislate for the Territories but not for the States. South Australia, New South Wales and Queensland followed suit and a considerable amount of crown land was returned. Finally the fiction of *terra nullius* was officially overturned by the High Court of Australia in the 1992 Mabo case (Reynolds, 1996). This decision establishes Aboriginals' and Torres Strait Islanders' continuing ownership rights where they have not been extinguished by the crown and do not conflict with the rights of other owners or leaseholders. Although the matter remains contested, a settlement which may serve something of the function of the New Zealand Treaty of Waitangi, on which to rest indigenous citizenship, is closer than at any time in the last two centuries.

The legacy of dispossession and protective policies remains the most urgent single issue for the Australian welfare state. Many Aborigines and Torres Strait Islanders live in conditions as bad as poor families in the poorest countries (see Table 4.1). The effects of marginalisation are evident in poverty, poor housing, high levels of suicides, deaths in custody, violence, ill-health and a life expectancy around 20 years less than non-indigenous Australians. Australia has been taken to task by international human-rights organisations for this grim situation and there are now some signs of change. For example, there is a concerted effort in the health field and special support schemes to encourage Aboriginal children to remain at school and to support them through tertiary education. These policies, while still inadequate, have made some impression. For example Aboriginal and Torres Strait Islander enrolments in universities reached half the rate they should be on a population basis, an important advance on earlier times.

Universal or Selective?

Australia mainly eschewed universal welfare policies and from the national inception in 1908 of income security, provisions (age and invalid pensions) have been selective. In the 1920s/1930s a universal insurance-based system with contributions from workers and employers was discussed, culminating in the passing of the National Insurance Act 1938. However, it was never implemented, ostensibly because of concern about finances that would be needed for the war effort. This outcome reveals much about Australian political history, and Kewley (1977, pp. 161–2) suggests that the financial concerns merely allowed 'latent opposition to the scheme to become manifest'.

At the time, comprehensive planning was treated with suspicion, a contributory scheme was seen by workers effectively to involve a cut in pay, and it was unpopular with employers because of the cost, while the medical profession was implacably opposed to the medical coverage which was on a panel basis. Soon after, in the 1940s, further income-maintenance provisions – widows' pensions and unemployment, sickness and special benefits – were implemented in the same selective mould as the age and invalid pensions. Thus this period in Australia showed little of 'the moralism, the broad vision of social reform, the comprehensive multi-functional planning and mass excitement about the new "welfare state" that were obvious in Britain' in the Beveridge reforms' (Jones, 1990, p. 39).

The principle of universality (or near-universality) has been more acceptable in relation to support for children. A maternity allowance, established in 1912 (abolished in 1976), involved a payment of five pounds to both married and unmarried mothers on the birth of a live child – but excluded Aborigines and most Asians and Pacific Islanders. While this was clearly consonant with concerns to increase the European population, it was couched in terms of children's well-being (Kewley, 1973, pp. 103–5). A second 'universal' payment, child endowment, was introduced in 1941, and was more inclusive, though was not paid in respect of nomadic Aboriginal children. Consonant with the drivers of a wage-earners' welfare state, child endowment was developed as a means of diverting pressure from wage demand (Watts, 1987, pp. 53–5). Payment was made to the mother in respect of each biological or adopted child, except the first (from 1950 the first child was covered) to the age of 16 years (Kewley, 1977, pp. 196–200). This payment was modified and integrated into a much more comprehensive, but selective, system of child support in 1987.

Australian education consists of government and non-government schools with most of the latter under religious auspices. In 1995, the government system catered for 71 per cent of the students and had 74 per cent of the schools (ABS, 1997). Universally-available education took shape from 1872 (in Victoria), as the six colonial governments successively established 'free, secular and compulsory' education for children aged six to 14 (later raised to 15 or 16, depending on State or Territory). Their vision for a brave new world spurred governments to act as both 'financial and administrative controller' of public education well before the state adopted a similar role in Britain (Branson and Miller, 1979, p. 57). New Zealand took a similar approach in 1875. In the early days of the system, though, 'free' at times meant means-tested, and attendance was often not enforced (Buckley and Wheelwright, 1988). Also, while primary and later secondary education were free, tertiary education has generally been fee-paying with the talented poor provided access through scholarships and means-tested living allowances, which were extended to students in the last two years of secondary schools in 1983. The Whitlam Labour government made tertiary education free in 1975, as part of a raft of universally-oriented reforms, though this only lasted until 1987.

A controversial universalising policy of the Whitlam government was the provision of state aid to non-government schools, aimed at the large but under-resourced Catholic system (in 1995, accounting for about two-thirds of enrolments in non-government schools). The subsequent Fraser Coalition government, however, gradually diverted some funds to even the most favoured private schools which, modelled on British 'public' schools, have educated society's elites since the 1850s. The next Labour government modified this, but what started as a redistributive project, ultimately began to threaten to residualise the state system as public education effectively suffered reductions in available funds in the late 1980s and 1990s at the same time as having to deal with more students. This occurred because the government succeeded in raising retention rates to the final year of secondary schooling from around 40 per cent in the early 1980s to over 70 per cent in the 1990s. With government schools under pressure, private schools attracted more students, the proportion rising from 22 per cent in 1974 to 29 per cent in 1995 (ABS, 1997, p. 69).

A similar residualising process also happened to the public housing programme, which between 1945 and 1970 accounted for 36 per cent of all housing constructed in Australia. Purchase was facilitated by low deposits and low-interest government-guaranteed loans. By the 1980s, there was little building of public housing and the housing stock left in government hands amounted to 6 per cent of all housing. This was the basis of a welfare rental housing programme for social security recipients; in addition, rental subsidies were provided to some poor families and individuals to defray the cost of private rental (Paris *et al.*, 1985; ABS, 1998).

Australia was late in establishing a universal health system. After two failed attempts, a national system, Medibank, was put in place in 1976. This was partly funded by a taxation surcharge, but this was not intended to cover the full costs and has always been topped up from consolidated revenue. Hence it does not thoroughly challenge Australia's non-contributory tradition. Developed by the Whitlam Labour government, Medibank was progressively undermined by the Fraser Coalition government. It was revived and renamed Medicare by the 1983 Hawke Labour government. Predictably, a process of reversal started with the election in 1996 of the Howard Coalition government, though its electoral popularity precluded its abolition. Nonetheless, see-saw processes such as this led Castles (1989) to declare that Australia has a 'reversible' welfare state.

A recent radical break with Australia's history of largely selective provisions funded from consolidated revenue is seen in the establishment, in the early 1990s, of a universal superannuation scheme. Originally conceived by Labour as part of a strategic Income and Prices Accord ('the Accord') with the trade unions, to substitute for claims for higher wage rates, it is consistent with labourist traditions of promoting occupational welfare. Employers remain responsible for all compulsory contributions (initially 4 per cent of wages, rising to 9 per cent by 2002), as a planned compulsory employee contribution was never pursued. The charge applies in respect of all employees between 18 and 65 years who earn more than A$450 per month (Sharp, 1995). Other workers, and those without cover, remain eligible for existing safety-net provisions. When the programme matures in 2030, it is predicted that a retiree on average weekly earnings (with a consistent employment record) will receive about 60 per cent of their pre-retirement income compared with current age pension rates of 25 per cent (Castles, 1994).

Redistribution

From its early history, the fragmentary available evidence suggests that Australia had less poverty, a more equal income distribution, more opportunities for employment and a less pronounced social hierarchy than most other societies (Encel, 1970; Mendelsohn, 1979) – overlooking the fate of Indigenous Australians. It is also likely that inequality fluctuated wildly with the state of the economy (Kingston, 1988), though the ideology of equality persisted (Thompson, 1994). More precise evidence is available for the twentieth century. A 1976 OECD survey, for example, which considered pre- and post-tax income inequality in 12 developed countries (including Canada, Germany, Japan, Sweden, the United Kingdom and the United States, also represented in this book), concluded that 'Australia and Japan, in that order, rank as the least unequal countries on most measures' (Mendelsohn, 1979, p. 67), though had New Zealand been included it is likely to have outranked Australia.

From 1908, with age and invalid pensions means-tested but relatively generous, and taken up by over 30 per cent of the age cohort, considerable redistribution was achieved. Until the 1940s, probably only provisions in Germany and Denmark were more generous (Jones, 1990, p. 24; Castles, 1994). That a contribution to social insurance was not required, left workers with scope to buy a house, something which has over the century led to wealth being more evenly distributed. This is demonstrated by a study of Victorian male estates between 1860 when the gini coefficient was a highly unequal 0.972, and 1973–74 when it was a less unequal 0.746, largely on the basis of the family home (Mendelsohn, 1979, p. 66). Whereas in the UK the proportion of home ownership only reached 50 per cent in 1971, in Australia, it reached that figure in 1911. The rate peaked in the 1960s at 72 per cent, falling to around 70 per cent in the 1990s (Milligan, 1983; ABS, 1999).

There is evidence that income inequality started to increase in the mid-1970s as unemployment burgeoned – from 3 per cent in 1972 to 8.5 per cent in 1996, peaking at 11 per cent in 1991. Also middle-paying jobs, particularly in manufacturing, started disappearing in the wake of economic restructuring (Gregory, 1993), and a more deregulated industrial relations system encouraged enterprise and individual wage and salary bargaining allowing better-placed workers to improve their relative positions. Between 1982 and 1995, the top quintile of income units increased its share of gross income from 43.9 to 47.9 per cent, while the share of the bottom quintile dropped from 4.9 to 3.6 per cent (ABS, 1994, 1997). The gini coefficient for income rose from 0.40 to 0.44, and was still at this level in 1997 (ABS, 1994, 1999) having reached a low of 0.31 in 1973–74 (Mendelsohn, 1979, p. 65).

In the 1980s, Labour concentrated its efforts on compensating the poorest families for the effects of a restructured labour market. For the first time in the history of the Australian welfare state, assistance was paid, via assistance to children, to the working poor. These policies were successful in ameliorating some of the most negative effects of the increasing gap between rich and poor. Taken together, taxation and transfer payments increasingly benefited the very lowest income households with dependent children, though mostly only those with incomes of less than half the average weekly earning. The reduction in income inequality accounted for by tax and benefits in 1992 was greater than that achieved in all other OECD countries, though the USA, the Netherlands, Belgium, Germany, Denmark and the United Kingdom were not far behind (Whiteford, 1995, p. 78). At the same time, however, these strategies magnified the residual nature of the Australian welfare regime.

Table 4.2 highlights the links between poverty and employment, showing rates of poverty among couples aged 25–54 years according to their working status. This shows clearly that the redistributive effects of Australian welfare are no guarantee against poverty. There is a poverty rate of 50 per cent when neither partner is employed. It also highlights a new reality for Australian society – that two, preferably full-time, incomes per family is the only really effective way to avoid poverty. This is very different from the regulated male-breadwinner wage underpinning Australia's wage-earners' welfare state for most of the twentieth century.

Table 4.2   The distribution of work and the distribution of poverty among working-age couples, 1995–96

Earner status of partners[a]	Percentage of all couples	Poverty rate[b] (%)	Percentage of all poor couples
(O,O)	8.8	50.0	45.9
(P,O)	2.7	41.3	11.6
(F,O)	29.5	8.4	25.9
(P,P)	0.8	24.6	2.1
(F,P)	25.3	3.7	9.8
(F,F)	32.9	1.4	4.8
Total	100.0	9.6	100.0

Source: Saunders (1998), SPRC 90, p. 26.
Notes: (a) Earner status at the time of the survey. Estimates exclude the self-employed. Key: O = no earnings; P = part-time earner; F = full-time earner. (b) Poverty status has been based on disposable income over the previous (1994–95) financial year.

Welfare Reform and Retrenchment: 1970s–1990s

In terms of welfare-state development Australia has been out of step with international developments since the 1970s. Just as it was becoming widely accepted that there was a 'crisis of the welfare state' (Offe, 1984), the 1972/5 Whitlam Labour government attempted to extend Australia's welfare regime in a social democratic direction. As Whitlam (1985, p. 360) later reflected 'We wanted to establish a welfare apparatus which was devoid of class discrimination and could not be stigmatised as providing charitable concessions to the "deserving poor"'. Policies initiated included: the automatic adjustment of pensions in line with the consumer price index; a pension for mothers who had not been in a permanent relationship; a non-means-tested retirement pension for people over the age of 70; the abolition of university fees; a national health service, Medibank; and a local development programme, the Australian Assistance Plan (AAP), to stimulate development of local social services and community involvement.

Policy also became more inclusive and empowering of previously excluded groups. Aboriginal policy was changed, with the spur of activist pressure, to one of self-management, facilitating the development of Aboriginal and Torres Strait Islander-managed services. Policy relating to Australia's many ethic groups also changed to one of recognition of cultural diversity, under the rubric 'multiculturalism'. This afforded many groups a greater say in shaping the welfare regime. Women, too, achieved greater inclusion. The breadwinner plank of the wage-earner's welfare state was in principle, if not in practice, removed by an equal pay ruling which took effect from 1975. The wage regulation structures underpinning the wage-earner's welfare state since the beginning of the century ensured that the gap between men's and women's wage levels narrowed quite quickly. Women's full-time weekly earnings reached 84 per cent of men's, high by world standards, in the 1990s (O'Connor *et al.*, 1999, p. 96). A women's adviser to the Prime Minister was appointed in 1973, the first move in the establishment of a special women's bureaucratic cadre, referred to as 'femocrats', charged with the promotion of gender equality and working closely with women's pressure groups. This administrative strategy later gained international recognition as an effective strategy for promoting gender equality policies (Eisenstein, 1991).

Keen to steer policy, the Whitlam government skirted the constitutional limitations of federal powers by increasingly utilising tied grants, especially for health and education. There was an increase in social expenditure (see Figure 4.1) though this still left Australia near the bottom of OECD countries (Castles, 1989, p. 22). This pursuit of a more social democratic welfare state was short-lived, however. With the oil shocks of 1973, the international economic tide turned and the rate of growth of Australia's GDP fell, inflation spiralled and unemployment started to rise. In 1975 the crisis culminated in a highly controversial and unprecedented dismissal of the government from office by the Governor-General.

The Coalition won the subsequent election and though the Fraser government did pursue some neo-liberal economic directions, it did not fundamentally break with the past. The national health scheme was progressively
undermined through incentives to insure privately, but the basic structure
of the wage-earner's welfare state was left in place. Levels of grants to the
States were reduced, but not to pre-Whitlam levels. Neo-liberal policies
found expression in a concentration on fighting inflation and a 'razor gang'
which investigated functions to be 'privatised, rationalised or devolved to
the states' (Fenna, 1998, p. 158), but the government's final 1983 election
budget veered away from such policy directions. But this did not sway the
electorate.

Keen to be seen as in the economic vanguard and avoid the judgment of
economic mismanagement associated with the Whitlam term, it was ultimately the incoming Hawke and then Keating Labour governments
(1983–96, the longest Labour term ever), that introduced major neo-liberal
economic reforms to Australia including floating the currency, freeing up
financial and product markets, and a range of measures aimed at increasing
the efficiency of both the economy and government (Henderson, 1989).
Other reforms included the selective corporatisation and privatisation of government utilities and services (the most notable being the Commonwealth
Bank and the airline QANTAS), contracting out and introducing user
charges.

Whitlam's universal health service was reinstated but age pensions once
again became means-tested, this time with regard to assets as well as income,
and fees were reintroduced in 1987 for tertiary education. Labour's hallmark
was, however, evident in the ingenious way this was done. The Higher
Education Charge Scheme (HECS) involves fees at a fraction of their cost
and broadly related to later income potential. Repayments are deducted automatically through the taxation system, but not recouped until a substantial
earnings level is reached (if this level is not reached, there are no repayments). Interest is not charged but the debt is increased/decreased annually
according to the cost-of-living index.

At the end of its 13 years of government, Labour had both restructured
the economy and refurbished the welfare state, mostly in the classic
Australian residual way. Government spending generally, though not social
welfare spending, was reduced (see Figure 4.1). Government funds were certainly spread more thinly as there remained pressure on the social wage
through increased numbers of unemployed, aged, sole parents and because of
an expansion of health and education coverage. Labour market programmes,
too, were developed to deal with the unemployed, though only with modest
success. Child and other poverty was tackled, relying heavily on research and
technocrat systems (as seen in the HECS) to point the way to downward
income redistribution. Pension rates achieved 25 per cent of average weekly
earnings for the first time ever, having been at 22.5 per cent when Labour
came to office (Castles, 1994). Income was effectively transferred to the

poorest families, partly, for the first time in Australia's history, by providing
support to the working poor via an expanded means-tested children's
allowance.

Labour maintained a focus on Aboriginal rights and multiculturalism and
on greater equality for women. Effectively, women were redefined as workers
rather than dependants, and formal equality largely achieved, even though
the weight of history means the reality still lags (Bryson, 1992, 1994;
O'Connor *et al.*, 1999). Universal rights to unpaid maternity leave were
established, while federal and some state public servants receive full pay for
12 weeks. An abortive attempt to universally provide 12-weeks paid maternity leave for women workers, as part of 'the Accord', finished up, in 1996,
as a one-off tax-free means-tested maternity allowance (*ibid.*, pp. 84–5). The
'femocracy' was expanded and discrimination in education, employment and
services systematically targeted. Women's education levels increased dramatically, and by the 1990s women made up more than half the higher-education
enrolments. There was a more than 500 per cent increase in childcare provision during Labour's term (Whitehouse, 1998, p. 328) through the establishment of a state-supported network of child-care centres across the country
with means-tested fee relief for parents, and the extension of fee relief for parents using private centres.

Labour also undertook some restructuring of the wage earners' welfare
state, and finally eschewed the 'interventionist domestic defence strategies'
that were at its heart. Levels of tariff protection for industry were reduced,
continuing a process tentatively started by the Whitlam government in the
early 1970s (Castles *et al.*, 1996, p. 8). This did not only involve retrenchment, but was eased in by a 'watershed' programme of industrial restructuring designed to address the deficiencies in Australian manufacturing and to
generate jobs (Capling and Galligan, 1992). There was some modification of
the industrial-relations system, with enterprise bargaining encouraged alongside central controls of wages and employment conditions; the labour market
was not, however, deregulated. The contributory retirement pension scheme
introduced in 1992 was the one potentially revolutionary universal reform,
and was made possible because the unions had agreed to wage restraint in
return for an increased social wage, as part of the Accord.

During Labour's terms, State governments also implemented a range of
compatible neo-liberal policies. Degrees of enthusiasm varied according to
circumstances and political allegiance, with Victoria's Coalition government
the most radical. Nonetheless, state-administered welfare services took on the
mantle of economic rationalism. The bureaucratic processes, together with
their distinctive language of down-sizing, privatisation, deregulation, enterprise bargaining, purchaser/provider split, bench-marking, contracting-out,
casemix (remibursing hospitals according to number and type of patients), all
became familiar.

Whilst Labour's successor, the Howard Coalition government, shared a
commitment to neo-liberal economics, their way of translating this into

policy was quite different from Labour's. The Coalition showed an eagerness to enact more radical economic policies and attempted fundamentally to change the parameters of the wage-earner's welfare state. The attempted measures included altering the progressivity of the taxation system and radical deregulation of the labour market. Whilst some change was achieved, the radical edge of the policies was blunted by the Senate, in which the government was in the minority. The focus of expenditure restraint was also very different. As with the Fraser government, tax incentives were offered for those taking private health insurance. Though the popular national health programme was not directly attacked, the dental programme was retrenched (Leeder, 1999). Inclusive policies became a lower priority, reflected, for example, in a 40 per cent funding cut for the Human Rights and Equality of Opportunity Commission (Fenna, 1998, p. 325). The focus of the women's welfare regime was redirected away from the pursuit of formal equality towards more traditional family and welfare goals. The femocracy was reduced and mechanisms for measuring change retrenched.

The language of welfare services started moving away from rights, taking on a more victim-blaming tone and emphasising welfare dependency and 'mutual obligation'. In the words of the Minister for Family and Community Services, 'our very successful Work for the Dole Programme has started to change the expectation among some young people that the taxpayer owes them something for nothing' (Newman, 1999, p. 3). Other changes reflected the business orientation of the government, with for example the employment-placement services of the Commonwealth Employment Service privatised, and clients/recipients becoming 'customers'.

Future Prospects

After two decades of economic rationalism, Australia's welfare state is changed, but not as radically as, for example, New Zealand's. Also, in the new superannuation scheme there is considerably more scope for adequate income in retirement. A change which has received considerable public attention is the changed face of government. Public administration was transformed by managerialist procedures and a new market-rather than service-oriented jargon. At a societal level, the gap widened between rich and poor, largely as a consequence of two decades of intractable unemployment and because of greater inequality among the employed as a consequence of deregulation of the industrial relations system. Although there was intermittent moral panic about whether increasing inequality was resulting in the development of an underclass, this was not supported by the evidence, though if unemployment continues this could become a real issue (Bryson and Winter, 1999).

Labour in the 1980s and 1990s pursued a quite different welfare-state vision from the more social democratic approach of the 1970s Whitlam years.

Basic neo-liberal goals of reduction of state expenditure, deregulation of markets and economic restructuring were pursued. In the case of the employment market, deregulation was partial, with basic wage-award structures maintained together with the central role for unions. Labour also assisted in restructuring key industries whose tariff protection had been reduced or removed. The negative effects of neo-liberal policies for individuals and families were dealt with through Labour's traditional selective measures, and were focused on more effective targeting of support to the poorest.

Overall, though, the welfare state was refurbished rather than retrenched. Indeed, by the mid-1990s Australia's welfare regime showed signs of a greater maturity than at any other time in its history. This was particularly the case for indigenous Australians, though there is still far to go, and for women. Also the main new occupational welfare provision that Labour introduced, the superannuation scheme, has the potential to transform the very nature of the Australian welfare state. It could become the basis of a broader contributory social insurance system delivering more than its current goal of providing replacement income at much higher levels for an ageing society. Ultimately, an extended scheme could cover a range of other contingencies now covered by the social security system, including unemployment, as well as filling gaps such as universal paid maternity leave.

A debate that became pertinent after Labour lost office was whether it may effectively have prepared the way for a Coalition retrenchment of the welfare state even beyond the routine processes of reversal seen in the past. Had Labour in Australia, as has been suggested by Castles and Shirley (1996) for Labour in New Zealand, acted as a grave digger for the welfare state? It seems likely the answer is no. There have been reversals but the Coalition has had difficulty in achieving its radical economic restructuring goals. This has not necessarily been due to Labour's efforts, but rather to the complexity of Australia's bicameral parliamentary system (at both national and State levels – only Queensland has a unicameral system) and its proportional voting system for the Senate. This makes change a more measured process than was the case in New Zealand, with its unicameral, first-past-the-post system prior to the electoral reform of the late 1990s. The federal Coalition government has had to take note of voters' negative response to the radical neo-liberal economic programme, something which was reflected in the fall of Victoria's Coalition government in 1999.

The definitive analysis of the effects of the Howard Government's policies on Australia's welfare regime will only really be made after it loses office. But it is possible to suggest a radical scenario for the next Labour government based on the retirement-income scheme introduced by the Hawke/Keating governments. This may indeed render them the gravediggers of the historic, but problematic, Australian wage-earner's welfare state – to be replaced with a new more universal and comprehensive system, and resulting in Australia losing its status as a distinctive antipodean form of liberal welfare state.

References

ABS (1994) *Australian Social Trends 1994*, Catalogue no. 4102.0, Australian Bureau of Statistics.

ABS (1997) *Australian Social Trends 1997*, Catalogue no. 4102.0, Australian Bureau of Statistics.

ABS (1999) *Australian Social Trends 1999*, Catalogue no. 4102.0, Australian Bureau of Statistics.

ABS/AIHW (1999) *The Health and Welfare of Aboriginal and Torres Strait Islander Peoples*, Australian Bureau of Statistics/Australian Institute of Health and Welfare.

AIHW (1997) *Australia's Welfare 1997*, Australian Institute of Health and Welfare, Canberra, Australia.

Beilharz, P. (1989) 'The Labourist Tradition and the Reforming Imagination', in R. Kennedy (ed.), *Australian Welfare History*, Macmillan.

Beilharz, P., Considine M. and Watts, R. (1992) *Arguing about the Welfare State: the Australian Experience*, Allen & Unwin.

Branson, J. and Miller, D. (1979) *Class, Sex and Education in Capitalist Society*, Sorrett Publishing.

Bryson, L. (1992) *Welfare and the State: Who Benefits?*, Macmillan.

Buckley, K. and Wheelwright T. (1988) *No Paradise for Workers: Capitalism and the Common People in Australia 1788–1914*, Oxford University Press.

Burke, T. (1998) 'Housing and Poverty', in R. Fincher and J. Nieuwenhuysen (eds), *Australian Poverty Then and Now*, Melbourne University Press.

Castles, F. G. (1985) *The Working Class and Welfare: Reflections on the Political Development of the Welfare State in Australia and New Zealand, 1890–1980*, Allen & Unwin.

Castles, F. G. (1988) *Australian Public Policy and Economic Vulnerability*, Allen & Unwin.

Castles, F. G. (1989) 'Australia's Reversible Citizenship', *Australian Society*, September, pp. 29–30.

Castles, F. G. (1994) 'The Wage-Earners' Welfare State Revisited: Refurbishing the Established Model of Australian Social Protection, 1983–93', *Australian Journal of Social Issues*, 29(2), pp. 120–45.

Castles, F. G., and Shirley, I. F. (1996) 'Labour and Social Policy: Gravediggers or Refurbishers of the Welfare State', in F. G. Castles, R. Gerritsen and J. Vowels (eds), *The Great Experiment: Labour Parties and Public Policy Transformation in Australia and New Zealand*, Allen & Unwin.

Costar, B. and Economou, N. (eds) (1999) *The Kennett Revolution*, University of New South Wales Press.

Department of Social Security (1998) *Annual Report 1997–98*, Department of Social Security.

Dickey, B. (1980) *No Charity There*, Nelson.

Eisenstein, H. (1991) *Gender Shock: Practicing Feminism on Two Continents*, Allen & Unwin.

Encel, S. (1970) *Equality and Authority*, Cheshire.

Esping-Andersen, G. (1990) *The Three Worlds of Welfare Capitalism*, Polity Press.

Fenna, A. (1998) *Introduction to Australian Social Policy*, Longman.

Friedman, M. (1962) *Capitalism and Freedom*, University of Chicago Press.

Friedman, M. and Friedman, R. (1979) *Free to Choose*, Macmillan.

Gregory, R. G. (1993) 'Aspects of Australian and US Living Standards: The Disappointing Decades 1970–1990', *Economic Record*, 69(204), pp. 61–76.

Henderson, D. (1989) 'Perestroika in the West', in J. Nieuwenhuysen (ed.) *Towards Freer Trade Between Nations*, Oxford University Press.

Henderson, R. (1975) *Poverty in Australia*, Australian Government Publishing Service.

Jones, M. A. (1990) *The Australian Welfare State*, 3rd edn, Allen & Unwin.

Kalisch, D. (1995) 'The Contribution of Family Payments to Family Incomes: Developments since the 1970s', *Social Security Journal*, June, pp. 87–97.

Kewley, T. H. (1977) *Social Security in Australia*, Sydney University Press.

Kingston, B. (1988) *The Oxford History of Australia, Vol. 3: 1860—1900*, Oxford University Press.

Langmore, J. and Quiggan, J. (1994) *Work for All: Full Employment in the Nineties*, Melbourne University Press.

Lee, J. and Strachan, J. (1998) 'Who's Minding the Baby now? Child Care under the Howard Government', *Labour and Industry*, 9(2), pp. 81–102.

Leeder, S. R. (1999) *Healthy Medicine*, Allen & Unwin.

Macarthy, P. G. (1976) 'Justice Higgins and the Harvester Judgement', in J. Roe (ed.), *Social Policy in Australia*, Cassell.

Markus, A. (1994) *Australian Race Relations*, Allen & Unwin.

Mendelsohn, R. (1979) *The Condition of the People*, Allen & Unwin.

Milligan, V. (1983) 'The State and Housing: Questions of Social Policy and Social Change', in A. Graycar (ed.) *Retreat from the Welfare State*, Allen & Unwin.

Newman, J. (1999) 'The Future of Welfare in the 21st Century', Ministerial address to National Press Club, Canberra, 29 September.

O'Connor, J., Orloff, A. S. and Shaver. S. (1999) *States, Markets, Families: Gender, Liberalism and Social Policy in Australia, Canada, Great Britain and the United States*, Cambridge University Press.

Offe, C. (1984) *Contradiction of the Welfare State*, Hutchinson.

Paris, C., Williams, P. and Stimson, R. (1985) 'From Public Housing to Welfare Housing', *Australian Journal of Social Issues*, 20(2), pp. 105–17.

Pember Reeves, W. (1969) [1902] *State Experiments in Australia and New Zealand*, Macmillan.

Reynolds, H. (1996) 'Segregation, Assimilation, Self-Determination', in J. Wilson, J. Thomson and A. McMahon (eds), *The Australian Welfare State: Key Documents and Themes*, Macmillan.

Saunders, P. (1994) *Welfare and Inequality*, Cambridge University Press.

Saunders, P. (1998) *Global Pressures National Responses: The Australian Welfare State in Context*, SPRC Discussion Paper no. 90, Social Policy Research Centre University of New South Wales.

Shaver, S. (1982) 'The Non-Government State: The Voluntary Welfare Sector', Paper delivered to Conference, *Social Policy in the 1980s*, Canberra, 28–30 May.

Smyth, P. and Cass, B. (eds) (1998) *Contesting the Australian Way: States, Markets and Civil Society*, Cambridge University Press.

Stevens, F. (1984) *Black Australia*, Aura Press.

Titmuss, R. (1974) 'The Social Division of Welfare: Some Reflections on the Search for Equity', in *Essays on The Welfare State*, Allen & Unwin.

Thompson, E. (1994) *Fair Enough: Egalitarianism in Australia*, University of New South Wales Press.

Watts, R. (1987) *The Foundations of the National Welfare State*, Allen & Unwin.

Whiteford P. (1995) 'Families, Benefits and Taxes: Support for Children in a Comparative Perspective', *Social Security Journal*, June, pp. 49–86.

Whitlam, G. (1985) *The Whitlam Government 1972–1975*, Penguin.

Wilson, R. (1997) *Bringing them Home*, Report of the National Inquiry into the Separation of Aboriginal and Torres Strait Islander Children from their Families. Commonwealth of Australia.

CHAPTER 5

New Zealand: The Myth of Egalitarianism

JUDITH A. DAVEY

Overview and history

In many ways, the development of social policy in New Zealand parallels that in other developed countries, but it also embodies unique features. New Zealand/Aotearoa is a bi-cultural country, founded on a treaty between the indigenous Maori and British settlers. Meeting welfare needs in this context provides a continuing challenge. Based on economic prosperity and an egalitarian ideology, New Zealand developed a comprehensive welfare state in the 1950s and 1960s, known for social experimentation. But, more recently, the country has taken welfare reform based on free-market principles and economic rationalism much further than many European countries. Well within the space of a lifetime there has been a shift to a minimalist approach to welfare, with extensive targeting and 'user-pays' policies. Given this background, New Zealand provides interesting examples of social policy change and the influences which bring change about.

The Treaty of Waitangi and Maori Society

During the early period of contact between Maori and Europeans, Maori controlled the land and resources (RCSP, 1987, p. 3). European settlement began to challenge this position and resulted in the signing of the Treaty of Waitangi between the British Crown and Maori tribal chiefs in 1840, now recognised as the founding document of New Zealand. Its three articles firstly ceded governance to the British Crown; secondly assured the Maori of continuing possession of and authority over their lands and property; and thirdly gave Maori the 'rights and privileges of British subjects'. The Treaty promised a balance between colonisation and indigenous rights which, as pressures for European settlement grew, it was unable to deliver (Orange, 1987). Traditionally, Maori society was based on collective organisation (Cheyne *et al.*, 1997, p. 147); individual identity and rights existed only through membership of ancestral groups – extended families and tribes. Relationships to land and natural resources such as fisheries were very important, which ran against the British emphasis on individual rights and private ownership and led to wars over land in the middle of the nineteenth century. Wars, disease and growing European immigration meant that Maori were a minority in their own country by 1880. This early history continues to influence New Zealand society and social policy.

The 19th Century: Settlement and Social Policy

Oliver (1988) saw nineteenth-century social policy as synonymous with facilitating European settlement. This included the transfer of land into settler ownership; bringing Maori into the 'civilising influences' of the cash economy; the construction of infrastructure such as roads and railways; and assisted immigration. The more traditional sectors of social policy involved a 'colonial Poor Law'. Those who could not afford to pay for health care depended on a hospital system, which also provided custodial care for the old, chronically ill and 'feeble-minded' (Oliver, 1988). The characteristics of the settler population – predominantly male and highly mobile – meant that care of old people became a problem and led to the introduction of an old-age pension in 1898, a decade before this happened in Britain (Cheyne *et al.*, 1997). Until the 1850s all New Zealand schools were privately-run and funded. The present national system of free, secular and compulsory education came with the Education Act of 1877. Other policy innovations included Female Suffrage in 1893, the first in the world at national level. A Department of Labour was created to oversee working conditions, and in 1894 the Industrial Conciliation and Arbitration Act was passed. This strengthened the bargaining position of trade unions and set up an Arbitration Court which exercised a dominant influence on wages and conditions of work for 75 years. The concept of the 'family wage' was a means of supporting families through wage structures, and laid the basis for a 'wage-earners welfare state' (Castles, 1986). However, it seriously disadvantaged women workers until the passing of the Equal Pay Act in 1972.

The Early 20th Century: The Emergence of State Welfare

Moving into the twentieth century, the New Zealand population became more settled and urbanised and policy shifted from development to welfare (Oliver, 1988). Pensions were extended to cover widows in 1911, miners in 1915 and the blind in 1924. Concern about housing led to several pieces of legislation, including the Housing Act of 1919. Emphasis was placed on home ownership; and as early as 1919, 53 per cent of homes in New Zealand were owner-occupied, when the equivalent figure in Britain was 10 per cent (Ferguson, 1994). Progress was made in child welfare and child health and the 1926 Family Allowances Act introduced a means-tested benefit for the third and subsequent children. Free secondary education became available for all children in 1936.

The Flowering of the Welfare State

The modern welfare state in New Zealand is usually dated from the Labour government of 1935–49, which passed the Social Security Act of 1938 (Cheyne *et al.*, 1997, p. 36). Welfare benefits were all means-tested except for a small universal superannuation. Free medical care through hospitals was financed through taxation, although the medical profession defended their right to charge patients directly. A wide range of measures was set in place to assist families: family benefit was made universal and later could be capitalised to provide housing finance; and housing assistance was delivered through the State Advances Corporation, which began a rental housing construction pro- gramme as well as continuing to provide mortgage finance (Wilkes and Shirley, 1984, p. 219).

The Labour government's welfare provisions remained substantially in place for more than 40 years, 'often questioned, sometimes examined, but only marginally altered' (Oliver, 1988, p. 25). These policies created expecta- tions that government would intervene to prevent distress and promote well- being, and electoral power was exercised on this basis. In the 1950s and 1960s, New Zealanders enjoyed economic prosperity which underpinned some of the highest living standards in the world. There was full employment (in 1956 only five unemployment benefits were being paid) and high health standards. New Zealand prided itself on having the lowest infant mortality rates in the world. High fertility levels and immigration led to a population growth of nearly 70 per cent between 1945 and 1971 (from 1.7 million to 2.9 million).

The government took a strongly interventionist role in economic as well as social policy. The economy was managed in detail by the state, with controls over exchange transactions, domestic credit, interest rates, incomes and prices, import licenses and tariffs (Oliver, 1988, p. 33). In the industrial-relations area there was compulsory union membership and General Wage Orders, which applied across the economy (Deeks and Boxall, 1989, p. 182).

The Unravelling of the Welfare State

In 1972, the Royal Commission on Social Security concluded,

> we have not been persuaded that our social security system should be radically changed at this time … no alternative which we examined is likely to do better. (Royal Commission, 1972, p. 32)

But things were beginning to change, socially and economically. After many years during which markets for primary produce – butter, meat, wool – seemed inexhaustible, Britain's intention to join the EEC was a threat. The 'oil shocks' had serious effects, and unemployment grew from 1 per cent of the labour force in 1966 to 7 per cent in 1986 (EMG, 1989, p. 12). Means-tested benefits fell behind wage increases and the cost of living, and inflation grew to peak at over 15 per cent per annum in the later 1970s (EMG, 1989, p. 11).

At the same time, cultural consensus in New Zealand was being eroded (Cheyne *et al.*, 1997, p. 38). Television was introduced in 1960, and air travel promoted rapid communication and international mobility. New social movements such as neo-feminism, environmentalism and the civil rights movement had their impact. The Maori population became urbanised (McClure, 1998), which led to social dislocation; but a cultural renaissance began, pointing out the relative disadvantage of Maori, and calling for the redressing of grievances and honouring of the Treaty.

But even as these changes were threatening the New Zealand welfare state, there were still significant additions to its structure. In 1973 the Domestic Purposes Benefit (DPB) was introduced for unsupported parents, and in 1972 the Accident Compensation (ACC) scheme came in to provide medical benefits and income replacement for accident victims. For a short time, against the general policy thrust in New Zealand, a contributory retirement income scheme was introduced, but quickly replaced by a tax-funded universal scheme when the National Party was re-elected in 1975. All three policies were to have long-term implications.

Changes and Reforms of the 1980s and 1990s

The 1984 general election was a landmark for social policy in New Zealand. A Labour government was elected and inherited serious economic problems (Dalziel, 1994), and it responded with a programme of neo-liberal reforms similar to Thatcherism in Britain and Reaganomics in the USA (Cheyne *et al.*, 1997, p. 41). Deregulation of the financial sector was rapid, exchange controls were lifted, agricultural subsidies were withdrawn and trade was liberalised. The state sector was restructured (Boston *et al.*, 1996, p. 99), and several departments with commercial operations were turned into state-owned enterprises (SOEs), for example in telecommunications and postal services, broadcasting and electricity generation (Le Heron and Pawson, 1996, p. 214). New Zealand followed the global trend of privatisation, with the sales of Air New Zealand and Postbank in 1988, followed by the Bank of New Zealand, state forests and Telecom (Le Heron and Pawson, 1996, p. 220). There was a shift to indirect taxation, with a flat-rate goods and services tax (GST) introduced in 1986 at 10 per cent and later increased to 12.5 per cent. These represented a movement away from the progressive approach to taxation, and reduced its redistributive impact.

In its restructuring of social policy systems, the Labour government favoured devolution. Its Maori policy gave tribal authorities considerable control over service delivery; and similar process took place in education, giving considerable autonomy to school Boards of Trustees. The 1989 Area Health Boards Act created 14 regionally-based largely elected bodies, subject to the new public sector accountability rules (Le Heron and Pawson, 1996, p. 221). However, pressure on government welfare and health spending was growing. In an attempt to rein back the generosity of National's universal superannuation, Labour introduced a tax surcharge on additional income above a certain level. This proved extremely unpopular, even though only a small proportion of superannuitants had to pay it.

One of the manifesto commitments of the Labour government was to hold a Royal Commission on Social Policy. This was set up in 1986, but its emphasis on universalism and state responsibility was obviously out of tune with the times and it had little, if any, influence on policy (RCSP, 1988).

The National Party continued the thrust for radical policy change when they won the 1990 election. Within weeks they announced cuts to welfare benefits, and the 1991 Budget brought sweeping changes to health, housing, education and income support in the direction of much greater targeting, 'user pays' and exhortations to self-reliance. This government had no qualms about tackling labour-market reform and passed the Employment Contracts Act, which swept away the century-old wage-setting system, replacing it with contractual arrangements between employers and employees which also stripped the unions of their traditional powers and status (Cheyne *et al.*, 1997, p. 43). The principles forming the basis for social policy reform under National were fairness, self-reliance, efficiency and greater personal choice (Boston and Dalziel, 1992, p. 7), but their interpretation differed from traditional welfare state dogma. 'Fairness' was seen as strict targeting determined by genuine need; self-reliance' suggested that individuals be encouraged to take care of themselves and their families (set in opposition to welfare dependency); 'efficiency' was defined as value for money; and 'choice' entailed the encouragement of alternative providers of health, education and welfare services. 1991 Budget policy put these principles into action (Shipley, 1991).

In addition to cuts in most welfare benefits, stricter eligibility criteria were introduced, such as age limits and stand-down periods. Major changes to retirement income were announced, including income-testing. However, after an electoral outcry (and some financial recalculations) some of these were reversed and the surcharge was reintroduced, at a higher level. Lifting of the age of eligibility for superannuation from 60 to 65 was retained, to be completed in stages by 2001. Health-care policy was substantially overhauled (Upton, 1991). The area health boards were replaced by four Regional Health Authorities (RHAs) which were made responsible for contracting-out all health services to a range of providers – public (public hospitals were re-created as Crown Health Enterprises), private, voluntary and Maori.

This had the effect of separating funding and provision. Health-care subsidies were to be delivered by means of a Community Services Card issued on an income-tested basis to all age groups. Part-charges were introduced for hospital services (but subsequently withdrawn for in-patients after difficulties in implementation). The ACC scheme retained its basic 'no-fault' concept, but has been amended to reduce employers' contributions, to introduce an employees' premium and abolish lump sum compensation payments.

In the 1970s, central government, through the Housing Corporation (HCNZ) provided half of new house mortgages. Housing assistance had become progressively more targeted, but in 1990 there was still income-related mortgage interest rates, and income-related rents. 'State housing' accounted for about a quarter of rented dwellings. The 1991 Budget changes replaced all forms of housing assistance with a single cash payment – the Accommodation Supplement (Shipley, 1991, p. 55). This is available to renters in both public and private housing, to boarders and also to mortgagors (thus meeting the 'choice' objective). The supplement is calculated on the basis of income, household size and location. At the same time, state tenants were to be charged market rents (introduced in stages) and would become eligible for the Accommodation Supplement. These reforms have been largely implemented, with progressive increases in the supplement which was inadequate in many instances. Changes in education policy applied mainly to tertiary institutions (Shipley, 1991, p. 69). Primary and secondary schooling continued to be 'universally available free of charge', although parents generally have to supplement government funding with 'voluntary fees'. However, tertiary students' allowances became more tightly targeted, with eligibility depending on parental income (both parents) up to the age of 25. The government abolished fees for tertiary education and instead funded institutions directly. This meant that institutions set their own fees. A student loans scheme was introduced to cover fees, course and living expenses.

The implementation of this wide-ranging programme moved New Zealand well along the track towards a residual model of the welfare state (Spicker, 1995, p. 70). The objective of ensuring that all citizens are 'able to feel a sense of participation in and belonging to the community', articulated by the Royal Commission on Social Security in 1972, has been replaced by a 'modest safety net' for those unable to meet their own needs (Boston and Dalziel, 1992, p. 1). The *quid pro quo* has been personal income tax cuts, introduced in 1996 and 1998.

In 1993, New Zealanders voted to change the electoral system to mixed-member proportional representation (MMP). The 1995 general election was conducted under this system and resulted in a centre-right coalition government. In a few areas there was some retreat from the minimalist stand on social policy. Health services for children under the age of six were made free, and the tax surcharge for superannuitants was abolished. However, rifts in the coalition soon became apparent, and the partnership was dissolved in mid-1998. A National minority government ruled somewhat precariously until the 1999 general election, when it was replaced by a centre-left coalition which promised further changes in retirement income policy.

Basic Themes and Characteristics of Social Policy in New Zealand

Consequences of History and Geography

The development of social policy in New Zealand has been, and continues to be, strongly influenced by the country's history and geography; the colonial heritage affected the nature and timing of early welfare innovations. Immigration policy has played an important part in population change and composition; mass migration of British settlers and intakes from the Pacific Islands in periods of labour shortage, has given way to greater variety in sources of immigrants. Policy now emphasises the potential economic contribution of applicants – work skills and asset-holding – rather than their racial or geographical origins. Thus the population is becoming more racially and culturally diverse.

Maori, as indigenous people, played a significant part in setting the parameters for European settlement. They suffered discrimination and injustice in the nineteenth century but recently have had greater success in demanding their rights though the Treaty of Waitangi. From being a colony, then a 'British farm', New Zealand has developed an individual identity which is beginning to incorporate expressions of its bi-cultural heritage.

The country is nevertheless a small society of under 4 million people and a small economy, distant from markets. There are some advantages in this. New Zealand has been protected from the consequences of overpopulation and has developed a 'clean, green' image. The negative side is that the country is vulnerable to and comparatively helpless in the face of international influences. Economic trends (and protectionist tendencies) in countries which import its products, impinge on New Zealand's prosperity, as the recent Asian downturn has shown. In social terms, New Zealand has a dominant culture derived from Britain and strongly influenced by the USA, but is geographically closer to Asia. Influence on policy directions is mainly from the former sources, as the above discussion has shown, although New Zealand has shown innovation, and has taken economic rationalism further than many countries dared.

The Myth of Egalitarianism

The colonial heritage is also the origin of New Zealand's image as an egalitarian society, where 'Jack is as good as his master'. Many immigrants left Britain to escape class discrimination. The pioneering lifestyle was certainly one of opportunity, but also of hardship and struggle, often without the family support which had been left behind. The welfare state of the 1940s to the 1970s, with its high living standards, impressive health records and high rates of home ownership, delivered standardised services to a population which was assumed to be homogenous.

New Zealand did not follow the British path of delivering social services through local authorities and did not adopt the social insurance approach to income replacement. Few benefits have been income-related, the majority are flat-rate, paid from general taxation rather than from contributions to separate funds. This made New Zealand, along with Australia, anomalous in the classification of welfare states (Esping-Anderson, 1990, pp. 74–5). Castles (1996, pp. 89–95) links this distinctive approach to social protection with the wage-setting system; the 'wage-earners' welfare state' provided the primary level of support, with benefits as a secondary safety net. Supplementation for dependants on the basis of need assisted families, and the encouragement of home ownership protected retired people from poverty.

Cheyne *et al.* (1997) challenge the myth of egalitarianism and social consensus on several grounds. Underlying the veneer of unity they see sexism, racism and an agenda of controlling the poor. Certainly the image of exemplary race relations, which New Zealand cultivated, did not acknowledge Maori grievances, and Maori language and culture were subjugated by assimilationist policies. Support through the 'family wage' discriminated against women workers.

The myth is comprehensively exposed by recent trends in income distribution. Stephens, Waldegrave and Frater (1996, p. 105) found that median household disposable income fell in real terms by 17 per cent between 1983/4 and 1992/3, and this decline was felt especially in the lower deciles. This has come about by a combination of factors, especially unemployment, but also policy measures. The 1991 cuts reduced the household income of beneficiaries from 72 per cent of mean household income to 58 per cent (Cheyne *et al.*, 1997, p. 185). Tax changes have been regressive, including the shift to indirect tax; personal income tax cuts were introduced with the aim 'to assist, strengthen, and empower low-and middle-income families'. Dalzell (1996, p. 13) shows, however, that households in the top 40 per cent of income distribution enjoyed well over half of the gain. Moreover, the structure of the tax changes (and associated family support delivered through the taxation system) does not assist beneficiary families, but rather is designed to create work incentives. As a result, poverty as defined in non-government surveys (there is no official 'poverty line') is apparently increasing. In 1993, 10.8 per cent of households were below the poverty line determined by Stephens, Waldegrave and Frater (1996, p. 109), compared to 4.3 per cent in 1984. Sole parents and large families have the highest incidence of poverty and levels are higher for Maori and Pacific Islanders than for the European-descent population. The same authors conclude that the social security system is effective in reducing poverty among retired people and households without children, but less so for those with dependent children.

The 'Welfare Burden'

The myth of egalitarianism has been replaced by the looming monster of the 'welfare burden'. It arises from social, economic and demographic change and also an ideological swing. Certainly increases in numbers of beneficiaries and welfare expenditure are impressive and frightening. In 1996, 400,000 (21 per cent of) working-age people were dependent on welfare benefits (including dependent spouses), compared to 8 per cent in 1985 (DSW, 1996, p. 5). In 1996, 30 per cent of children lived in benefit-dependent families compared to 12 per cent in 1985. As a percentage of GDP, benefit expenditure doubled between the 1970s and the 1990s (Treasury, 1990); although total benefits and pensions expenditure only increased from 7.6 per cent of GDP in 1950 to 8.3 per cent in 1990, with a dip to 4.9 per cent in 1970 (author's own calculations).

Population ageing is driving up the cost of New Zealand superannuation and it now accounts for half of income support expenditure. The story of retirement income policy since 1976 has been attempts to cut back the government's liabilities. Increasing life expectancy will be reinforced by cohort dynamics as the 'baby-boomers' reach their 60s from around 2010; and as well as income support, older people are likely to require high levels of health investment.

Social change in patterns of family formation and dissolution is driving demand for the domestic purposes benefit. Numbers grew to 17,000 within five years of its introduction and stood at 97,000 by 1991. Cuts in that year levelled out the growth curve, but its upward trend has resumed. Sole parenthood, 90 per cent of which means women alone with their children, is perceived as problematic in New Zealand, as elsewhere. The problem has variously been perceived as moral (demise of the family and sexual irresponsibility); relating to deficient parenting (children of 'broken' families are seen as achieving less well and lacking a male role model); poverty-related (sole parenthood is strongly linked to low incomes); or as one of unwarranted state dependency. Consistent with the latter, incentives and sanctions are now being applied to increase rates of participation in paid work by lone parents.

Unemployment arises from economic trends and structural changes, and its consequence is welfare dependency, with 140,000 unemployment beneficiaries in 1997. A certain amount of take-up of invalids' benefit is probably also employment-related. People with physical or social disabilities can compete less well when the labour market is tight. Unemployment, sickness and invalid benefits were cut in 1991 and eligibility rules were tightened. In October 1998, unemployment and sickness benefits became the Community Wage, for which beneficiaries are expected to work for 20 hours a week. This is intended to promote work skills and habits and to facilitate a return to paid employment. Many critics see the scheme as unrealistic, with the dangers of job displacement and lack of worker protection, issues raised with respect to other versions of 'workfare' (Finn, 1999).

Welfare dependency is being attacked in New Zealand with policy and ideological weapons borrowed from overseas, especially from the USA. The 'welfare to work' emphasis is exemplified in the new Department of Income and Work, which incorporates the income-support functions of the Department of Social Welfare, work-related disability services and the job-search services of the Ministry of Labour.

Privatisation, Contracting and Pluralism

References to privatisation and the selling of state assets have already been made. The programme is continuing, most recently in the form of public share-floats for airports, ports and electricity companies, but not without controversy. In the social policy area the process has mainly been confined to corporatisation, contracting and the funder-provider split, illustrated most clearly in health services reform.

The four Regional Health Authorities purchased services for their populations using financial allocations from the Minister of Health and guidelines for funding priorities (Le Heron and Pawson, 1996, p. 222). Contracts for services were let in a competitive market which included public, private and voluntary providers; dominant among these were the Crown Health Enterprises (CHEs). The rhetoric promised greater efficiency and better access, but in many areas this has not been fulfilled. Duplication of effort in the RHAs emerged and bureaucracies burgeoned, so that they were eventually combined into a single Health Funding Authority in 1998 (which still operates on a contractual basis). Many CHEs found themselves in financial difficulties. There were strong protests from senior medical staff and the commercial requirements on hospitals have recently been relaxed. Waiting lists and waiting times for elective surgery have proved intractable and a new 'booking' system remains controversial. Fears about access to surgery in particular made private medical insurance more popular. After reaching peak coverage of about 50 per cent of the population, however, the figure has fallen to under 40 per cent mainly because of sharply rising premiums. On the positive side, the contracting system has brought greater diversity into health provision and improved coordination between primary and secondary services. The number of Maori health providers has grown rapidly, helping to address disparities in health between Maori and non-Maori populations. The funder–provider split and competitive contracting have also been applied to other policy areas such as community and personal services and education. New providers have responded to the call for bids, providing greater choice, but also variation in the quality of services. Pluralism is growing and competition widespread, epitomised most recently by increasingly undignified advertising for students by tertiary education establishments.

New Zealand has always had a strong voluntary sector, and the current environment has given it a new role and prominence. Voluntary agencies range from multi-million dollar enterprises with well-developed bureaucracies – IHC (dealing with intellectual handicap), Barnardo's and Presbyterian Support – to informal support and self-help groups. They differ considerably in their capacity to perform in the competitive environment and to catch the ear of government. Long-established agencies, such as the Plunket Society and the Foundation for the Blind, have become more or less institutionalised in the policy system, while others are less influential. Much of the criticism of policy changes in income support and housing has come from church-based organisations (for example the Council of Christian Social Services, or the Salvation Army).

People in New Zealand, as in many similar countries, meet their needs through a variety of systems (RCSP, 1988, vol. 2, pp. 773–92). Families and communities provide the majority of personal care; and the private sector, sometimes with government subsidies, is playing a growing part and the insurance market seems set to expand with increasing emphasis on self-reliance. A special New Zealand feature is service delivery through Maori, especially tribal, systems. Local and regional government play little part in social policy in New Zealand, but this is not to underestimate their contribution to well-being in providing basic services. Thus, as pointed out by Cheyne *et al.* (1997, p. 26), the role of the state in providing for well-being should not be overestimated. As central government becomes less interventionist and seeks to reduce welfare spending, so welfare pluralism becomes the dominant paradigm.

The Maori Dimension and Bi-Culturalism

The Maori people did not die out or become assimilated as was expected at the turn of the century; their numbers recouped and they became urbanised. They never forgot the Treaty of Waitangi and continued to petition the British Crown for redress. However, the outcomes for Maori of fifty years of welfare-state policies have been far from egalitarian. By the 1990s, Maori represented 14 per cent of the population but well over 14 per cent of people unemployed, living on benefits or low incomes, in prison or dying prematurely. Maori education and health standards lag well behind those of the total population. Standardised, even universal provision did not deliver the equality promised by Article 3 of the Treaty.

A Maori revival, calling for self-determination and the redress of grievances, grew around the issue of land rights in the early 1970s. This had much in common with the reassertion of indigenous rights elsewhere in the world. The call found a sympathetic ear in the Labour Government (1973–75) which set up a tribunal to consider claims relating to the Treaty of Waitangi. The resolution of claims has become a goal of governments on both sides of the political spectrum, and large sums of money have been involved in recent settlements. By 1997 they had involved over NZ$600 million of assets, including land, fisheries, forests and geothermal resources, as well as cash. The Treaty has also been invoked in the process of privatisation of state assets. When Radio New Zealand became a state-owned enterprise in 1988, the Maori Council took a case to the High Court claiming that Article 2 of the Treaty required protection of the Maori language. This resulted in higher allocation of funding for Maori radio and TV.

The relative disadvantage of Maori has led to the development of alternative methods of service delivery, intended to be more culturally appropriate and hence more effective. This includes several important educational initiatives. Te Kohanga Reo are early childhood education centres, using the Maori language and with a strong dimension of cultural revitalisation and parent education. Kura Kaupapa Maori (total immersion Maori schools), bilingual schools and bilingual classes have become more common in the 1990s. They cover only a small proportion of Maori children, but produce good educational results. There are, nevertheless, still fears for the survival of the Maori language, despite it having been made an official language.

Maori initiatives in the health services include cultural support in hospitals, education of the health workforce in cultural sensitivity, and the encouragement of Maori nurses, community health workers and medical personnel (through reserved training places and scholarships). Health clinics have been established on marae (Maori community centres), and special preventive programmes targeted at Maori such as smoking-cessation, asthma management, diet improvement and ante-natal care. Some of these, along with remedial services, are now provided by tribal organisations.

Future Prospects

Many challenges confront social policy in New Zealand. Some arise from historical and geographical circumstances, some are shared with similar nations. Globalisation in all its forms will continue to impact on the future of New Zealand and on the policy environment. One challenge which is easy to anticipate arises from population ageing; as noted by the Periodic Report Group (PRG, 1997), the New Zealand government has a 'window of opportunity' before the baby-boomers reach retirement age. During this time it must set in place a system of retirement-income support which is sustainable and equitable (both intergenerationally and in terms of current society). Economic trends and the economic assumptions which underlie policy are crucial in this area.

The same is true for employment prospects. By the end of the twentieth century, unemployment rates were rising again and the then government continued to put its faith in economic growth to produce jobs. However, the vulnerability of the New Zealand economy makes this an area of great uncertainty, made more crucial by the declared objective of moving a large proportion of welfare beneficiaries into paid work.

Political uncertainty internally is another issue. Most areas of social policy have undergone fundamental and continuing change since 1984. Greater stability in areas such as health-service provision, retirement income and employment are crucial for maintaining standards of living and if people are to plan their futures. An emphasis on self-reliance, salient in social policy since 1990 and implicit in some policies before that date, requires people to take more individual responsibility for their future. But people need stability and certainty if they are to do this.

The main features of provision in New Zealand for the areas of income support, health and education services, housing, social services and other services, are now summarised below.

Key Features of Welfare Provision

Income Support

(a) Main income replacement benefits

	Purpose, coverage and eligibility
New Zealand Superannuation	Payable to persons at the qualifying age (rising from 60 to 65). Residential qualification applies
Unemployment Benefit (from 1 october 1999, Community Wage)	Payable to unemployed persons 18 or over and married people 16 and over with dependent children, able and willing to undertake suitable work. Numbers include *Independent Youth Benefit* (for those aged 16 or 17 who cannot live with their parents or be supported by them), *Job Search Allowance* and *55 Plus Benefit*
Domestic Purposes Benefit	Payable to single parents and some full-time caregivers of disabled people
Invalids' Benefit	Payable to persons 16 years and over, permanently and severely restricted in their capacity for work due to disability
Sickness Benefit	Payable to persons 16 years and over, temporarily incapacitated for work
Veterans Pensions	Pensions for persons who served with New Zealand forces and whose disability is related to war service

(b) *Supplementary Payments*

	Purpose, coverage and eligibility
Special Needs Grants	One-off payments to meet essential and specific emergency needs. Some grants have to be repaid. Available to beneficiaries and non-beneficiaries
Special Benefit	Paid to beneficiaries and non-beneficiaries who do not have enough income to meet ongoing essential expenses
Accommodation Supplement	Assists people with limited income and assets to pay accommodation costs
Disability Allowance	Reimburses people for costs that they incur because they have a disability
Handicapped Child Allowance	Non-means-tested payment to parent or guardian of a seriously disabled child who lives at home and requires constant care and attention
Child Care Subsidy	Financial assistance to low-income families with children under five to pay for childcare services

Note: Numbers are at 30 May 1998. Expenditure is for the year ending 30 May 1998.

Health Services

Primary care services	Access
General practice	Average GP charge NZ$30–40. Subsidies for Community Services Card (CSC) and 'high-use' card holders of NZ$15 for adults and NZ$20 for children
GP care for children 5 and under	Subsidies are intended to cover all GP consultation fees and prescription costs (but may not always do so)
Pharmaceuticals	Subsidies available to reduce maximum charge to NZ$3 for CSC holders and NZ$15 for others, although a premium charge is payable for some products
Laboratory services	No charge
Diagnostic services	No charge

(*Continued*)

Health Services

Dental services	No charge for children seen by dentists or in school dental clinics. Otherwise fees set by providers apply to everyone
Maternity care	No charge except for private specialists
Secondary care services	*Access*
Hospital in-patient services	No charge
Specialist out-patient services	No charge
Day-patient services	No charge
Mental health services	No charge

Education Services

Service	*Description*
Early childhood care and education services	Age range 0–4. The leading services (in numbers of enrolments) are childcare centres, kindergartens, Playcentres, Te Kohanga Reo (Maori pre-schools), home-based childcare, Pacific Island groups, various funding regimes and establishment grants
Primary and intermediate schools	The age of compulsory schooling is 6–15 but most children attend at 5. Primary schools cover the age range 5–12 and Intermediates 10–12. Schools are bulk-funded for operational grants and are moving to bulk-funding for teachers' salaries
Secondary schools	Age range 13–16 (compulsory) and beyond (post-compulsory). "Integrated" primary and secondary schools have the same system of control, management and funding as state schools. Most of these are Roman Catholic
Correspondence school	Primary and secondary education for students unable to attend a school because of isolation, suspension, medical or psychological problems, pregnancy or living overseas. Free apart from adult students
Special schools	For students with special needs, e.g. sensory disabilities, severe learning or behavioural

(Continued)

Education Services

	problems. There are also special education classes in mainstream schools. Schools receive extra funding for special needs students
Universities, polytechnics, colleges of education, Wananga (Maori tertiary institutions)	Admission based on school performance with open entry from age 25. Government provides the institutions with partial tuition subsidies based on EFTS calculated annually by the Ministry of Education. These are being gradually reduced to reach 75 per cent of tuition costs by 2000. Student allowances are means-tested on joint parental income to age 25. Interest-bearing student loans are available to cover fees, course costs and living expenses

Housing

Tenure	Per cent of private dwellings	Comment
Owned with mortgage	37	Obtained mainly from the private sector, especially banks
Owned without mortgage	32	High rates of mortgage-free ownership among older people (80 per cent for people 70 and over)
Total owner-occupied	*71*	
Rented in private sector	16	The vast majority rented from private individuals, small landlords owning under 10 properties
Rented in public sector	6	5 per cent Housing NZ or other central government agency; 1 per cent local authorities
Rented (landlord unspecified)	3	
Total rented	*25*	
Occupied rent free	4	Housing attached to work-places, farms
Total	*100*	

Source: 1996 Census, National Summary, Table 30.

Social Services and Other

Service/programme	Description
Child Support	Operates under the Child Support Act of 1991. The Child Support Agency, part of the Inland Revenue Department, accepts applications, assesses amount of support, collects payments through the PAYE system and pays them out. Payments are passed on to the Government if the recipient is receiving a welfare benefit and to the custodial parent if they are not
Family Assistance	Paid through the Inland Revenue Department, this consists of *Family Support*, which is calculated based on a family's income and the ages and number of the children; *Guaranteed Minimum Family Income* and *Independent Family Tax Credit*. These last two are extra payments for non-beneficiaries
Disabled Persons Community Welfare	Operates under DPCW Act 1975 – car loans, rehabilitation allowances etc. Home-based care for older people and people with disabilities – home alterations loans, appliances and equipment
Children and Young Persons Service (CYPS) Department of Social Welfare	The CYP Act 1989 set up a system of Family Group Conferences to deal with care and protection cases. The service also provides information and referral services, family support services and custodial and guardianship services. The Youth Justice service operates under the same act and deals with offenders up to and including age 16
Community Funding Agency (CFA) Department of Social Welfare	Allocation and delivery of funding and support to community-based social and welfare service providers, for example, child and youth support programmes – life skills training, OSCAR (out-of-school hours care). Counselling and therapy for families and individuals. Family Service Centres – programmes for at-risk families. Home-based support and assistance – social work. Includes special Maori programmes, emergency housing and women's refuges. To merge with CYPS in 1999

References

Boston, J., Martin. J., Pallot, J. and Walsh, P. (1996) *Public Management: The New Zealand Model*, Oxford University Press.

Boston, J. and Dalziel, P. (eds) (1992) *The Decent Society? Essays in Response to National's Economic and Social Policies*, Oxford University Press.

Castles, F. (1985) *The Working Class and Welfare*, Allen & Unwin.

Castles, F. (1996) 'Needs-Based Strategies of Social Protection in Australia and New Zealand', in G. Esping-Anderson (ed.), *Welfare States in Transition: National Adaptations in Global Economies*, Sage.

Cheyne, C., O'Brien, M. and Belgrave, M. (1997) *Social Policy in Aotearoa/New Zealand: A Critical Introduction*, Oxford University Press.

Dalziel, P. (1994) 'A Decade of Radical Economic Reform in New Zealand', *British Review of New Zealand Studies*, 7, pp. 49–72.

Dalziel, P. (1996) *Poor Policy: A Report for the New Zealand Council of Christian Social Services on the 1991 Benefit Cuts and the 1996 Tax Cuts*, Council of Christian Social Services.

Deeks, J. and Boxall, P. (1989) *Labour Relations in New Zealand*, Longman Paul.

DSW (1996) *Strategic Directions: Post-election Briefing Paper*, Department of Social Welfare, Wellington.

EMG (1989) *The Economy in Transition: Restructuring to 1989*, Economic Monitoring Group, New Zealand Planning Council.

Esping-Andersen, G. (1990) *The Three Worlds of Welfare Capitalism*, Princeton University Press.

Ferguson, G. (1994) *Building the New Zealand Dream*, The Dunmore Press Ltd.

Finn, D. (1999) 'A Job for the Unemployed: Lessons from Australian Welfare Reform', *Journal of Social Policy*, 28(1), pp. 53–72.

Le Heron, R. and Pawson, E. (eds)(1996) *Changing Places: New Zealand in the Nineties*, Longman Paul.

McClure, M. (1998) *A Civilised Community: A history of Social Security in New Zealand 1898–1998*, Auckland University Press.

Oliver, W. H. (1988) 'Social Policy in New Zealand: An Historical Overview', *The April Report* (Report of the Royal Commission on Social Policy) vol. 1, pp. 3–45.

Orange, C. (1987) *The Treaty of Waitangi*, Allen & Unwin/Port Nicholson Press.

PRG (1997) *1997 Retirement Income Report:* A Review of the Current Framework Interim Report, Periodic Report Group.

RCSP (1988) *The April Report*, Report of the Royal Commission on Social Policy, Government Printer.

Royal Commission (1972) *Social Security in New Zealand*, Report of the Royal Commission of Inquiry, Government Printer.

Shipley, J. (1991) *Social Assistance: Welfare that Works*, GP Print Ltd.

Spicker, P. (1995) *Social Policy: Themes and Approaches*, Prentice Hall–Harvester Wheatsheaf.

Stephens, R. Waldegrave, C. and Frater, P. (1995) 'Measuring Poverty in New Zealand', *Social Policy Journal of New Zealand*, 5, pp. 88–112.

Treasury (1990) *Briefing for the Incoming Government*, The Treasury.

Upton, S. (1991) *Your Health and the Public Health*, GP Print Ltd.

Wilkes, C. and Shirley, I. (edn) (1984) *In the Public Interest: Health, Work and Housing in New Zealand*, Benton Ross Ltd.

CHAPTER 6

Japan: Bidding Farewell to the Welfare Society

TAKAFUMI KEN UZUHASHI

Overview

Population

Japan is one of the Far East countries sometimes referred to as the 'Asian Tigers' of the Pacific Rim. The country consists of four principal islands on which 123 million people live. Since the area of the country is fairly small, about 377,800 square kilometers, Japan is densely populated by Western standards. This high population density is a feature not only of Japan but also of some other Asian Tigers such as South Korea, Singapore and Taiwan. Why they are so densely populated is not clear – although some have claimed the production of rice as a staple food is a possible cause, as a given amount of rice can feed more people than other grains and yet rice production is relatively labour-intensive. Whatever the cause, however, the resulting population density has been a key feature structuring the development of economic and social policy within these countries. What is more, in recent years the issue of population has been attracting more and more attention in Japanese policy planning. This attention is not so much related to the number of the people, however, but rather to the structure of it. That is the 'problem' of aging. Japan has seen a growth in the proportion of older people in its population, which has been much more rapid that that of many other comparative countries, as Table 6.1 demonstrates,

Furthermore, ageing Japan will be super-aged by the year 2020, when this proportion is projected to be 26.9 per cent. This aging is also combined with a declining fertility rate. The current fertility rate (1997) in Japan is 1.39, far below the replacement level of 2.1. It is obvious that this ageing along with the lowering fertility rate will have a huge impact on social policies in Japan.

Economic Growth

The other key element structuring policy development in Japan has been the country's rapid economic growth. The scale of growth in the fifty years up to

Table 6.1 Aging populations, some international comparisons

	UK	USA	Sweden	France	Japan
Number of years for population aged 65 and over to move from 7 per cent to 14 per cent	46	69	82	114	24

the mid-1970s was quite remarkable – the miracle of the Japanese economy – based especially on the export of popular consumer goods such as cameras, radios, TV sets and cars. GDP per capita in the year 1997 was US$34,000, one of the highest in the world. This rapid economic growth also went hand in hand with massive changes in industrial structure within the country. The agricultural and fishery sector, which in 1968 employed 21 per cent of the total workforce, employed only 5 per cent in 1997 – fewer than in the construction industry. Yet in 1997, 22 per cent were working in the manufacturing industry, 25 per cent in the service industry.

As a result of these changes, many people have moved from rural areas to urban cities, where a lot of large-scale firms were founded. In particular, large urban capitals like Tokyo, Osaka, Yokohama, Fukuoka and Kobe have been created. This has also resulted in major changes to family structure, with urban dwellers experiencing different family types to those of their parents in rural districts. There has been a decline in the prevalence of traditional, three-generation, Japanese families, which in tandem with the decline in fertility, discussed above, has resulted in an overall fall in family sizes. The three-generation family type used to be 19.2 per cent of all types in 1966, but has declined to 11.6 per cent in 1996. On the other hand, the nuclear family type and single-unit family are on the rise. The average number in a family was about five until the mid-1950s, but had been reduced to 2.8 by 1997.

These changes have altered the need for social security, which must now accommodate a modern urban life rather than an agricultural rural life. People living in cities no longer expect to rely on the traditional family care and support when in need; for example in the case of child rearing or caring for the elderly. Thus the need for welfare provision by the state has begun to grow and grow. The economic growth which Japan experienced during the period of urbanisation could afford to fund these welfare costs, and this has resulted in massive changes in social policy over the last fifty years. But the journey to a welfare state has not been a painless one. It took a long time for Japan to create a modern welfare system, and the country is still facing some difficulties as a result of both internal and external pressures. This was especially the case after the late 1970s when the growth rate declined and government budgetary restraint reached crisis levels. As we shall see, this appeared to trigger a watershed for welfare development in Japan; and it is notable that the idea of a Japanese-type of 'welfare society' emerged in this period, supporting the case for welfare retrenchment. We will return to these issues towards the end of this chapter.

Brief History

Before the Second World War

Japan bade farewell to its feudal economic and political systems and paved the way for the creation of a modern capitalistic nation at the time of the Meiji Restoration in 1867. After that the government abandoned previous 'close-the-door' policies and sought to tackle two new goals which were regarded as essential to avoid the country being colonised by Western powers:

- The encouragement and development of manufacturing industries; and
- The creation of a strong military.

The 130 years since 1867 is usually divided into two periods. The first is up to the end of the Second World War in 1945, and the second is thereafter. These two periods differ from each other in respect of both political systems and economic life and ideas. In short, after 1945, Japan restarted as a democratic nation departing forever from its past militaristic regime. We do not have space to explore social policy in the pre-Second World War period in detail here, but two points must be mentioned.

First, social policy developed relatively late. But even under the military regime, few social policy measures were enacted in the earlier period. Health services, for example, began to be provided in 1927 on the basis of insurance (Employees' Health Insurance, EHI), although this covered only employees in large firms. Pension schemes (the Employees' Pension Insurance, EPI) were introduced in 1942, covering similar kinds of workers; and as with other late-developing capitalistic countries, Japan sought to adopt an insurance basis for provision, aiming to imitate the carrot-and-stick ideas of Bismarckian social insurance schemes.

In Japan it was civil servants in central government and military members with their families who were the first priorities to be covered by the insurance protection (pension and health services) run by the state. These were followed later by local civil servants and employees in large firms. However, it was only later, in the post-Second World War period that other groups of workers and farmers were covered.

Second, the meaning of the term social policy was differentiated. In 1897, early on in comparative terms, the Japanese Social Policy Association was founded with the aims of social amelioration and reconciliation of classes. The main issue the Association discussed at this time, however, was Factory Acts. This symbolically shows the importance that was initially put on the welfare of the working people. This too was a feature of social policies in the late-developed nations; and it was only after the end of the Second World War that the idea of citizenship as a focus for policy was introduced.

Even today the concept of social policy in Japanese (shakai-seisaku) has a different meaning to that in English. It refers to specific protections for working people as well as more general schemes for citizens; for instance, the Labour Standard Law and industrial relations policy. On the other hand, social security (shakai-hosyo in Japanese), which could be understood as an integration of social assistance and social insurance, seems to be similar to the term social policy in English. It embraces not only income maintenance but also schemes for health services and personal social services. Yet housing policy and education are not included in social policy or in social security in Japan.

After the Second World War

From the end of the Second World War to the peace treaty of 1951, Japan was under the joint sovereignty of the Allied Forces and the Japanese government. During that time a range of innovative measures were implemented which included the establishment of the new Constitution, reform of farmland and the dismantling of saibatsu (financial groups). These measures amounted to a significant element of democratisation in the country. The fifty years after this are usually divided into three periods:

1 Arrangement of national minimum;
2 Expansion; and
3 Reform and Retrenchment.

Arrangement of National Minimum (1945–1950s)

During this period most of the welfare implemented followed a US model, except for social insurance provision, where the Beveridge Report was reputed to have had a huge influence on policy-planning. In the year 1955, a government White Paper, from the Economic Planning Agency, declared that Japan was no longer a postwar economy. And in the political arena, too, the year symbolised significant change when the newly amalgamated conservative party (Liberal Democratic Party) came into power, remaining so for the next 39 years.

In more practical terms, this immediate postwar period saw the introduction of new welfare acts and social insurance schemes. There were three welfare acts (one of which was then extended): the Livelihood Protection Act 1946 (the old act – means-tested social assistance; the Children's Welfare Act 1947; the Disabled Welfare Act 1949; and the Livelihood Protection Act 1950 (the new Act – widening its scope and creating the right of appeal). There were also a number of insurance schemes: the Unemployment

Insurance Act 1947; reform of the Employees' Pension Insurance (EPI) in 1954; reform of the National Health Insurance (NHI, a residual flat-rate scheme managed by local authorities) in 1959; and the National Pension Insurance (NPI, a residual flat-rate scheme managed by local authorities) of 1961.

As a result of these changes, 1961 is referred to in Japan as the year when the whole of the people were covered by pension and health insurance.

Expansion (1960s–1970s)

In the 1960s the priority of government policy in Japan was the promotion of national economic growth rather than the further development of social policy and social welfare (see Campbell, 1992). The prevailing ideology of policy-makers was, as it were, to increase the size of the cake more rapidly, rather than to share it more fairly. Thus, only in the late 1960s and early 1970s, after successful economic growth had been achieved, did any expansion of welfare occur. Major changes included: the Elderly Welfare Act 1963; the introduction of the Fund of Employees' Pension Insurance in 1966; the reduction of health charges borne by insured persons – from 50 per cent of the whole medical bill to 30 per cent (NHI) – in 1968; the introduction of Children's Allowance 1972 – the last-implemented social security provision; the reduction of health charges borne by the insured employee's family in 1973 – from 50 per cent of the whole medical bill to 30 per cent (Employees' Health Insurance, EHI); free medical services for the elderly aged 70 and over in 1973; indexing introduced on a sliding-scale system to employees' pensions (EPI), also in 1973; and increases in various insurance benefits (EPI, NPI, the non-contributory Welfare Pension) in 1973.

As a result of these changes, 1973 is called the first year of welfare in Japan.

Reform and Retrenchment (1980s to date)

In the last two decades of the twentieth century, however, welfare provision in Japan has been subject to many of the pressures for reform and retrenchment which have been experienced in many other advanced industrial countries. This has led to the introduction of a number of changes aimed at responding to the need for financial tightening and the growing proportion of older people in the population at the beginning of the twenty-first century.

- 1982 – The Elderly Medical Services Act, which abolished free medical services for the elderly aged 70 and over;
- 1982 – reformed regulation of the Livelihood Protection Act, which strictly checked fraud;

- 1984 – reformed EHI, which introduced a charge to be borne by the insured person of 10 per cent of the whole medical bill;
- 1985 – reduction of the charge borne by the state, from 80 per cent to 70 per cent, of the running costs of social welfare facilities;
- 1986 – reformation of NPI and EPI by reduction of benefits, and widening its scope through the newly-established Basic Pension Scheme;
- 1994 – reformation of EPI (change of entitlement age from 60 to 65).

Partly as a result of the changes driven by the pressures of an aging population, the year 1986 is referred to as the first year of pension reform.

Outline of Japan's Social Security Programmes

Pensions

Pension schemes, as with health services mentioned above, are mainly organised on the basis of insurance in Japan. All citizens are expected to join the mandatory and contributory insurance schemes to provide for their old age. Until 1985, there were several different kinds of occupational and statutory pension schemes, organised on an industry basis. For instance, workers in private firms, civil servants, the self-employed, sailors and national railway workers were expected to join their own independent pension schemes. However, there were a number of problems with such a system. First, there were gaps between, or inequalities within, the level of provision and insurance premiums. Second, at times of rapid change in industrial structure, as has been the case in many industries, some insurance schemes faced serious financial problems. For instance, the schemes for sailors and national railway workers were on the verge of bankruptcy in the 1980s.

Pension reform in 1986 introduced a new, flat-rate, basic pension scheme which every insured person of each occupational pension was supposed to join. Since then, public pension schemes have been of a two-storied structure. Basic pension is the first floor of protection, and each income-related occupational pension is the second floor – with membership of such secondary provision being mandatory. These reforms also integrated the sailors' pension into EPI and implemented measures for mutual financial cooperation among pension schemes. As a result, therefore, the ten occupational schemes which existed before 1985 had, by 1997, been integrated into one basic pension and six occupational schemes.

Furthermore, since 1986, the wives of male workers (or more accurately the non-working spouses of all workers), who used to be able to join NPI voluntarily, have been required to join the basic pension scheme. However, they are entitled to benefits with no additional charges or contributions. Thus the principle of 'one pension for one person' was established as part of the reform process.

Health Services

As a nation Japan has one of the highest levels of longevity by international standards. Life expectancy in 1996 was 77.1 for men and 83.6 for women. And there can be little doubt that the development of health insurance schemes, which have improved access to modern medical treatment, have contributed to this phenomenon. Public (mandatory) health insurance is in practice divided into several independent schemes. However, they can be classified broadly into two groups. The first includes occupational schemes (EHI and some Mutual Aid Associations, MAA); for these, premiums are fixed on an income-related basis. The second is flat-rate residual provision (NHI), administered by local authorities and covering farmers, the self-employed and retired people.

Therefore, when people see a doctor, they pay a charge, and the charge-rate is determined largely as follows: under EHI and MAA, the insured person pays 20 per cent of the health bill (10 per cent until 1997); dependents on examination pay 30 per cent of the health bill; and dependent on hospitalisation pay 20 per cent of the health bill. Under NHI, all persons pay 30 per cent of the health bill. Older people, aged 70 and over, pay certain charges when examined or hospitalised – Yen 500 for each examination, and Yen 1100 for one-day's hospitalisation (170 Yen ≡ £1 sterling, 2001 prices).

Social Assistance

Social assistance schemes in Japan are based on the Livelihood Protection Act, and as in most countries, this protection is means-tested. The level of benefits is fairly generous, but the numbers of recipients are relatively small and have actually declined within the last forty years (see Eardley *et al.*, 1996). In the year 1955, 1.9 million people were recipients but by 1996 this had fallen to 0.9 million; this is only 0.71 per cent of the population, a much lower proportion than in other advanced countries. Questions may be asked, therefore, about this low, and declining, percentage of recipients of social assistance, and there seem to be several reasons for it.

For a start, the legislation stipulates that support and maintenance by applicants' relatives should be regarded as the first port of call in the meeting of basic needs. In line with this, the welfare bureaucracy administering the scheme checks all applications under stringent income and asset tests. Receipt of the social assistance benefits is supposed to be literally a measure of last resort, and therefore this administration provokes a deep sense of stigma amongst applicants and recipients – and, more generally, amongst the public at large (see Gould, 1993). This is inevitably likely to lead to low levels of take-up; and, although there is no official governmental survey of take-up levels, some critics have argued that it is as little as a quarter of eligible people.

The fall in the number of recipients over the last forty years is probably also largely attributable to rises in the standard of living, and the spread of pension cover. However, in the late 1980s this fall has been much sharper – from 1.4 in 1985 to 0.9 million in 1990. This may rather be the result of stricter administrative procedures, referred to in official parlance as 'proper or appropriate measures'. By the 1980s the two main categories by household type in receipt of assistance benefits were older people and lone parents, by proportion 4.2 per cent and 9.1 per cent respectively.

Child Allowances and Personal Social Services

Child allowances were the last form of social security provision to be implemented in Japan. The reason for this delay was that, prior to their introduction, there had existed a similar, but non-statutory allowance, paid by private firms to their employees. And even after implementation, these two kinds of allowances can coexist, at least for employees in large-scale enterprises. There are two problems with statutory child allowances, however. The first is that the level of benefit is fairly low, especially for the first child. The second is that only families with children under three are entitled to receive it. For this reason the scheme is sometimes referred to as the 'baby and toddler's allowance'.

Personal social services in Japan mainly consist of services for the elderly, the physically and mentally disabled, lone-parent mothers and child-care services. We cannot cover these in detail here, although for discussion of lone-parent protection see Bradshaw *et al.* (1996). However, it is important to note that in 1990 the administration of these social welfare services was changed, with local authorities (cities, towns and villages as administrative units – about 3,300 in total) becoming responsible for various services to the elderly and the handicapped.

Education and Housing

As we mentioned earlier, education and housing are not generally regarded as part of social policy or social security in Japan. Nevertheless, the key features of such provision are shown in Boxes 6.1 and 6.2.

Box 6.1   Education (All figures are for 1994–95)

State Education

6–14 Compulsory elementary (6–11) and compulsory junior high school (12–14), mainly funded by local government, with a long-established national curriculum controlled by the Ministry of Education.

(Continued)

(Box 6.1   Continued)

15–17 Optional senior high school, subject to entry requirements – 96.7 per cent of junior high-school graduates go on to this level (including private schools).

18+   Optional higher education, subject to entry requirements, in four-year university or two-year junior college places, funded by central or local government – 36.1 per cent of senior high-school graduates go on to this level (including private schools).

Private Education

5–18+   Fee-paying access to private schools, privately funded and controlled, mostly subsidised by the state – the proportion of students going to private schools at each level is: elementary school, 0.8 per cent; junior high school, 4.9 per cent; senior high school, 30 per cent; junior college, 92.5 per cent; University, 73.4 per cent.

Pre-School Education

49.3 per cent of 3–5s go to nursery schools, either public (20 per cent) or private (80 per cent), all with a half-day programme controlled by the Ministry of Education – called kindergarten in Japan.

31.7 per cent of 3–5s go to full-time day nurseries, either public (54 per cent) or private (46 per cent), controlled by the Ministry of Health and Welfare.

Box 6.2   Housing

Owner-Occupied (1998 – 69.0 per cent population)

Dwelling bought for cash price on open market; most purchasers borrow a large proportion of the cost as a mortgage from a bank repaid over 20 or 25 years.

Public Renting (1998 – 4.4 per cent population)

Local authorities are major landlords. Dwellings are for low-income residents; tenants pay monthly rents which are low compared to private renting.

(Continued)

(*Box 6.2   Continued*)

Private Renting (*1998 – 18.7 per cent population*)

Tenants pay monthly rent to a private landlord, based on the market rate for tenancies; there is no rent subsidy to the low paid and unemployed.

Social Housing (*1998 – 1.7 per cent population*)

Housing associations – private bodies with public regulation and subsidy; no rent subsidy to the low-paid and unemployed.

Company House and Official Residence
(*1998 – 3.3 per cent population*)

Dwellings for employees and civil servants – provided as part of corporate welfare; rents are fairly low.

Features of the Japanese Welfare State

The Scale of Social Security

We examine here the level of resources which go into the three main sections of social security consisting of medical services, pensions and others (see Figure 6.1). The costs of social security in Japan comprised up to 17 per cent of the GDP in the year 1995, and this proportion has almost doubled in the last twenty years – from 9.5 per cent in 1975. But the level is still not high compared to other countries (see Figure 6.2). When comparing the proportions for each section of expenditure, medical services had been at the top of the three until the year 1980; but since 1981 pension expenditure has been at the top – 51.8 per cent in 1995. What is more, viewed from a comparative perspective, the proportion of 'others', which mainly consists of social assistance, child allowance and personal social services, is remarkably small. This low level of provision is certainly one of the distinguishing features of Japanese welfare provision. However, the expansion of elderly care services towards the twenty-first century and the Elderly Care Services Insurance Schemes which will be implemented in the year of 2000, alongside other factors, are likely to alter the picture to some extent and are expected to boost the proportion of 'others' in the early years of the next century.

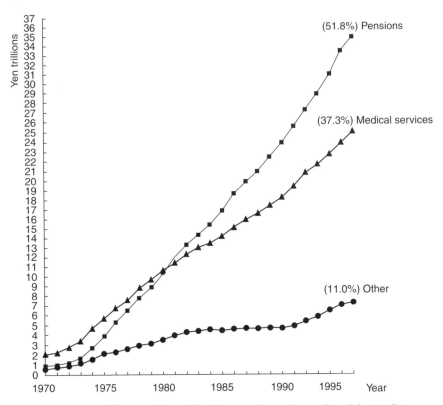

Figure 6.1 Composition of the three main sections of social security

Source: National Institute of Population and Social Security Research, *Shakai Hosho Kyuhu-hi*, 1998.

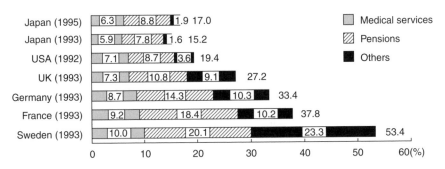

Figure 6.2 Ratio of social security benefits to national income

Source: National Institute of Population and Social Security Research, *Shakai Hosho Kyuhu-hi*, 1997.

Table 6.2 Income distribution and redistribution

Year	Gini coefficient (pre-transfer)	Gini coefficient (post-transfer)	Net redistributive effect	Redistributive effect by tax	Redistributive effect by social security
1961	0.390	0.344	11.8%	—	—
1966	0.375	0.328	12.6	3.7%	8.7%
1971	0.354	0.314	11.4	4.4	5.7
1974	0.375	0.346	7.8	2.9	4.5
1977	0.365	0.338	7.4	3.7	1.2
1980	0.349	0.314	10.0	5.4	5.0
1983	0.398	0.343	13.8	3.8	9.8
1986	0.405	0.338	16.5	4.2	12.0
1989	0.433	0.364	15.9	2.9	12.5
1992	0.439	0.365	17.0	3.2	13.2

Source: Ministry of Health and Welfare, *Survey of Income Redistribution, each year.*

Income Distribution and Redistribution

Patterns of equality and inequality in Japan underwent significant change in the latter part of the twentieth century. Table 6.2 shows the income distribution, as expressed by gini coefficient, and the redistribution effect through tax and social security provision. This table tells us a number of things. First, in the 1960s, during a period of high economic growth, income distribution in Japan became more equal; second, from 1973 to 1975, during a period of economic turmoil caused by the oil shock, this pattern was reversed for a short while; and third, in the late 1980s, during the so-called 'bubble economy', this trend towards inequality was accelerated. This last change was mainly the result of changes in asset-based incomes; and even since the bubble 'burst' in the early 1990s, this trend has still been continuing.

Therefore, although the total redistribution effect has been increasing over the last 30 years, income distribution before tax and social security transfers began to move in the opposite direction to a significant extent. In other words, the efforts to redistribute have not been able to offset trends towards greater initial inequality. The result of this is that income equality after transfers in the year 1992 was smaller than that in 1960; and this has led some people to argue that Japan is losing its advantageous position as an egalitarian society.

Of course, cross-national comparisons of income distribution are very difficult to make for a number of well-known reasons. The variability of statistical bases and the different definitions of survey units make direct comparisons difficult. These problems have been resolved to some extent by the establishment of large-scale international data sets such as the Luxembourg Income Study (LIS). Japan was asked to join the LIS project, but the Japanese government rejected the proposal for domestic legal reasons. Therefore it is not easy to identify how equal or unequal Japanese income distribution is in comparison to other countries. At one time the dominant view in Japan was that it was one of the most egalitarian of advanced societies; but, taking the recent trends towards inequality and reduced levels of redistribution seen in Table 6.2 into consideration, this optimistic view is under revision.

The Japanese Welfare Regime

Although interest in the character of Japan's welfare system has been growing among Westerners, there is still confusion as to the nature or typology of the Japanese welfare state. The reasons for this are twofold. First, as Japan's data is not included in the LIS it cannot be proven what 'outcome' social policy in Japan is bringing about in terms of poverty alleviation and income redistribution. Second, scholars in Japan have not attempted to clarify the character of Japan's welfare state using commonly accepted analytical frameworks.

One means of seeking to classify Japanese welfare provision, which has become quite popular (see Jones, 1993), is to regard the East Asian nations such as Japan as Confucian welfare states. However, this is a somewhat misleading approach: first, because such a general anthropological grasp cannot explain the drastic changes of the way of life, and the way of thinking, which people in Japan have experienced over the last fifty years; and second because even if the mutual care and support provided by family members in three-generation households still remains, it is not influenced by the Confucian ideology in any sense, but rather is peculiar to the traditional rural society. Thus in practice rapid industrialisation has taken over traditional family welfare. Therefore any attempt to classify the Japanese welfare regime must utilise the methodologies and typologies developed by modern comparative analysis, notably Esping-Andersen (1990), Castles (1985) and Mishra (1990) – the three most influential scholars in this field. Esping-Andersen is the only one of the three to examine Japan, and according to his decommodification index (1990, p. 52) Japan is classified as a corporatist regime, though the differences from liberal Great Britain are very narrow.

In terms of the following indices, which are supposed to be key features of corporatist welfare states such as Germany, France and Italy, Japan can be said to belong to them:

- *Stratification* (status-differentiated social insurance schemes, occupational grouping) and *guiding principles* (hierarchy, authority and direct subordination of the individual to the patriarch or state);
- *Preservation* of traditional family structures;
- *Ranking* by a decommodification index; and
- *Redistributive* impact.

On the other hand, Japan has much in common with liberal welfare-state regimes in terms of a strong sense of stigma, modest level of benefits (in particular child benefits) and liberal work ethics. Ragin (1994) therefore places Japan in a sub-type of 'corporativistic countries that lean toward the liberal world'. But this is the only half the story, as a discussion of unemployment rates and levels of social security expenditure reveals.

Esping-Andersen refers to the importance of policies to pursue full employment as the crucial character of social-democratic regimes. If this is right then Japan, where the unemployment rate is very low (3.4 per cent in 1997) might be characterised as a social-democratic, liberal and corporatist welfare regime – obviously a self-contradictory conclusion. And, strictly speaking, even if Japan has enjoyed full employment, that does not necessarily mean that it has a social democratic regime. Esping-Andersen also emphasised that full employment was a precondition for social-democratic regimes to afford high levels of social security expenditure,

> On the one side, the right to work has equal status to the right of income protection. On the other side, the enormous costs of maintaining a solidaristic, universalistic, and de-commodifying welfare system means that it must minimize social problems and maximize revenue income. This is obviously best done with most people working, and the fewest possible living off social transfers. (Esping-Andersen, 1990, p. 28)

While Esping-Andersen points out the 'supplementary' relationship between full employment and high social expenditure as shown above, it is Castles who implies that there can be a 'substitutive' relationship between them,

> real welfare outcomes are not necessarily solely a function of the extent of income maintenance expenditures. They also depend crucially on the level of employment, the level of remuneration accruing from employment and the resulting distribution of primary income from employment. (Castles, 1985, p. 82)

Therefore, in order to understand Japan's characteristics it is necessary not only to apply the standard, widely-accepted rulers, but also to develop innovative ways of assessment and categorisation. In this respect, Mishra (1990), with his emphasis on full employment, is helpful. Mishra seems to argue that a policy for full employment basically proceeds alongside a progressive social security policy, but this is not necessarily the case as Figure 6.3 shows. The figure is divided into four quadrants using the average social security expenditure of seven countries in 1970 and 1989, 14.5 per cent, and the average unemployment rates of the seven countries in 1970 and 1989, 3.9 per cent. In the fourth quadrant of the figure, where Sweden remains located and where Austria used to be, we can observe the supplementary relationship – that is, full employment can afford to maintain a high standard of social security expenditure. The first quadrant, where no countries were located in 1970 but Great Britain, Austria and Canada are located in 1989, might be regarded as somewhat unstable because the precondition of compensating the high social security costs by full employment is lacking. In the third quadrant, where Great Britain and Australia used to be and Japan still remains, a low unemployment rate and low

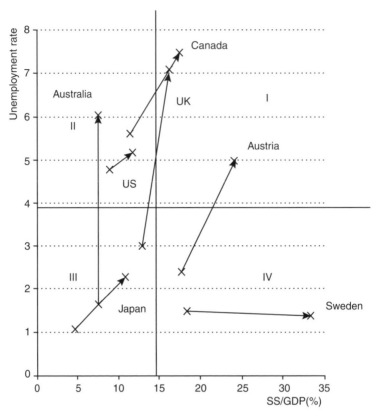

Figure 6.3   The cost of social security, from 1978/80 to 1987/89

Source: International Labour Organization data adapted from *The Cost of Social Security,*
11th International Inquiry, 1978–1980 and *The Cost of Social Security,*
14th International Inquiry, 1987–1989.

social expenditure coexist. This suggests that full employment is shouldering
the function of social security – that is, that there is a substitutive relationship.

After experiencing a 'crisis' in their welfare states many countries shifted
towards the upper-right in Figure 6.3 – undergoing a rise in unemployment
and an increase in social expenditure. In these conditions, Japan's uniqueness
becomes more and more prominent throughout this period. If 'shouldering or
substituting the role of social security by full employment', could be regarded
as 'workfare', then Japan could be classified as a *workfare* state.

Welfare Reform and Retrenchment

Financial Deficits

Most of the advanced nations in the OECD have been facing serious financial
(budgetary) deficits in the last quarter of the twentieth century, and Japan is no

exception to this. The government has tried to improve the budgetary balance several times; for instance, in 1989 value added tax (VAT, called the consumption tax in Japan) was introduced and in 1997 its rate was raised from 3 per cent to 5 per cent. But this did nothing to improve the situation. More recently, in 1997, the government enacted a Financial Structure Reform Act with the goal of controlling the ratio of deficits to GDP to within 3 per cent by the year 2003 (from 5.4 per cent in 1997). But the prospects for realising this are not bright.

This financial problem has emerged since the recession following the oil-price shocks of the mid 1970s. It is important to notice that this oil-price crisis coincided with a period of welfare expansion in Japan – 1973 was the first year of welfare. This has led some critics to suggest that the second year never came, but this is an exaggeration. However, after the late 1970s the government began tightening controls over social security expenditures, and welfare retrenchment was started.

Welfare Retrenchment

Owing to financial tightening throughout the 1980s and 1990s, every field of Japanese social security underwent thorough reform, and this is still ongoing. Some critics have described this process as 'the complete cut down of welfare'; but the reality is not so simple, because the motive for reform is twofold. Facing financial problems is one factor; but at the same time the country is seeking to prepare for the coming aging of the Japanese population. Measures have been implemented in the field of pensions and health services where the keynote is retrenchment; and in the field of personal social services new measures for financial funding aiming to widen the scope of beneficiaries, particularly amongst the elderly, have been implemented – as represented by the introduction of the Elderly Care Services Insurance Scheme.

A number of objectives and techniques are common across these various reforms:

- The reduction of financial expenses by central government. This has occurred in every part of social security schemes, particularly in pensions and medical services. And in some cases, as the other side of these measures, local authorities have been asked to contribute more funding to maintain protection. This can be seen in social assistance benefit, the child-rearing allowance for divorced and unmarried single mothers, and the running costs of welfare facilities such as nursing homes for frail older people.
- The levelling down of benefits. This has been most prominent in the pension reforms of 1986. The benefits of the Mutual Aid Association (MAA) were reduced to dissolve the inequality between civil servants and employees of private firms; and the benefits of EPI itself were also sharply reduced to cope with current financial difficulties and to secure future financial stability for the scheme.

- The raising of user or client charges. This has been most prominent in the health services, typically shown by the abolition of free medical services for the elderly aged 70 and over in the year 1982.

The Elderly Care Services Insurance Scheme

It is estimated that in the year 1993 there were around two million frail older people in Japan needing some intensive care services. This number is projected to rise to 2.8 million in 2000, and to 5.2 million in 2025. This is an inevitable consequence of the rapid aging of the country's population; and it is no exaggeration to say that the issue of how to provide adequate and effective care services to these people has now become of the greatest interest among the public. Up to now the trend has been for significant numbers of frail older people to be placed in hospitals – often called long-term social hospitalisation. This is a product of shortages of welfare facilities, insufficient delivery of home-help support in their residences, and the declining capacity of families to care. This is not an effective or an efficient response. What such people need is not medical treatment but care services; and yet the cost of the former (medical treatment) is usually more expensive than the latter (care services). However, it is no simple matter to turn to family care for older people. Even with direct aid for helpers, the burden of care is extraordinarily heavy and carers are often exhausted by it. What is more, this form of care has a significant and damaging gender dimension, because most of the carers are women such as wives, daughters or daughters-in-law.

It is within this context that the Elderly Care Services Insurance Scheme has been developed and is due to be implemented in the year 2000. Its key features are:

1 Insurer: local authorities – cities, towns and villages as administrative units.
2 Insured: people aged 40 and over (people aged 65 and over are called the first insured; people aged 40–64 are called the second insured).
3 Fund: 45 per cent – public fund (central government 22.5 per cent; prefecture 11.25 per cent, cities, towns and villages 11.25 per cent); 45 per cent contribution by the insured; and 10 per cent charges borne by the service users.
4 Services provided: institutional welfare services and domiciliary welfare services.
5 Insurance premium: estimated at about Yen 3,000 monthly

The insured form two groups according to their age. Those aged 65 and over are entitled to care services in circumstances where they are 'frail' (recognised as being in need for care by the organisation which is set up by local authorities), regardless of reasons for this need. People aged 40–64 are entitled to similar services if their frail conditions arise as a result of one of 15 specific diseases. These conditions are classified into five degrees, each of which has a maximum budget within which the family can choose the kind and amount of the care services. Unlike similar insurance schemes in Europe, cash is not provided to the family.

There have been fierce arguments as to how care services for frail older people should be delivered in Japan. Delivery through social assistance schemes was considered as an option, which would mean provision financed by tax revenues rather than by contributions from insured citizens. In respect of the right of entitlement, however, delivery through the insurance mechanism was thought to be superior to social assistance schemes because of the stigma attached to assistance discussed above.

However, the insurance system is not a panacea. Firstly, there is a concern that people who cannot afford to pay the monthly contribution would be automatically deprived of benefits, as seen in National Health Insurance (NHI) and National Pension insurance (NPI). Secondly, there is the problem that in some districts people cannot expect to have sufficient quality and quantity of services – what some critics have dubbed 'insurance schemes without delivery of services'. But even with these anticipated problems, the implementation of the Elderly Care Services Insurance Schemes means that people enter the welfare market (which is called silver market in Japan) with high purchasing power (Yen 4.8 trillion). This huge demand will stimulate the supply of care services in which the private sector will come to play a more and more important role.

Pension Reform

Pension schemes in Japan are facing difficulties from the aging of the population; and, in contrast to the relatively bright future for elderly care services, the outlook here seems more pessimistic. The proportion of the retired older generation to the active working generation, which was 11.7 per cent in 1970, rose to 25.0 per cent in 1997 and is projected to reach 50.2 per cent in 2025. If the pension schemes were run on a fully-funded basis, then these demographic changes would not affect the pension finance. This used to be the case in Japan, but during the expansion in the 1970s provision was changed to a pay-as-you-go base, so that most of the insurance premiums paid by active working people are transferred to pensioners. As early as 1986, the so-called first year of the pension reform, measures were taken to raise insurance premiums and to reduce the benefit level.

In 1997, the Ministry of Health and Welfare (MHW) presented a document called *Plans of Pension Reform: Five Options*. Three of the five options proposed raising insurance premiums and cutting benefit. Under these plans premiums would be raised from the current 17.35 per cent of income (based on a fifty–fifty contribution from employers and employees) to 26–34 per cent, and benefit reductions of 10–40 per cent were proposed. The current expected level for a model married couple, who joined the pension insurance plan forty years ago, is Yen 230 thousand per month – about 62 per cent of the average net income earned by working people. Another option was to maintain the current level of benefit with twice the present premiums; and still another proposed to replace the public pension (EPI) with private and personal pensions run on a fully-funded basis. In such circumstances many Japanese people, especially those of the younger generation, are worried about the future of the public pension fearing that their own benefits could depreciate to a considerable extent.

Another plausible alternative, which is not referred to in the official pension reform proposals, is to transfer more tax revenues into the insurance finance. This could maintain benefit levels and keep premiums at current levels. However, it would encounter strong opposition from the Ministry of Finance, which is now devoted to tackling the financial deficit. Furthermore, tax-raises of any kind are unpopular among the public because of their distrust concerning the expenditure of tax revenues. Nevertheless, the future of pension reforms depends on how this balance between taxes, premiums and benefits can be resolved.

Future Prospects

Since the late 1970s, and throughout the 1980s, the argument that Japan was developing a new type of 'welfare society' was the basis of official social policy. This had a widespread impact on the implementation of various measures for welfare reform, and was very influential on both policy-makers and academic commentators.

The nature of the Japanese type of welfare society, as formulated in the late 1970s, can be summarised as having three distinguishing characteristics:

- First, families are ready to give good care services to older relatives in their homes.
- Second, Japanese companies are providing a high level of corporate welfare to their employees.
- Third, the average saving rate of households is high enough to prepare for the longevity of life.

Therefore, in Japan, a welfare society rather than a welfare state has been realised. This is very different from the model in most Western advanced countries, and makes it unnecessary for the state to provide high levels of welfare benefits as in Western welfare states.

Ironically, however, it is now not clear that such a welfare model is seen as appropriate for future policy development towards the twenty-first century. Government policies in the last ten years, from the Gold Plan for the Longevity Society of the MHW to the Elderly Care Insurance Services Schemes, have been based to an increasing extent upon the assumption that the old idea of a welfare society is becoming bankrupt, and changes in the stance of government are inevitable.

Nowadays, as seen in the previous section, families can no longer afford to give care services to their members; the scale of the family becoming smaller and more women are increasingly engaged in paid work. Corporate firms in the process of downsizing and restructuring have been sparing expenses for corporate welfare. And, in addition, the savings rate in Japan is projected to decline with the process of population aging. These changes will not change the character of the Japanese welfare society overnight, of course, but over time the differences between Japan and other advanced nations are likely to get smaller and smaller.

However, by bidding farewell to a welfare society, Japan does not necessarily proceed towards a welfare state. Under the pressure of ageing and tight financial conditions it is difficult even to maintain current levels of expenditure on benefits such as pensions and health services. In other words, with the exception of the elderly care services, people cannot expect more from social security in general, and will be expected to make full use of their abilities for self-help. The idea of Japanese welfare society may be out-of-date at the end of the twentieth century, but a set of alternative policies and a new prospect have not yet emerged to replace it.

References

Bradshaw, J. *et al.* (1996) *The Employment of Lone Parents: A Comparison of Policy in 20 Countries*, Family Policy Studies Centre.

Campbell, J. (1992) *How Policies Change: The Japanese Government and the Aging Society*, Princeton University Press.

Castles, F. (1985) *The Working Class and Welfare: Reflection on the Political Development of the Welfare State in Australia and New Zealand 1890–1980*, Allen & Unwin.

Eardley, T. *et al.* (1996) *Social Assistance in OECD Countries: Synthesis Report*, Department of Social Security Research Report no. 46, HMSO.

Esping-Andersen, G. (1990) *The Three Worlds of Welfare Capitalism*, Polity Press.

Gould, A. (1993) *Capitalist Welfare Systems: A Comparison of Japan, Britain and Sweden*, Longman.

Jones, C. (1993) 'The Pacific challenge: Confucian Welfare States', in C. Jones (ed.), *New Perspectives on the Welfare State in Europe*, Routledge.

Mishra, R. (1990) *The Welfare State in Capitalist Society: Policies of Retrenchment and Maintenance in Europe, North America and Australia*, University of Toronto Press.

Ragin, A. (1994) 'A Qualitative Comparative Analysis of Pension Systems', in T. Janoski and A. Hicks (eds) (1997) *The Comparative Political Economy of the Welfare State*, Oxford University Press.

CHAPTER 7

The United Kingdom: Rolling Back the Welfare State?

PETE ALCOCK AND GARY CRAIG

Overview

Welfare policy in Britain in the twenty-first century can be traced back to the early years of the nineteenth century, and indeed beyond that to the onset of industrialisation and capitalist economic relations in the seventeenth century. However, we cannot explore such a distant history here (see Digby, 1989); but it is sufficient to gain an understanding of current, and prospective, welfare policies to see the ways in which these emerged from the key political, economic and ideological developments within the twentieth century. This historical context can be loosely divided into six broad stages of development:

- *Early Reform* – during the first two decades of the last century a new role for the state in providing welfare services for a wider range of citizens was introduced in a number of key areas. These included: social security through state insurance for pensions, unemployment and sickness; primary education (up to 12) in local state schools; the establishment of a ministry of health; and the beginning of the building of public sector houses to rent.
- *Responding to Recession* – between the two world wars Britain, in common with most other western industrial nations, experienced severe economic recession. Although there was some piecemeal growth in welfare services during this period the pressure of social need meant that in many areas limited public provision could not meet expected public demand, leading to some cuts (for instance, in social security benefits in 1930) and much suffering.
- *The Postwar Welfare State* – in the late 1940s, following the end of the Second World War, the newly-elected Labour government engaged in the most significant and rapid period of welfare reform in the century. During this period, as we shall discuss below, public services providing near universal coverage for most welfare needs were introduced with widespread

popular and political support. The period is often regarded as leading to the establishment of a 'welfare state' within Britain.

- *Incremental Growth* – throughout the 1950s and 1960s a political consensus over the desirability of state welfare was allied to a long period of economic boom, and this resulted in gradual growth in welfare provision and welfare expenditure within the services established by the postwar reforms. Between 1951 and 1976 welfare spending on education, health and social security grew as a proportion of gross domestic product (GDP) from 11 to 22 per cent.
- *Containment and Retrenchment* – In the mid-1970s the long postwar boom came to an end and economic and political priorities altered sharply in Britain. In the 1980s, Conservative governments openly hostile to the collective values of state welfare provision were in power, the proportionate rise in welfare spending was halted and significant reforms were introduced to privatise and marketise welfare provision.
- *The New Welfare Mix* – at the end of the twentieth century state welfare provision remains significant and widespread, despite the cutbacks of the 1980s. Nevertheless other private, voluntary and informal forms of welfare provision have been openly encouraged and major changes have been introduced into public welfare provision, leading to a new mix of welfare services; and this more eclectic approach has been embraced by the new Labour government elected in 1997, which has championed a 'third way' between state monopoly welfare and private market provision.

The changes outlined here are discussed in more detail in books examining the history of welfare development in Britain, in particular Glennerster (2000), Thane (1996), Timmins (1996), and Page and Silburn (1998). Despite the shifts in both policy and ideology, however, there are significant continuities within British welfare policy, especially when compared with policy developments in other countries throughout the developed world. Britain provided an interesting case of the Anglo-Saxon welfare model, sometimes also referred to as the 'Beveridgean Welfare State', which contrasts starkly with the more residual approaches found in the USA, Canada and Australia, and the 'social state' model adopted in Germany and other continental European countries.

From this perspective, British welfare provision is associated most closely with the major national reforms of the late 1940s and the establishment of universal, redistributive, national welfare services. The clearest exposition of the rationale behind these reforms was provided by the Beveridge Report of 1942. In his report Beveridge outlined a plan for a peculiarly British social insurance scheme for social security, based on all-inclusive flat-rate benefits; but he also talked about the need for comprehensive health and education services and for state support for full employment (for men). His ideas were largely taken up by the postwar Labour government; and, despite the reforms which have been made since then, the basic structure of much of the Beveridge vision remains in place in the country.

Of course the development of the British welfare state was not just a product of the intellectual vision of policy-makers such as Beveridge; welfare policy changes were the result of political struggles, economic changes and ideological conflicts. And these struggles and conflicts remained powerful motors for continuing reform during the last half of the twentieth century. These changes involved shifts in political principle as well in welfare practice and they resulted in cutbacks and cancellations as well as extensions in welfare services. Throughout these changes, however, a number of key issues remained of significant importance, as we shall see below.

The British Welfare State

Beveridge and Keynes

The British welfare reforms of the 1940s were based upon both policy and political alliances. In policy terms the creation of the welfare state involved significant changes to both economic and social policy. Beveridge's report on social insurance envisaged a commitment to social policy provision through the state in order to guarantee that key welfare needs were met for all citizens. He characterised this graphically as the combating of five great social 'evils' – want, disease, ignorance, squalor and idleness. These were to be removed from postwar society through new policy initiatives – comprehensive social security protection, free state education, a national health service, public housing for all who wanted it, and employment for working-age men (see Timmins, 1996).

The social policy changes needed to deliver on these promises, and more, were introduced by the postwar Labour government. However, the latter promise in particular involved a change also in economic policy, to utilise state involvement and state investment to boost economic activity and ensure full employment. This broad strategy of 'demand management' had been advocated by a contemporary of Beveridge's, the economist Keynes. The marrying of such strategies for economic growth with the public provision of social welfare was referred to by some as the Keynes/Beveridge approach (see Cutler *et al.*, 1986). Of course, welfare reform also supported and was supported by economic growth, for instance, providing a healthier and better-educated workforce for the growing manufacturing industries. It was a virtuous circle which seemed over the next two decades to have produced the success of well-being for all within a broadly capitalist economy; and, although it was not without its critics, even socialist commentators have pointed to the ways in which welfare policy could co-exist with capitalist economic growth (Gough, 1979).

It is perhaps not surprising, therefore, that this joint policy approach attracted ideological and practical support across a wide spectrum of political opinion. In particular the Keynes/Beveridge approach was supported by both the major parties of government – indeed it even attracted a pseudonym,

Butskellism, based on an amalgam of the names of the Labour Chancellor of the Exchequer, Gaitskell, and his Conservative successor in 1951, Butler. Butskellism within the political sphere meant that, despite changes in government, social policy development would continue along similar lines to cement welfare policy within the British social order in the latter half of the twentieth century – although, as we shall discuss shortly, it came under strong challenge in the last quarter.

National or Local Welfare?

One of the major themes of the postwar welfare reforms in Britain was the establishment of national services with guaranteed minimum standards for all – symbolised in the titles of the National Health Service (NHS) and National Insurance (NI) scheme. However, much of the development of public welfare provision in the country in the earlier part of the century had been pioneered not by national, but by local or municipal government. Public provision for education, health, housing, social security and personal social services all had their roots in local government initiatives. What is more, despite the radical character of much of the postwar welfare reforms, the practical policy aim was to base the delivery of the new national welfare services on the infrastructure of existing, local, welfare provision. Beveridge himself was clear in his view that the reformed public services would draw on the principles and the practices of previous welfare provisions. Decisions therefore had to be taken about how far the British welfare state of the 1940s should be based upon a 'nationalisation' of past local activity.

In some measure this is what happened – especially in the cases of the NHS (which took local hospitals into national control and marginalised the role of local government) and the NI scheme (which replaced all existing private and public social insurance cover with a compulsory scheme run by central government). But in practice this process of nationalisation was not as far-reaching as the political rhetoric of the time might have suggested.

The other three major public welfare services remained (or were placed) in local government hands. State education up to age fifteen was to be provided for all children; but was to be managed, as before, by municipal government through local education authorities (LEAs). The building of public housing for rent had been pioneered by local authorities early in the twentieth century and remained under their control, although now subject to national standards and supported by new central government subsidies. Social services, or social work, provision for vulnerable adults and children was placed on a new statutory footing in the 1940s as a state-funded public service, administered by local government.

In practice, therefore, the organisational basis of the postwar welfare state in Britain was a combination of central and local administration. National standards were set and national funding provided for all services; but management, and political control, of some remained at local government level. And, although this involved some reduction in the range of responsibilities of local government, it meant that it remained responsible for a growing proportion of public expenditure. As demand for improved services for education, housing and social care grew, so too did expenditure on these – both absolutely and as a proportion of public spending.

In the 1980s and 1990s, when public expenditure was being cut back, this led to conflict between central and local government over spending on these local services. Local authorities, especially those controlled by the then opposition Labour party, did not welcome the planned spending reductions. When central subsidies were cut, they sometimes replaced these by raising higher local taxes. However, this was outlawed by central government, leading to political conflict and a breakdown of central/local relations, resolved only by central government taking a greater degree of control over the management of local authority services.

Therefore, although the welfare reforms of the 1940s involved some nationalisation of locally-controlled services, welfare provision in Britain remained balanced between local and central control. This balance has remained throughout the rest of the century, although central control over local administration of services has been accentuated.

Universalism and Selectivity

One of the defining characteristics of the Beveridge welfare state was its formal commitment to the universal provision of welfare services. This can be found most obviously in health, education and social services where access to the main features of public provision is free for all citizens, irrespective of means, social status or contributions paid. In practice, however, there are charges for some aspects of these services (such as provision of medicines on prescription, first introduced in 1950), and there is evidence that social barriers of gender, 'race' or disability have prevented all citizens from pursuing their rights to all services (see Williams, 1989). Nevertheless the principle of universalism remained strong in the UK throughout the second half of the century, associated most significantly with the National Health Service (NHS), which even Margaret Thatcher was keen to assert was 'safe in our hands' (Timmins, 1996, p. 393).

Access to public rented housing has also been open to all on a universal basis; and as the numbers of such houses grew in the decades following the 1940s the proportion of people renting grew to a peak of around 30 per cent in the early 1970s. Social security provision following the war was also couched in universal terms, with the NI scheme expected by Beveridge to provide comprehensive protection for all outside the labour market, and NI benefits paid at a flat rate to all claimants. However, entitlement to them was based upon the condition that certain contributions had been made towards the scheme and, as with other social insurance schemes, this meant that in practice some were not protected.

Beveridge was aware of the danger of exclusion from the NI scheme and for this he proposed the retention of a means-tested assistance scheme (National Assistance). This meant that some element of selectivity was included as a key feature of the British welfare state, with assistance benefits being targeted onto poor citizens who had to undergo a formal test of means to establish that they had no other sources of support. The expectation of Beveridge and others was that such selectivity would play a minor, and declining, role within British welfare provision; but in practice this has proved to be far from the case. Dependence upon means-tested benefits, such as National Assistance (now called Income Support), grew within social security from 1 million people in 1950 to over 10 million in the mid-1990s; and selectivity through means-tested has been extended into other areas of state welfare – in particular through rebates or exemptions on rents and service charges in housing, health, education and social care.

A Mixed Economy of Welfare

The postwar welfare reforms had the primary aim of establishing comprehensive state welfare services in Britain. However, in practice this comprehensive approach did not imply the creation of a monopoly over service provision. The retention of an alternative of privately purchased health care or education was a key element in the political compromise over these services, and *private market* provision has remained a small, but in recent times expanding, feature of welfare for the well-off, backed up in some areas by personal insurance protection.

State health and education services also interact with private markets in other ways:

- through the purchase of equipment (drugs and books) from private manufacturers, and
- through the use, especially since the 1980s, of private contractors to supply catering and other services.

Private market provision has also grown in importance in social security and social care, with:

- private and occupational pensions to supplement basic state support,
- support from employers for sickness and maternity support, and
- residential provision for vulnerable adults in private nursing homes.

In housing private ownership or private renting has always been the dominant form of provision within the country, with owner-occupation in particular growing dramatically from 26 per cent in 1945 to 68 per cent in the mid-1990s, whilst private renting has declined to around 10 per cent.

British welfare provision has always been characterised by a mix of public and private market provision, therefore, with the role of markets growing towards the end of the twentieth century. However, welfare is not only a mixture of state and market. There are also important elements of voluntary and informal provision.

Voluntary sector organisations have played a key role in providing some welfare services which are between both state and market. These range from major national bodies such as the National Society for the Prevention of Cruelty to Children (NSPCC) to local community centres and playgroups, and altogether they have an annual income of over £13 billion and employ millions of workers and volunteers (see Kendall and Knapp, 1996).

Informal welfare is more difficult to quantify and define, and yet in volume terms it is probably more important. Informal care and supervision in the family and community provides the major means of support for most children and up to 6 million vulnerable adults. In the 1990s 'community care' at family or neighbourhood level has been championed by government as an alternative to public residential provision for many sick and disabled people. And, although some state support exists to assist with home-based care, expectations upon family members to care for their relatives when in need remains a major, if sometimes hidden, feature of the mixed economy of British welfare.

Redistribution

For many of the Fabian and social democratic reformers who had supported the development of state welfare in Britain, a major goal of public social policy was the redistribution of resources from rich to poor – what Tawney, had dubbed a 'strategy of equality'. Redistribution can be achieved by state welfare policy both through the direct transfer of cash by taxation and social security and through the indirect transfer of benefits in kind through the differential use of welfare services.

In practice there is evidence that the post-war welfare reforms achieved redistribution of both kinds, especially in the early decades after the war. Of course measuring the distribution of resources over time is a notoriously difficult activity, given the relative lack of comparable statistical information. Nevertheless, in 1950 Rowntree repeated the study of poverty in the city of York (carried out earlier in 1890 and 1930) and found much reduced levels of poverty (Rowntree and Lavers, 1951). More recently, research funded by the Joseph Rowntree Foundation (JRF) (Hills, 1996) has traced relative incomes over four decades since 1960 and found evidence of a gradual decline in inequality up to 1980 (see Figure 7.1).

What Figure 7.1 also reveals, however, is the stark rise in inequality after 1980 – leading to a doubling of the proportion of the population on low incomes. This is evidence of some reversal in welfare policy in the 1980s and early 1990s. Inequality in incomes can be offset to some extent by differential

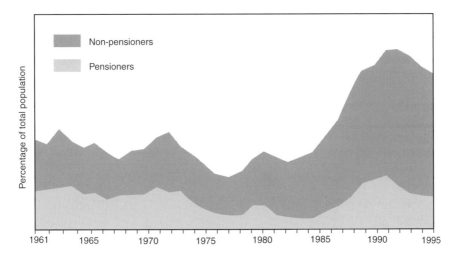

Figure 7.1   Number of individuals below half average income, based on income before housing costs

Source: Joseph Rowntree Foundation (1998).

benefit from welfare services, however, and there is some evidence that poorer citizens do benefit more from welfare services (sometimes referred to in Britain as the 'social wage'), although this has been subject to debate in some quarters (for instance, Le Grand, 1982). Nevertheless, if equality is a goal of social policy within the UK, it is perhaps only one of many, and has not always been consistently pursued.

Redistribution through welfare also operates in other ways. In particular there is the aim of redistributing income across the life cycle, which has always been both a direct and indirect goal of state intervention as exemplified through the provision of child and family benefits and pensions, and through the differential use of services such as education (young) and health (old). In a study of what they called 'welfare dynamics', Falkingham and Hills (1995) argued that such life-cycle redistribution was as important in quantitative terms as was the 'Robin Hood' redistribution from rich to poor.

Welfare Reform and Retrenchment

Economic Crisis

The steady growth in welfare provision and social expenditure in the decades following the postwar reforms in Britain were accompanied, as they were in all developed countries, by a period of sustained economic boom. In a growing economy meeting increased demands for welfare from expanding public services was a relatively painless process; and, as we can see in Table 7.1 below,

Table 7.1   *Expenditure on welfare (education, health and social security),
1900–95*

	1900	1921	1941	1951	1961	1971	1981	1991	1995
Expenditure £ billions, 1996 prices	3.6	8.8	12.7	28	43.7	75.1	112	147	169.8
Expenditure as percentage of GDP	2.6	6.4	5.6	11.2	13.2	17.3	22.2	22.6	24

Source: *Adapted from Glennerster and Hills, 1998, tables 2A.1 and 2A.2, pp. 25–6.*

expenditure grew dramatically over three decades in both absolute and relative terms.

In the mid-1970s, however, the long boom came to an abrupt end, precipitated by the oil price rice of 1973. This had significant consequences for social policy throughout the world, as the other chapters in this collection reveal. In Britain, however, its consequences were particularly far-reaching, especially as they were accompanied at the end of the 1970s by the election to power of a right-wing Conservative government which openly rejected the Butskellite consensus on welfare and argued that the response to the crisis required a significant change in direction for social policy. In essence, therefore, Britain then became a paradigm example of changing welfare policy.

The problems caused for social policy by the economic crisis of the mid-1970s have been analysed by a wide range of welfare theorists. In Britain, however, it was a 'new-right' analysis which seemed to hold sway, especially amongst the leading members of the Thatcher governments of the 1980s. Part of their criticism was encapsulated in the 'overload thesis' developed by Bacon and Eltis (1976), which in simple terms argued that welfare needs would exert an ever-upward pressure on social expenditure and that at times of economic stagnation this would crowd out capital investment leading to an ever-worsening crisis in growth. The response to this, the new right argued, was to cut welfare expenditure in order to provide resources for capital investment to grow; and such cuts in planned expenditure were forced on the UK government in the 1970s by the International Monetary Fund (IMF).

The new-right critique also had ideological and political dimensions, which were taken up in the 1980s by the Thatcher governments, who justified attempts to cut social spending by arguing that in any event public provision of welfare was too extensive, encouraging dependency on the state and restricting choice and diversity in the delivery of services. It was this broader assault on state welfare which made the British experience of reform and retrenchment so dramatic. In Britain, it might be argued, social policy changed direction after the crisis of the 1970s with reforms of state welfare that went beyond the mere curtailment of costs – although in practice reductions in costs were not really achieved anyway, and the reforms led to changes in the structure and operation of state welfare services rather than the whole-sale abandonment of them.

Targeting

One area in which the Thatcher governments sought to achieve change in welfare policy was in the distribution of resources through the state. The new-right critiques took issue with many of the universal features of the postwar welfare state and argued instead for selectivity – or, as they put it, the targeting of (limited) resources onto those in need.

It was in the social security area where some of the major moves towards greater targeting took place, especially in the 1980s. Entitlement to NI bene-fits was cut back and the scope of means-tested benefits increased, particu-larly after the extensive reforms introduced in 1988. The result of this was a doubling (from 4 to 8 million) of the numbers of people dependent upon the major social assistance benefit, Income Support, and an increase in overall dependency upon a means-testing to affect around a third of the population.

Of course other welfare services with a more universal nature do in fact benefit lower-income groups most. And in practice, despite the rhetoric, little was done in the 1980s or 1990s to introduce more targeting in health, edu-cation or social services, although other changes were made. In public hous-ing there was a shift towards more targeted expenditure both by design (by shifting public subsidies from overall building costs to means-tested support for rent payments – Housing Benefit) and by default (because the sale of public houses to tenants meant that those remaining in the state sector were disproportionately from the poorest groups). In the 1980s the cost of Housing Benefit rose from almost £3 billion to almost £7 billion; and by 1994 76 per cent of public tenants were in the bottom 40 per cent (by income) of the population (Glennerster and Hills, 1998, pp. 153, 183).

In other areas of social policy targeted policies were also pursued with more vigour after 1980, although the principles underlying such an approach had their roots in the 1960s and early 1970s. This is particularly true of urban policy and economic regeneration under which additional public resources were provided for deprived or declining neighbourhoods, especially in the inner cities. There is considerable debate about the extent to which such targeted expenditure does in practice benefit local poor people, espe-cially when, as in the 1980s, much of it is spent in practice on property build-ing and renovation. A major government review of the evidence here was somewhat equivocal about the achievements of such activity (Robson, 1995); but the targeting approach still remains popular within British social policy.

For those who believe that targeting of resources will reduce poverty and inequality by concentrating resources onto those in need, however, the evi-dence from Britain provides little confirmation. As we saw in Figure 7.1, poverty and inequality grew most rapidly in the 1980s, at a time when the new targeting policies were being pursued most vigorously. Of course there are other reasons outside of social policy for the growth of such social exclusion over this period – in particular the impact of economic recession leading to reduced wage levels and increased unemployment. But this merely underlines more strongly the need to analyse, and to develop, social policies within the context of economic trends and pressures.

Privatisation

The pursuit of initiatives to privatise state welfare provision by the Thatcherite governments was a product both of economic policy priorities (to reduce commitments to spending) and of social policy shifts (to encourage people to provide for themselves and to promote 'choice'). In fact, however, both of these proved to be elusive goals. As we shall see shortly, public expenditure did not decline in real terms, and the advantages of private welfare remained a 'choice' that only a small minority were willing or able to take up.

The earliest and most high-profile attempt at privatisation was the introduction in 1980 of the 'right to buy' their rented dwellings for public tenants. This was a controversial measure at the time, although it is now supported by most shades of political opinion; but it was popular with tenants. Within a decade over a million houses has been transferred over to private ownership; and by 1995 1.7 million, over a quarter of the stock, had been bought, reducing the proportion of people within the sector from 30 to 20 per cent. In 1988 the right to transfer into private ownership was extended to whole estates, which would then move from a municipal to a private landlord. This was potentially a further-reaching measure, although by the mid-1990s only just over 200,000 dwellings had been transferred.

Privatisation in housing was not confined to the transfer of existing dwellings, the government also sought to encourage new building by private, rather than state, providers. In particular this was pursued through state support for housing development by housing associations (private landlords and philanthropic agencies, subject to state control and subsidy). Of course, housing association building still consumed public resources; but by the end of the century such building had almost entirely replaced direct public expenditure on construction by central and local government.

Privatisation was perhaps easiest to pursue in the housing field, where the bulk of provision has always been in private hands. In other areas of welfare policy both the goals and the achievements of policy were less extensive. In education and health encouragement was given to the small private markets which had survived the welfare state reforms of the postwar years. There was some growth here, in particular through the expansion of private medical insurance which grew from covering 3.6 per cent of the population in 1970 to 10.6 per cent in 1995 (Glennerster and Hills, 1998, p. 98) – still only a small minority. In social services, growth in private provision was more dramatic, especially in residential care for older persons, although this too was indirectly supported by public expenditure in the form of means-tested support for the cost of charges in private nursing homes.

It was in social security where the pursuit of privatisation was perhaps most controversial, however; and yet here too some significant changes were made. First, occupational welfare was expanded through the transfer of responsibility for support for sickness and maternity protection from the state to employers. Second, individual private provision for pensions was openly encouraged after 1988, leading to a big growth in providers, many of whom, it later transpired, were offering rather dubious pension investments. Over the 1980s the number of people covered by private pension schemes grew from around 1.5 million to around 14 million, although these figures included some small policies into which no current contributions were probably being made (Glennerster and Hills, 1998, p. 284).

Despite the limited nature of many of the privatisation ventures of the 1980s in the British welfare field, some shift in the welfare mix did take place over the period, reducing the proportionate role of directly provided state services. By the end of the 1980s, however, the ideological shifts in social policy were also being extended into state welfare itself, through the attempt to introduce private market principles into public welfare services.

Marketisation

The Thatcherite attacks on state welfare provision in the 1980s were motivated not only by a desire to reduce public expenditure in order to meet economic policy goals, they were also informed by an ideological belief in the superiority of markets as a means of allocating resources in response to needs. After their third election success in 1987, the government carried forward this belief into a series of reforms within the welfare state to convert the public delivery of welfare services onto a market basis. These changes were referred to as the introduction of *quasi-markets*. These quasi-markets were most widely used within those state services which themselves remained very largely in public hands despite the reforms introduced elsewhere after 1980 – education, health and social services. In all three the overall aim was to give the consumer of public services 'choice' over access to these by creating a semi-artificial competition between different public sector providers.

This can be seen most simply in the area of education. Prior to the reforms parents were largely constrained to sending their children to the local school provided for them by the local council. After 1988 this changed and parents could choose to send their children to any school which would accept them; and, in making this choice, they had access to information about examination performance which the schools were now required to provide. Schools were thus encouraged to compete with each other for pupils, and those which felt constrained in this by the policies of their local council were permitted to 'opt-out' of local control and receive public support direct from central government – another move towards the centralisation of welfare discussed earlier. Of course for many parents – and their children – these choices were more hypothetical than real. Most schools had a full quota of pupils in any event and would only take those from the local area, as had been the case before. But for those with the commitment, and resources, to shop around (including the Labour Party leader and later Prime Minister, Tony Blair) there was the chance now to get your children educated in the state sector at the school of your choice, a privilege previously only available to those paying fees in the private sector.

In education, quasi-markets did at least place the principle of choice in the hands of public service users. In health and social services, however, their introduction took on a more complicated form. This is because it was felt that consumers of health and social services would not be in a position to make sufficiently informed choices about the service options which may be available to them – patients do not know what drugs they need or what operations they should undergo. Therefore the 'choice' for service users here is exercised on their behalf by professionals employed by the state, in practice doctors and social workers. In the new quasi-market structure, however, these professionals became *purchasers* who use a budget allocated to them on behalf of their clients to purchase the services which they require from other public service *providers*, such as hospitals or residential care homes. In health, therefore, the move to quasi-markets led to a separation between purchasers and providers, with the latter being encouraged to compete for business, from the former. In social services, purchaser and provider roles were frequently separated, and providers included voluntary and private sector agencies – such as residential care homes – as well as public sector bodies, with social workers aiming to choose the optimal deal for their clients.

Whether the introduction of quasi-markets into state welfare provision in Britain has led to the improved efficiency and customer responsiveness which was initially hoped for is rather questionable. Certainly there is as yet no hard evidence of improved services, and there are many practitioners and commentators who have pointed out that the management of quasi-markets may in fact have diverted much needed resources from public service delivery – in short doctors must also now be accountants. Nevertheless, the quasi-market reforms fundamentally altered the nature of many public services in the UK and are unlikely to be reversed in the foreseeable future.

A New Welfare Mix

At the end of the century, therefore, Britain had developed a new and more mixed economy of welfare. Many of the major features of the postwar welfare state remained, including universal (largely) free access to education and

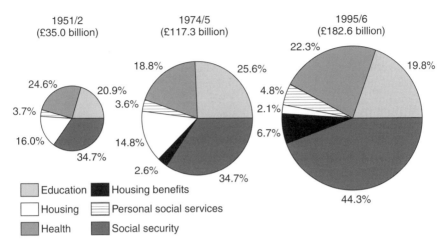

Figure 7.2 The size of the welfare state

Source: Glennerster and Hills, 1998, p. 314.

health, national insurance protection for (most) workers; and public support for the vulnerable and disabled. However, public support now operates alongside – and increasingly in partnership with – private and voluntary sector welfare provision. For instance, in housing or social services users can choose between state, voluntary or private providers; and in social security many use private or occupational investments to supplement basic state benefit protection.

What is more, these changes have not prevented a gradual growth in the scale and scope of state welfare. This can be seen from Figure 7.2, which compares the size and distribution of state welfare in the second half of the century. Table 7.1 shows in more detail how this pattern has developed over the century as a whole for three major areas of public welfare, both in terms of real expenditure and as a percentage of GDP. What the table reveals is that, despite their apparent policy aims, the Thatcherite governments of the 1980s were not able to prevent a continuing real growth in spending on public welfare. However, they were able over the 1980s to arrest the gradual growth in the share of national resources devoted to welfare, although this began to expand again in the 1990s. Whether these could be regarded as successful or desirable achievements is, of course, the subject of much political dispute in the country. A summary of the main features of welfare provision is given at the end of the chapter.

Future Prospects

Following the economic recession of the 1970s, welfare policy in Britain experienced two decades of reform and retrenchment. The changes made may not have altered many of the basic features of state and private welfare established during the major reforms of the 1940s, but they have restricted the expansion of state welfare services and restructured their management and delivery. They have also led to a small but significant increase in private and voluntary sector welfare provision, changing the balance of welfare provision in ways which may be difficult, if not impossible, to reverse. At the same time as this has been taking place, however, demographic, economic and cultural changes have created pressures for improved welfare services in many areas. In his review of changes in public welfare policy over the last quarter of the century, Glennerster (1998) referred to this as 'welfare with the lid on'.

Britain has entered the twenty-first century, however, with a New Labour government under whom the prospects for future social policy may be somewhat different from the retrenchment of the Thatcher years. Nevertheless, in the short term at least, the prospects for future welfare policy in Britain have been very largely determined by the recent past. Labour inherited the new mixed economy of welfare constructed over the past two decades. To change this would require some time, but in any event the new partnership between public and private provision has been largely welcomed by Labour, and they have made it clear that they do not wish to see a return to some of the expensive and monopolistic state services of the past.

The Labour government thus embraces the notion of a new welfare mix for the twenty-first century and they reject any simple return to state collectivism. At the same time, however, they are also keen to distance themselves from the anti-state, private market rhetoric of the new right. A new welfare mix does include a positive, and major, role for the state, and does not imply the unilateral pursuit of market-based solutions to all social problems.

Not surprisingly, therefore, the government have sought to characterise their future vision for social policy as a 'third way', between state collectivism and unfettered private markets. And in pursuing this vision they have adopted a long-term perspective looking towards the early decades of the new century. This longer perspective has led to changes in economic policy – an attempt to move away from the cycle of 'boom and bust' by passing major economic policy decisions over to independent specialist bodies. But it is also evident in early social policy planning. Major areas of policy development such as pension provision, social care needs and support for housing costs have been subject to long-term policy review; and a paper on welfare reform, published in May 1998, adopted a planning frame extending up to the year 2020 to establish a 'new contract' for welfare between the state and the people.

Despite the long-term nature of some policy planning, however, the new government in Britain has made some relatively rapid early policy changes. Most significant here is a package of measures generally presented as promoting the move 'from welfare to work'. The measures include a new job training scheme (targeted mainly at the young unemployed), tax credits for low-income families, and the introduction of a statutory minimum wage. Underlying these new measures is a clear and open belief in the role of labour market participation as the major (indeed the only) means for tackling the problems of poverty and welfare dependence.

This is a prime example of the UK commitment to public/private partnership in social policy, and of the government's rejection of the state collectivist 'solutions' of the past. It has also been accompanied by a comprehensive review of public spending in all welfare services, and the commitment to increase state expenditure in real terms in particular in the areas of education and health. Whether this new third way will succeed in reversing the growing poverty and inequality which had been experienced in the country over the previous two decades is, of course, open to debate – and the government is not without its critics on both the right and the left. Nevertheless, the prospects for British social policy in the early twenty-first century do suggest that the near future for welfare provision in the country may be somewhat different from the more recent past.

Key Features of Welfare Provision

Social Security

Social Insurance

- NI contributions from employees and self-employed where paid between lower and upper earnings limits, supplemented by employers and general taxation.
- NI benefits:
    - Retirement Pensions, including SERPS, earnings-related supplement since 1978.
    - Incapacity Benefit, for long-term sick and disabled.
    - Job-Seekers' Allowance, for 6 months unemployment.

Social Assistance

- Income Support, means-tested benefit for economically inactive.
- Job-Seekers' Allowance, means-tested benefit for unemployed after 6 months.
- Family Credit/Working Families Tax Credit, means-tested supplement to wages for families.
- Housing Benefit, means-tested supplement to rent payments.

Universal Benefits

- Child Benefit, to carers of all children.
- Disabled Living Allowance, to meet costs of care and mobility for severely disabled.

Private Market Benefits

- Personal and occupational pensions, widespread coverage.
- Mortgage protection for private house owners, limited coverage.

(Continued)

National Health Service

Public Health Care – free access

- Purchasers – primary health care, general medical practitioners.
- Providers – acute health care, hospitals, ambulance services, etc.

Health Promotion – state funded

- Health authority and municipal partnerships.

Private Health Care – private medical insurance

- Private consultants, private hospital beds.

Education

State Education

- 5–16, compulsory primary (5–11) and secondary (11–16) education in LEA-controlled or direct-grant schools – national curriculum and generic examinations.
- 16–18, optional further education in schools or further education (FE) colleges for generic or vocational qualifications.
- 18+, optional further education in FE colleges – no financial support.
- 18+, optional higher education in universities, subject to entry requirements – financial support through grants and loans.
- 18+, part-time or occupational education in FE colleges or universities.

Private Education

- 5–18 fee-paying access to exclusive primary and secondary schools, privately funded and controlled.

Social Services

Children's Services

- Statutory, local authority social service departments (SSDs), responsible for monitoring child care and abuse, with power to remove vulnerable children to foster parents or residential homes.
- Voluntary, third-sector agencies (Childline, NSPCC, Barnardos) offering support or residential care for vulnerable children.

Adult Services

- Statutory, local authority SSDs responsible for assessing need and establishing provision for 'community care' for vulnerable adults. Limited NHS hospital care for cases of acute mental illness.

(Continued)

- Voluntary and private, residential and day-care services for vulnerable adults run by a range of public and private bodies, access through private fees or through local authority community care assessment.

Housing

Owner-Occupied (1995 – 66.8% population)
Dwelling bought for cash price on open market (or from public landlord under 'right to buy'). Most purchasers borrow a large proportion of the cost as a mortgage from a bank, repaid over 20 or 25 years.

Public Renting (1995 – 18.9% population)
Local authorities are major landlords, most property built between 1945 and 1980. Tenants pay weekly rent based on cost of managing and maintaining dwelling. Rents subsidised for the low paid and unemployed.

Private Renting (1995 – 9.9% population)
Tenants pay rent to private landlord based on market for tenancies. Rents subsidised for the low paid and unemployed.

Social Housing (1995 – 4.3% population)
Housing associations – private bodies with public regulation and subsidy – now replacing public landlords for new properties. Tenants pay rent based on cost of dwelling. Subsidies low for the paid and unemployed.

References

Bacon, R. and Eltis, W. (1976) *Britain's Economic Problem: Too Few Producers*, Macmillan.

Beveridge, Sir W. (1942) *Social Insurance and Allied Services*, Cmd 6404, HMSO.

Cutler, T., Williams, K. and Williams, J. (1986) *Keynes, Beveridge and Beyond*, Routledge & Kegan Paul.

Digby, A. (1989) *British Welfare Policy: Workhouse to Workfare*, Faber & Faber.

Falkingham, J. and Hills, J. (eds) (1995) *The Dynamics of Welfare*, Harvester.

Glennerster, H. (2000) *British Social Policy Since 1945*, 2nd edn, Macmillan.

Glennerster, H. (1998) 'Welfare with the Lid on', in H. Glennerster, and J. Hills (eds), *op. cit.*

Glennerster, H. and Hills, J. (eds) (1998) *The State of Welfare: The Economics of Social Spending*, 2nd edn, Oxford University Press.

Gough, I. (1979) *The Political Economy of the Welfare State*, Macmillan.

Hills, J. (ed.) (1996) *New Inequalities: The Changing Distribution of Income and Wealth in the United Kingdom*, Cambridge University Press.

Joseph Rowntree Foundation (1998) *Findings: Income and Wealth: the Latest Evidence*, JRF.

Kendall, J. and Knapp, M. (eds) (1996) *The Voluntary Sector in the UK*, Manchester University Press.

Le Grand, J. (1982) *The Strategy of Equality*, Allen & Unwin.

Page, R. and Silburn, R. (eds) (1998) *British Social Welfare in the Twentieth Century*, Macmillan.

Robson, B. *et al.* (1994) *Assessing the Impact of Urban Policy*, Department of Environment.

Rowntree, B. S. and Lavers, G. (1951) *Poverty and the Welfare State*, Longman.

Timmins, N. (1996) *The Five Giants: A Biography of the Welfare State*, Fontana.

Thane, P. (1996) *The Foundations of the Welfare State*, 2nd edn, Longman.

Williams, F. (1989) *Social Policy: A Critical Introduction*, Polity Press.

CHAPTER 8

Sweden: Between Model and Reality

TAPIO SALONEN

Swedish Society

No other country has so often served as a role model in international social policy comparisons as Sweden. In the second half of the twentieth century, in particular, it has been singled out as a welfare state with distinctive characteristics. In the mid-twentieth century Sweden was presented as an attempt to find a 'middle way' between capitalism and socialism (Childs, 1947), and in later years it has been considered a prototype of the institutional welfare model (Mishra, 1981). In the modern literature on the emergence and characteristics of Western welfare states, Sweden has been categorised as the most developed example of a universal welfare state (Flora *et al.*, 1986; Esping-Andersen, 1990). However, the underlying assumptions for yardsticks of this kind have often been a blurred mix of normative ideas and empirical data. Some scepticism about such 'Swedocentrism' (Shalev, 1983) – a tendency to use Sweden without reflection as a role model for other countries – is therefore in order. Undoubtedly there is some justification for analysing Sweden as a distinct country in the broad field of social policy, but it is a mistake to uncritically confuse the popular role model of Sweden with the variability seen in real life.

Although Sweden, by international standards, has undoubtedly reached relatively high levels of citizen-related social-policy benefits and rights, this does not mean that these aspirations to universalism apply in all situations or for all groups. And we shall explore these nuances in an examination of the complex and rapidly changing development of the Swedish welfare state. The core of the model of Sweden as an institutional welfare state lies in the interplay between these three policy areas:

- social security
- public service
- labour market policy

In many prominent macro-analyses of modern welfare states there has been a narrow-minded focus on social security provision between countries. This is most likely due to easier access of comparable data here. However, Sipilä *et al.* (1997) have convincingly demonstrated the missing story of 'the secret Scandinavian social care model'. Furthermore, a deeper understanding of the specific Swedish features must also take the influence of labour market policies into account. Esping-Andersen (1994b, p. 76) has clearly pointed out that the unique composition of the Swedish model has been its capability to combine measures to promote productivity in markets with preventive social policies. This strategy presupposes a strong interventionist state which manages at the same time to maintain a balance between, on the one hand, active labour market policies aiming at full employment and, on the other hand, universalistic welfare reforms. These three general elements of the Swedish welfare state will therefore serve as a guiding order throughout this chapter.

Sweden shares many of its characteristic features in the development of the welfare state with its neighbouring countries in northern Europe. Sometimes they are jointly described as a 'Nordic' or a 'Scandinavian' model of modern welfare states (Titmuss, 1974; Eriksson *et al.*, 1987; Kautto *et al.*, 1999). In terms of living conditions in everyday life, the distribution of income equality and public services, there is strong evidence that these Nordic countries form a distinct group in international comparisons (Vogel, 1997). Sweden, together with Denmark, Norway and Finland, undoubtedly demonstrate examples of higher degrees of state interventions based on relatively high taxes and public expenditures. But of course there are also clear variations between these neighbouring countries which are due to their differing historical circumstances. For example, the impact of international economic trends has affected the countries' abilities to uphold welfare ambitions quite differently in the last decades of the twentieth century. Kautto *et al.* (1999) show that all the Nordic countries have introduced reform changes due to recent economic pressure, but it is unclear whether they have adopted similar patterns in their efforts to renew social policies in the next century.

The Development of the Swedish Welfare State

In contrast to many other countries, Sweden has not witnessed dramatic change in the development of the modern welfare state. On the contrary, the Swedish road to an advanced variant of the welfare state developed gradually over the last 120 years without involvement in wars or revolutions. To understand the birth and development of the Swedish welfare state, therefore, we must analyse it in connection with underlying political and economic driving forces.

Until the end of the nineteenth century, Sweden was a poor backward agrarian country on the outskirts of Europe. Years of famine and hardship had forced nearly one million Swedes to emigrate overseas from the mid-nineteenth century until the First World War. The industrialisation of Sweden took place long after the boom in continental Europe, but the transformation of Swedish society in the twentieth century was exceptionally swift and with an extraordinary impact unmatched in earlier centuries. In this single century Sweden has both entered and left the industrialised production-dominated society. The standard of living among the Swedish population, reckoned in narrow material terms, has on average risen at least 12-fold.

A more thorough analysis of this exceptional phase in Swedish history has to take account of many intertwining factors in the spheres of production, economics, politics and sociocultural behaviour. Distinct periods in the evolution of the modern welfare state in Sweden are not self-evident or indisputably identified. One often forgotten overall factor explaining the breakthrough of extended social policy reforms in Sweden has to do with its strong centralist and nationally homogeneous traditions. No matter who – kings, clergy, bourgeoisie or political parties – has been in power in Sweden, the last few centuries have reflected a prolonged tradition of compromise and coalition in a relatively homogeneous society, in terms of religion, ethnicity and language. For national and universal policy development this has been a significant advantage.

The Liberal Reform Era

The emergence of the Swedish welfare state has often been associated with the Social Democratic Party's entry into government in the 1930s. A more fair and reasonable starting-point to consider is the vigorous reform period which followed the rapid industrialisation at the turn of the century. Between the 1880s and the First World War there was far-reaching reform activity which resulted in the first social insurance for working people. These reforms (sickness benefits, injury insurance and old-age and invalidity pensions) were shaped in a context where liberal reformers dominated the political scene in competition with a growing labour movement. This early Swedish social policy discourse had clear connections with the German Bismarckian influence, but 'was simultaneously less despotic, less etatist and less elitist' (Olsson, 1990, p. 83). One propelling motive was obviously to achieve a peaceful development of the evolving labour market. Many of the modern features of the welfare state were adumbrated in this early reform period but were only revived and implemented in the mid-twentieth century. Many social policy ideas, such as universal security for all people, were already recognised as guiding policy principles, and some observers therefore rightfully claim that the welfare state in fact emerged at the start of the twentieth century (Edebalk, 1996). However, this reform era came to an end due to the international recession following the First World War.

The People's Home Reform Era

The inclusive reformist strategy initiated by the Social Democratic Party, when it came to power in 1932, was first introduced by Prime Minister Hansson in a famous parliamentary speech in 1928:

> The basis of the home is community and the feeling of togetherness. The good home knows no privileged or disadvantaged individuals, no favourites and step-children. There, one does not look down upon another; there, nobody tries to gain an advantage at the cost of another, the strong one does not hold down and plun-der the weak. In the good home equality, consideration, helpfulness prevail. Applied to the great people's and citizens' home, this would mean the breaking down of all social and economic barriers, which now divide citizens into privileged and disadvantaged, into rulers and dependants, into rich and poor, propertied and miserable, plunderers and plundered. (Quoted in Olsen, 1992, p. 98)

This strong vision of a society treating all individuals in an equal way was the overall political concept that informed nearly half a century of parliamentary dominance by the Social Democrats (1932–76), underpinned by a set of inte-grative links that have promoted cooperation and coalition across Swedish society.

In the *political* arena the Social Democratic Party was concerned to pro-mote extended solutions in cooperation with other political parties. This was true for electoral reasons in the 1930s and 1940s with the Farmers' Party, but was also promoted later as a general principle of political practice. This specific kind of consensus-based political cooperation was named 'Harpsund democracy' (after a rural estate used for government purposes). In the mid-twentieth century this strategy was broadened to gain support from a grow-ing number of white-collar workers. Even in the late 1970s and at the beginning of the 1990s, when Social Democrats were in opposition, major policy decisions drew on consensus planning.

In the *labour market* arena we find another crucial pillar in creating this historical compromise. Until the beginning of the 1930s the labour market had been characterised by tensions and social unrest, with a high frequency of strikes and lockouts (Korpi, 1978). After the electoral victory of the Social Democrats in 1932 the industrial leaders were motivated to avoid further legislative interventions. Instead, SAF (the Swedish Employers' Federation) reached a Basic Agreement with LO (the blue-collar Trade Union Confede-ration) in 1938, known as the Saltsjöbaden procedure, which promoted peaceful order in the Swedish labour market. Many strategic policy decisions were shaped in a tripartite understanding between the Social Democratic government and the contestants on the labour market.

The shaping of the 'Peoples Home' strategy influenced reforms in all major political areas: education, housing, working life and social security. The long-term goal was to tear down barriers and eradicate conditions which shaped class-related inequalities. Within the Social Democratic Party there was initially no unified understanding as to how to achieve these aims. In fact, two conflicting reform strategies were represented in Social Democratic thinking and pragmatic decision-making; the first was the 'cash strategy' and the other the 'in-kind strategy'. While the former stressed the introduction of different kinds of allowances, the latter underpinned the importance of building up a broad supply-side arsenal of services in education, health and social services. The Minister of Social Affairs until 1951, Gustav Möller, was the most outspoken advocate of the more egalitarian strategy, while Alva Myrdal was the most pugnacious representative of a more elitist implementation of 'the good life' (Rothstein, 1984; Edebalk, 1996). Möller, however, was the most influential architect behind the Swedish welfare state. In fact he was the first to use the term 'welfare state' in a manifesto in 1928, long before it was internationally associated with Beveridge and the postwar programme for the UK. Möller's idea was that social insurance systems after the Second World War should be built on a universal minimum-standard model. This flat-rate principal was to guarantee everyone decent income security. In addition to this state-financed insurance, people could top up with supplementary insurance. Only after Möller had resigned was it possible for the Social Democratic government to accomplish an insurance package.

The Middle-Class Reform Era

This period from the 1950s to the 1970s is also called the 'golden age' of welfare states (Esping-Andersen, 1996), a period when welfare reforms were introduced in most Western industrialised countries. In Sweden this included particularly the involvement of the growing white-collar middle class in public systems. For instance, there were debates over pension reform in the 1950s, which marked a new direction for the Social Democratic reform scheme. The post-Möller era also opened up reform of social security, where flat-rate principals were combined with income-related benefits. This was the case in all major benefit systems in the mid-twentieth century; and it remained more or less unchanged until the end of the century.

Far-reaching Swedish active labour market policies also took shape in the 1960s. Instead of focusing on the passive measures which predominated in most other countries (including the other Nordic countries), labour market policies in Sweden complemented a Keynesian counter-cycle policy on the macro level with a more dynamic regulation of the labour force on the micro level. In the longstanding economic boom of the 1950s and 1960s, in particular, special policies were created to promote labour-force mobility, education and occupation flexibility. This active strategy has popularly been called the 'AMS policy', after the abbreviation of Arbetsmarknadsstyrelsen (the National Labour Market Board) which has been the central actor in promoting this policy. The Swedish welfare state took an active role in subsidising movements from the declining countryside to flourishing major cities and encouraging labour immigration.

This was the heyday of the Swedish mood of cooperation between organised labour movements and the national capitalist leaders. The growth in production permitted both high profits in markets and increasing revenues financing evolving welfare reforms; the building of one million apartments in a ten-year period (1965–74), for example, was one of the most ambitious political plans to be fulfilled. The material standard of living saw a general rise, promoting economic equality between different classes. The growing public sector also played an increasing role in the longstanding endeavour for full employment and equality between the sexes. Until the mid-1960s, the traditional housewife model had dominated Swedish households, but there was a subsequent rapid increase of women in the workforce. No other Western welfare state has witnessed such a rapid increase in the female employment rate, from around 50 per cent in the 1960s to 80 per cent in 1990.

The Transition to the Post-Industrial Era

In the last two decades of the twentieth century the relative homogeneity of the Swedish welfare state came under challenge from various pressures. The period has also been characterised in competing and different ways. For a start the era could also be divided into two specific periods with the deep recession at the beginning of the 1990s as a clear watershed. Until then the expansion of the welfare state had been forceful and combined with ambitions to uphold full employment for both sexes. However, many observers argue that the crisis in the 1990s can also be understood in terms of the changed conditions in economy and politics after the oil crisis of the 1970s. This economic crisis of the 1970s hit the Swedish economy but it did not in principle affect the long-term expansion of the welfare state. On the contrary, the public service area – especially in health care and care for children and the elderly – expanded enormously.

If Sweden really diverged significantly from the overall trends of Western welfare states, it was in the years of the late 1970s and the 1980s. Unlike most other countries, even Nordic neighbours like Denmark, the employment rates stayed high for men and rose rapidly for women. Esping-Andersen (1990) discerned this employment pattern as a growing gender division between the male-dominated industrial sector and the female-dominated service sector.

In several crucial areas in Swedish society, however, the former consensus-based contract was shattered. In the political arena the Social Democrats lost electoral ground and were in opposition between 1976–82 and 1991–94. And when in government the Social Democratic Party was dependent on support from other parties. Within the labour market the former highly centralised model of agreements was replaced by more uncertain decentralised negotiations. A starting-point for the abandonment of the earlier understanding between organised labour and capital (Olsen, 1992) was the proposal by LO to increase the power of employees over private companies by wage-earners' funds; and by the end of twentieth century the once strong tripartite corporative system had faded away in the face of increasingly global markets.

From the mid-1980s an overall shift of priority between full employment and monetary goals (low inflation) could be noticed at the governmental level. Since the Social Democratic postwar programme in 1944, full employment had been a political top priority. Due to the globalisation of the economy and neo-liberal influences, Sweden also followed the overall international trend towards deregulation of financial and business markets.

In the first years of the 1990s Sweden was hit by a crisis comparable with the great depression at the beginning of the 1930s. Unemployment went up from internationally extremely low levels, around 1.5 per cent, to rates above 10 per cent in a few years between 1990 and 1993. The job losses amounted to more than a half million, first in the industrial private sector, then in the public service sector. Huge deficits in public finances forced both Social Democratic and centre-right governments to introduce tough packages of budget cuts, and a broad range of retrenchments took place in most public areas between 1992 and 1997. When the Social Democrats came back to power in 1994 the public budget deficit was around 16 per cent of the GDP. A promise to balance the budget in 1998 was fulfilled, with a combination of firm cutbacks in social transfers and services and expanding income policies. In the last few years there has been a diverse trend; on the one hand further cutbacks in social benefits and service and on the other hand the restoration of benefits formerly affected by cutbacks and the introduction of special grants to secure quality standards in local social services, particularly in public schools, day care for children and especially the care of the elderly.

In the very last years of the twentieth century there were clear signs of recovery. Unemployment was reducing and public finances in balance again. Some of the reductions from the policies of austerity in social security and social services have been redressed; and at the beginning of the twenty-first century, the preconditions of the Swedish welfare state are quite different from those at its breakthrough after the Second World War. Sweden is no longer a small economically isolated country on the periphery. In its ambitions to form new sustainable societal contracts in a post-industrialised world there are new kind of challenges.

Some Characteristics of the Swedish Welfare State

Preconditions

One elementary circumstance is of course the *economic foundation* on which to build an extensive welfare state that is able to redistribute the growing wealth.

As already illustrated above, the shaping of the Swedish welfare state coincided with a strong long-term economic growth. The Swedish case also displays a more complicated interrelationship, with an expanding welfare system in itself promoting economic prosperity.

To follow Esping-Andersen (1994b), a distinct Nordic or Swedish model first came into existence in the 1970s and 1980s, 'with the shift towards active labour market policies, social service expansion and gender equalisation' (p. 10). Until the mid-1970s Sweden followed the average OECD rate of social expenditure, from which point the OECD countries as a whole have only marginally increased on this rate. As Table 8.1 shows, the Swedish figures boomed until the beginning of the 1980s. Thereafter, social expenditure has been more or less stable, at around one-third of the annual GDP. This does not mean, as we exemplify later, that social provisions came to a definitive halt in Sweden from the 1980s. Instead, it illustrates a more differentiated and dynamic composition of services and security in a budget-limited framework in recent decades.

A second precondition is the *political framework*. As described above, the formation of the Swedish welfare state can be explained by strong relationships between central actors in both politics and economics. In the literature this kind of power dimension is highly disputed. In the 'power resource theory' Sweden is frequently used as an obvious example of successful building of strong networks, bridging major conflicts in a capitalist society (Korpi, 1985; Esping-Andersen, 1985). This was at least the prevalent notion at the culmination of the industrial period.

A third circumstance in the Swedish case has been the strategy of an expansive public sector and large-scale policy interventions. For its success this modernistic approach has been reliant on the development of *expertise* and *professional organisations*. No other Western developed country has such a high proportion of the workforce employed in the public sector as in Sweden. A nation's *demographic* trends also play a significant role shaping

Table 8.1 Social expenditures as a percentage of GDP in Sweden, 1960–95

Year	Social expenditure (% of GDP)	% change over previous 5 years
1960	12	
1965	14	+2
1970	20	+6
1975	25	+5
1980	33	+8
1985	31	−2
1990	36	+5
1995	36	0

Source: Statistics Sweden.

specific provisions of welfare. Sweden seems to be ahead of most other Western countries in terms of its increasing elderly population, which rose from 10 to 18 per cent of the population between 1950 and 1990. In the same period the proportion of children has decreased, especially in the latter years of the twentieth century. The composition of Swedish households has undergone a gradual change, with an increase in single households and in the proportion of children with separated parents. Sweden has also now become a country of immigration, with over a million residents born outside the country. The pattern of immigration has changed dramatically from work-related immigrants from nearby countries (especially Finland) in the 1960s and early 1970s, to immigrants from non-Nordic countries, often as refugees, in the last decades of the twentieth century. Sweden has thus become a multicultural society and this challenges many traditional values.

A fifth basic precondition for a strong interventionist welfare state is of course its *legitimacy* among the population. Repeated surveys report strong support for an expansive welfare state, including high tax-based expenditures for basic public services (Svallfors, 1995; Statistics Sweden, 1997). Universal programmes tend to gain greater popular support than targeted programmes, and during the crisis years in the 1990s support for extensive welfare provisions seems to have grown among Swedish people in general.

Measures

- *Social security* Nearly every element of the Swedish social security system has gradually undergone a tightening of entitlement conditions and compensation levels in the 1990s. This 'insecurity shock' has especially hit households with weak economic positions; low-income families, especially single parents, newly-arrived immigrants and young people. At the end of 1990s there are clear indications that cutbacks in the crisis period have been followed by more expansive and generous provisions in the social insurance systems. A remaining question is whether the Swedish security system also reveals growing differentiation between insiders and outsiders.
- *Social service* In the 1990s there was extensive rationalisation in the *child care system*, with a higher children-to-staff quota, and employment within the sector has decreased. A study from the National Board of Health and Welfare shows that in 1996 the Swedish child-care system was taking care of 170,000 more children than in 1991, at no higher cost (Socialstyrelsen, 1997). A significant change in the child care system concerns unemployed families. Formerly child-care was a right for every child, but with higher unemployment and a financial crisis, child-care rights were denied to unemployed parents in many parts of the country.

  In *health care* and the *medical service sector* the most obvious changes in recent years concern the decrease of social insurance benefits and the rise of fees. In the municipal personal service system there have also been several changes, such as cuts in institutional care and continuous rises in patient fees.

The Swedish system of *care for the elderly* is probably the welfare sector in which the transformation of the welfare state has been most visible. At the municipal level, service charges have risen, and means tests have been more frequently applied. The outcome of these changes has been that proportionately fewer elderly people have received public service and care, with care measures more and more concentrated on those demanding the most care. The share of over 80s receiving care in institutional or home help decreased from 62 per cent in 1980 to 44 per cent in 1996 (Szebehely, 1998). Another significant change is the new legal framework which has facilitated a transition towards new administrative systems in local care organisations, such as purchaser–provider models, and outsourcing. The changing service patterns and the greater demands on the individual have increased the importance of the family and the personal network. The tendency in Sweden seems to be that relatives, especially daughters, now do much more caring work for the elderly than ten years ago – despite clear evidence that the majority of elderly people prefer personal care from public care-givers.

- *Labour market policy* In the 1970s and 1980s, in periods of a well-balanced labour market and low unemployment, the active *labour market programmes* in Sweden took care of 2–4 per cent of the labour force. In the crisis years of the 1990s this rate dramatically increased to 6–7 per cent and in the mid-1990s the total expenditure for labour market policy, including unemployment compensation, accounted for 6 per cent of GDP. According to many observers, labour market programmes tend to lose efficiency when the share of the labour force increases. In Sweden, too, it is clear that labour market programmes cannot easily create new jobs without the risk of squeezing out existing ordinary jobs. Labour market policies alone, even in the most ambitious Swedish version, are incapable of eliminating mass unemployment or securing stable economic growth.

  However, the picture of the Swedish labour market policies must be complemented with an intensified investment in the *education sector*. This can be noted at all levels of education. Nowadays nearly all young people complete a 12-year basic schooling. Special efforts have been in operation to upgrade adults without upper secondary level through the Adult Education Initiative. Since 1997 over 100,000 persons annually (equivalent to 2.5 per cent of the labour force), mainly unemployed, have participated in this special adult education. In the area of higher education a number of new regional *högskolor* have been established. These can be described as undergraduate colleges with no research and a clear concentration on technical education. The governments' intention has been both to strengthen the regional aspect of higher education and to use higher education as variant of active labour market policy.

Outcomes

During the last two decades Swedish living standards have increased significantly, and disposable income has increased by approximately 18 per cent since the mid-1970s, measured by consumption unit; most of the improvement took place in 1985–90. One important factor in this development over the last two decades has of course been the sharp rise of employment among women. In the 1990s this trend has been broken and standards are decreasing. However, the growth in living standards from the 1970s onwards has not benefited all parts of the population equally. From 1975 to 1995 the income differences between generations have been large, and in the 1990s they have grown significantly. In this period it is younger adults who have been most affected by the social and economic changes in society, and during the whole period they have experienced significantly lower increases in income than their parents. Statistics also show that the income for those aged between 18 and 22 has even decreased by 30 per cent since 1975. This means that the income gap between different generations grew gradually after the mid-1970s (Statistics Sweden, 1997).

The development described here concerning income and income inequality reveals that the 1990s has in some respects meant a clear shift in Swedish society. This is also the case with poverty. Around 1990 there was a significant shift towards increasing poverty rates; from 1983 to 1990, the proportion of the population living in poverty declined from 8 to 3 per cent, but by the mid-1990s the proportion had returned to 7 per cent. The groups most exposed to this new trend have been young people in general, immigrants and single parents without full-time employment. Poverty rates among pensioners have not increased during the 1990s (Statistics Sweden, 1997). A summary of the main features of welfare provision in Sweden is given at the end of the chapter.

Recent Patterns and Trends

Five issues sum up recent patterns and trends in the Swedish welfare state:

1   Degree of *universality/selectivity*. Principals of universal rights of security and service are more or less guaranteed in childhood and old age. In working age, however, the decline of employment in the 1990s has also demonstrated that the Swedish provision system is basically a performance-related system. Due to increased unemployment, the amount of non-qualified persons or persons with insufficient levels in the public provision systems has grown.
2   Patterns of *commodification*. In most public systems, both insurance and service, the labour work requisite has strengthened, which has turned the long-term trend of de-commodification to its opposite: re-commodification. In Sweden, as elsewhere, the flexibilisation of working life is an increasingly

common feature, supporting a renewed emphasis in the importance of paid work.

3   *Activation.* In contrast to earlier decades the activation policies in the crisis period of the 1990s have more often taken the form of selective work-to-welfare programmes. Sweden seems to have followed a general workfare trend in the Western world, with tightening of eligibility for means-tested assistance.

4   *Decentralisation.* Since the mid-twentieth century the Swedish welfare state has become more of a local welfare state. Growth has taken place in the traditional areas for local service provision: schools, health care, and care for children and the elderly; and, starting in the 1960s, responsibilities were transferred from central government to county councils and municipalities.

5   *Welfare pluralism.* The welfare mix has been recurrently referred to in analyses of the changing patterns in the advanced welfare states. In Sweden, welfare pluralism refers to a shift from formerly more homogeneous ways to control, finance and produce welfare services and distribute social insurance. In the 1990s, the dominant role of the welfare state came under some challenge on both ideological and practical levels, and there are signs that several actors were ready to try new ways to design and distribute welfare provisions and services (Sunesson *et al.*, 1997). However, the trend to privatisation in public services in Sweden is still very modest – even in the 1990s the share of private alternatives only increased from 4.2 to 8.5 per cent of all employed in the traditional public service sector (SOU, 1999, p. 133).

Future Challenges

A recent comparative study for the EU countries (Vogel, 1997) reveals a clear threefold cluster of welfare regimes, with the Nordic countries as a distinct category characterised by higher rates of female employment, a more equal distribution of incomes, higher degrees of state-provided social policies, and so forth. This study runs only to 1993/94, however, and has not been able to highlight the most recent changes in Sweden and elsewhere. Despite the sharp decline of the Swedish welfare state in the last few years, it nevertheless seems to be adequate to categorise it, together with the other Nordic countries, as a specific category of advanced welfare states. Many of its distinct characteristics are still there but perhaps not as essentially marked as before.

    The same kind of conclusion can be found in other contemporary analyses of the Swedish welfare state in the mid-1990s (Statistics Sweden, 1997; Kautto *et al.*, 1999). In some respects, however, the Swedish welfare state has changed its character. The mass unemployment shock accompanied by extensive welfare expenditure cuts and institutional changes has in some sense strengthened selective mechanisms in the Swedish welfare state (Sunesson *et al.*,

1997). This rollback of universalism has two aspects. One the one hand, residualism comes when universal systems are made unattractive for high- and middle-income citizens as benefits and coverage decrease, and private compensation appears more cost-effective. The clearest example of this is the increase of private pension insurance in Sweden. On the other hand, cutbacks in general programmes, for example housing benefits, directly lead to higher social assistance dependency on the local level. As a consequence of these changes the municipalities have acquired a more extensive responsibility for inclusion/ exclusion policies.

In some other European countries unemployment and social exclusion are being tackled by reducing working time. In Sweden, however, this has almost been a non-existent issue. The latest Act, from 1973, stated that the total working time in one week should be 40 hours. Since then no national reductions have been made, and during the last decade the actual working time per employee has increased. In the mid-1990s the total number of overtime hours in industry was much higher than it ever was in the 1980s. The national political initiatives that have been adopted have had weak results, and instead initiatives mainly come from local municipalities and private firms.

Another area of change is the organisation of unemployment insurance, which follows two separate tracks. The major concern is about the low compensation level for those included in the unemployment funds; and the minor debate focuses on people not eligible for any compensation at all. In the 1990s, with high unemployment, significant groups of the population, particularly young people, immigrants and single mothers (Socialstyrelsen, 1998), have never been able to qualify for unemployment insurance and have instead been referred to social assistance. This is a classical insider/outsider problem of inclusion and exclusion between a rights-based and a selective system. More recently, therefore, it has been argued that unemployment insurance protection should be reorganised onto a state-funded basis with a flat-rate benefit complemented by an income-replacement principle.

The basic problem in the current Swedish welfare state is how the work-oriented strategy, which has underlain the system, will function in a future labour market characterised by flexibility and insecurity. In the 1990s social rights throughout working years are increasingly dependent on the individual's achievement in terms of paid work, with universalistic principles eroded as a result of a diminishing labour market and a declining welfare state. In the short term, the development of the labour force and unemployment rates are major objectives in Swedish inclusion policies. In the longer term, greater equality in income and paid work, the capability to combine new labour market patterns with social citizenship rights, and so on, will have to be scrutinised.

At the turn of the millennium all major Swedish policy documents (that is, Budget Bills and the National Action Plan for employment) emphasise new ways of promoting growth and employment. The operative main target is to increase the percentage of people regularly employed to 80 per cent in 2004.

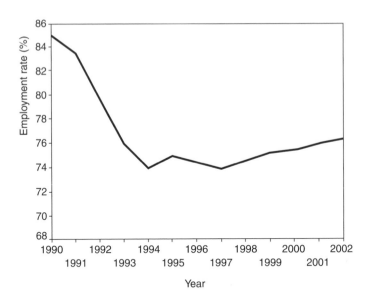

Figure 8.1   Employment rate in Sweden among persons aged 20–64,
1990–2002

Note: Figures for 1999–2002 are from the Ministry of Finance's forecast in the 1999 Spring Budget Bill.

Source: Swedish Ministry of Finance, May 1999.

In the last few years this rate has moved up again slightly, but it is still far from the high levels of late 1980s (see Figure 8.1). This reinforced 'activation principle' contains a broad spectrum of new policy measures. The official goal is to strengthen Sweden as a leading IT nation and to stimulate every individual to take an active part in the emerging knowledge-based society, based on themes like 'life-long learning', 'learning organisations' and individual 'skills development'. A great deal of effort has been expended on this, and to improve the employability of low-educated risk groups, a concentration on regular adult education is underway. In 1999 the government introduced a special tax credit for employers who hire long-term unemployed persons, and in the years 2000–2002 an ambitious plan for competence development throughout the whole of Swedish working life is to be launched. Every student will receive an e-mail address. In higher education the official goal is that at least 50 per cent of young people will have attended higher education – a massive growth.

It may of course be questioned whether this bold, knowledge-driven, welfare policy will be a success in gaining economic prosperity as well as equality in a post-industrial society. It is a great challenge for the Swedish welfare state to succeed in including marginalised groups in working life as well as the public welfare systems – especially when those at the bottom of the income and education distribution live more segregated lives in the most deprived housing areas and tend to be ethnically concentrated. For instance, employ-ment among non-Nordic citizens dropped dramatically from 66 to 39 per cent between 1990 and 1998.

Thus the complex nature of the advanced welfare state in Sweden is not easy to capture in simplistic terms, and some healthy scepticism is therefore recommended. The most optimistic interpretation of the Swedish case would argue that the crisis period in the 1990s was just a 'bump' in the road towards improvement of the universal welfare model. On the other hand, a more criti-cal view might argue that the universal model has never really existed and that many of its basic preconditions are in a state of hazardous change in the ongo-ing transition to a post-industrial society. The present transformation of the welfare state raises the same fundamental questions of equality, efficiency and power as in earlier stages of the emerging welfare state.

Key Features of Welfare Provision

Social Security

	Provisions
Social insurance, families and children	Parental cash benefit Maternity benefit Benefit in the event of adoption Child allowance
Health	Sickness benefit Benefits to close relatives and carriers of contagious diseases In-patient health care and general primary health care Private out-patient treatment financed by counties and municipalities Private dental treatment financed by National Social Security Office Other social measures such as ambulance service provided by counties and municipalities
Disability	Anticipatory pension as basic pension including supplements Anticipatory pension as labour-market pension Care allowance Disability compensation Rehabilitation benefit Support for buying a car
Old age	Old-age basic pension Labour-market supplementary pension

(*Continued*)

	Special supplements, including child and wife supplements Private service pensions from collective labour market insurance Partial retirement pension
Housing	Housing benefits for families with children Housing benefits to recipients of old age pension, wife supplement Housing benefit to young people

Social Assistance
Municipal means-tested social assistance
  Introductory compensation to refugees

Services

	Provisions
Education	Compulsory schooling free of charge for all children aged 7 to 16, including transportation and free lunch State grants for independent (private, non-profit) schools Additional home language training Three-year upper secondary school (98 per cent entry rate) Municipal adult education The Adult Education Initiative (*Kunskapslyftet*), special programme 1997–2002 to boost adult education and training Higher education
Social services	Municipal child care for children aged 1 to 6 years Municipal school-age child care Home-help services for old age and persons with disability Special housing for old age – group homes etc. Accommodation for old age – old people's homes, nursing homes etc. Municipal expenditure on special housing for elderly, including care, treatment etc. Municipal expenditure on support to the elderly in ordinary flats Transport service for elderly and persons with disability Psychiatric service and care Legal family case-work Youth counselling Family counselling Counselling and treatment for drug abusers

Labour Market Measures

- Unemployment insurance (union-based but state-funded)
- Expenditure on labour market support
- Support to start a business
- Educational supplements for labour-market training
- Vocational training benefit for labour market, job-seeking and rehabilitation
- Support for youth placements
- Removal grants

References

Childs, M. (1947) *Sweden: The Middle Way*, Yale University Press.
Edebalk, P. G. (1996) *Välfärdsstaten träder fram: Svensk socialförsäkring 1884–1955* [The Welfare State Emerges: Swedish Social Insurance 1884–1995], Arkiv.
Eriksson, R., Hansen, E. J., Ringen, S., and Uusitalo, H. (eds) (1987) *The Scandinavian Model: Welfare States and Welfare Research*, M. E. Sharpe.
Esping-Andersen, G. (1985) *Politics Against Markets*, Princeton University Press.
Esping-Andersen, G. (1990) *The Three Worlds of Welfare Capitalism*, Polity Press.
Esping-Andersen, G. (1994a) 'Jämlikhet, effektivitet och makt' [Equality, Efficiency and Power], in P. Thullberg and K. Östberg (eds), *Den svenska modellen* [The Swedish Model], Studentlitteratur.
Esping-Andersen, G. (1994b) *After the Golden Age: The Future of the Welfare State in the New Global Order*, UNRISD, Occasional Paper no. 7.
Esping-Andersen, G. (ed.) (1996) *Welfare States in Transition: National Adaptations in Global Economies*, Sage.
Flora, P. (ed.) (1986) *Growth to Limits: The Western European Welfare States Since World War II*, Vol. 1: Sweden, Norway, Finland, Denmark, de Gruyter.
Ginsburg, N. (1992) *Divisions of Welfare*, Sage.
Gould, A. (1996) 'Sweden: The Last Bastion of Social Democracy', in V. George and P. Taylor-Gooby (eds), *European Welfare Policy – Squaring the Welfare Circle*, Macmillan.
Hansen, H. (1998) *Elements of Social Security. A Comparison Covering: Denmark, Sweden, Finland, Germany, Great Britain, Netherlands and Canada*, The Danish National Institute of Social Research, no. 98: 4.
Kautto, M., Heikkilä, M., Hvinden, B., Marklund, S. and Ploug, N. (eds) (1999) *Nordic Social Policy*, Routledge.
Korpi, W. (1978) *Arbetarklassen i välfärdskapitalismen* [The Working Class in Welfare Capitalism], Prisma.
Korpi, W. (1985) 'Power Resources Approach vs. Action and Conflict: On Causal and Intentional Explanation in the Study of Power', *Sociological Theory*, no. 3, pp. 31–45.
Mishra, R. (1981) *Society and Social Policy*, Macmillan.
NOSOSKO (1998) *Social Protection in the Nordic Countries 1996: Scope, Expenditure and Financing*, Nordic Social-Statistical Committee, no. 9: 98.
Olsen, G. M. (1992) *The Struggle for Economic Democracy in Sweden*, Avebury.
Olsson, S. E. (1990) *Social Policy and the Welfare State in Sweden*, Arkiv.

Rostgaard, T., Holm, T., Jensen Toftegaard, D. and Byrgesen, Graff C. (1998) *Omsorg for børn og ældre – kommunal praksis i Europa* [Care for Children and Old Age – Local Practice in Europe], Socialforskningsinstituttet, no. 98: 19.

Rothstein, B. (1984) 'Gustav Möller, välfärdsstaten och friheten' [Gustav Möller, the Welfare State and the Freedom], *Tiden*, 81.

Shalev, M. (1983) 'The Social Democratic Model and Beyond: Two "Generations" of Comparative Research on the Welfare State', *Comparative Social Research*, no. 6, pp. 315–51.

Sipilä, J. (ed.) (1997) *Social Care Services. The Key to the Scandinavian Welfare Model*, Avebury.

Socialstyrelsen (1997) *Barnomsorgen sparar* [Savings in the Care of Children], Pressmeddelande 60, National Board of Health and Welfare.

Socialstyrelsen (1998) *Social Report 1997*, National Board of Health and Welfare.

SOU (Official State Inquiries) (1999) *Kommunkontosystemet och rättvisan – momsen, kommunerna och konkurrensen* [The System of Municipal Accounts and Justice – VAT, the Municipalities and Competition], Ministry of Finance, no. 133.

Statistics Sweden (1997) *Välfärd och ojämlikhet i 20-årsperspektiv 1975–1995* [Living Conditions and Inequality in Sweden – a 20-Year Perspective 1975–1995], Report no. 91, Statistics Sweden.

Stephens, J. (1996) 'The Scandinavian Welfare States: Achievements, Crisis and Prospects', in G. Esping-Andersen (ed.), *Welfare States in Transition: National Adaptations in Global Economies*, Sage.

Sunesson, S., Blomberg, S., Edebalk, P. G., Harrysson, L., Magnusson, J., Meeuwisse, A., Petersson, T. and Salonen, T. (1998) 'The Flight from Universalism', *European Journal of Social Work*, 1(1).

Svallfors, S. (1995) *In the Eye of the Beholder – Opinions on Welfare and Justice in Comparative Perspective*, Bank of Sweden Tercentenary Foundation.

Szebehely, M. (1998) 'Omsorgsstat i förändring – svensk äldreomsorg i nordisk belysning' [The Caring State in Transition – Swedish Old Age Care in a Nordic Light], in *Välfärden – verkan och samverkan* [Welfare – Outcomes and Cooperation], no. 1, Försäkringskasseförbundet.

Titmuss, R. (1974) *Social Policy*. Allen & Unwin.

Vogel, J. (1997) *Living Conditions and Inequality in the European Union*, Eurostat Working Documents, Population and Social Conditions, E/1997–3.

CHAPTER 9

Germany: Reform from Within

LUTZ LEISERING

What is 'Germany'?

Since the late nineteenth century, Germany has undergone more drastic changes, both of political regime and territory, than most other countries. During four decades after the Second World War I there were two diametrically opposed regimes coexisting within Germany. Imperial Germany, the Reich (1871–1918), was followed by the Weimar Republic, the first German democracy (1919–33), and by National Socialism, the Third Reich (1933–45). After a period of occupation, a democratic and capitalist West Germany, the Federal Republic of Germany (FRG), and a totalitarian and communist East Germany, the German Democratic Republic (GDR), were founded in 1949 and only reunited in 1990. These historical periods have left their marks on social policy as on other areas of policy. Yet, despite the changes, there were considerable institutional continuities across political regimes. Unification in 1990 was a takeover of the GDR by the FRG. On one day, all FRG legal and social institutions were imposed on the eastern part, including the basic institutional arrangements of social policy.

Since its foundation as a national state in 1871 Germany has been a federal state consisting of (currently) 16 states (*Länder*). Federalism was abandoned only during National Socialist and communist rule. This diversity stems from pre-1871 traditions when 'Germany' was split into numerous small states and principalities. The federal structure of the German polity is laid down in the Constitution of 1949 in Article 20 which cannot be changed even by a 100 per cent majority in parliament. A major aspect of German federalism is that education almost exclusively falls within the competence of the Länder. Unlike other countries, education is therefore not normally considered to be part of 'social policy' and, for example, does not figure in the social budget.

161

The Evolution of a Welfare State Model (1880–2000)

Germany came late to industrialisation, but pioneered modern state welfare. Several historical phases can be distinguished:

- *Laying the foundations* (1880–1918). In the 1880s, Chancellor Bismarck introduced social insurance systems to protect workers – and from 1911 white-collar workers also – against the risks of sickness, industrial injury and old age. These were paternalist and authoritarian reforms with a double edge both against the economic liberals of the day and the socialist workers' movement which were seen as a threat to the imperial regime. While Britons think of the late 1940s as the founding years of 'the welfare state', Germans think of Bismarck as the founding father of their social insurance state. Primary education had already been made compulsory in Prussia (the largest pre-1871 German state) in 1825. During the First World War, foundations were laid for modern industrial relations between trade unions and employers.

- *Democracy and economic crisis* (1918–33). The first years of mass democracy gave rise to substantial departures in social policy, such as the introduction of social rights in the new Constitution, the creation of a new branch – unemployment insurance – of social insurance, and social democratic policies in the municipalities, for example in the field of health and family services. However, massive economic and social problems and political confrontation led to societal breakdown and the emergence of National Socialism.

- *The National Socialist 'welfare state'* (1933–45). One of the original promises of the regime was to replace mass unemployment and misery by new welfare. The racist and authoritarian ideology left its mark on social policy, by orienting health, family and education policies towards eugenic aims, replacing trade unions and the labour party by a fascist organisation of industrial relations, the principle of self-government of social insurance by authoritarian rule, and by expelling Jews and critics of the system from the civil and welfare services. However, much of the basic institutional structure of social insurance remained intact or was even extended.

- *Establishing the postwar welfare state* (1949–66). After the Allied occupation, the two Germanies were founded in 1949. In the FRG, the major focus of this chapter, debates about a new, more egalitarian welfare state along the lines of Beveridge or the ideas of the German labour movement soon subsided. Instead, ingrained social policy institutions were restored by a centre/centre-right government led by the Christian Democratic Party (CDP), increasingly backed by the social democratic (SDP) opposition. Economic reconstruction, promoting house- building and integrating millions of migrants were the main social policy tasks of the early years, followed by a gradual expansion and reform of social security and the 1949 Constitution introduced which the welfare state (or rather the 'social state') as an unalterable principle of the FRG. The major 1957 old-age pensions reform act became the legitimating cornerstone of postwar welfare.

- *Modernising the welfare state* (1966–75). With the Social Democrats in government, an unprecedented expansion of social policy unfolded, provoking high hopes of social planning and active policies directed to enhancing 'the quality of life' for all groups in society, and not only for workers, as in traditional industrial social policy. Education boomed and a wide range of new or extended benefits and services was introduced, for example housing benefit, means-tested grants for students and active labour market policies. Keynesian economic policy and neocorporatist systems of negotiation between state, employers and employees were also introduced. It was also the formative period of social work as a semi-profession.

- *Consolidation and new expansion* (1975–*c.* 1995). Economic crisis and political challenges terminated the era of expansion. Fiscal constraints began to dominate policy-making, and social security systems were restructured rather than extended. Unlike Thatcher, however, Chancellor Kohl's neoconservatism remained largely rhetorical during his 16 years of office (1982–98). Benefits were cut repeatedly, but key structures remained intact. There were even new departures, especially benefits and social rights for families and mothers and, above all, the explosion of social spending triggered by the unique historical event of unification with the economically run-down East Germany in 1990. In 1996, social spending (not including education) reached an all-time peak of 35 per cent of GDP. After unification, social expenditure reached an historic scale of about two-thirds of the (East German) regional GDP. Without this effort, mainly flowing from annual transfers of some DM150 billion from west to east, the enormous problems of mass unemployment and social upheaval could not have been handled in a politically safe manner.

- *The socialist 'welfare state' – the GDR* (1949–90). The GDR, too, was a welfare state but counter-posed to the Western variety. It claimed to deliver more social security than West Germany. Rather than redistributing wealth produced in a market as in western states, the GDR model aimed to abolish the market altogether and establish a command economy oriented towards 'social' aims, for example by securing jobs for everybody, by massive subsidies of basic consumer goods and by tying housing, social services and pension entitlements to the workplace. The design of social services and benefits broke with the Bismarckian tradition even more than had the National Socialists. Centralised and uniform benefit schemes prevailed. In the early years, active discrimination policies against children from bourgeois families achieved higher equality of opportunity in higher education than in West Germany. However, social security benefits were low, social services – for example old-people's homes – were in poor condition and there was collective as well as individual (relative) poverty. In the late 1980s, the GDR became the first welfare state to collapse under the burden of its social services.

Bismarck's initial policies have left their mark till the present day, basic principles and forms of organisation having survived. However, the widespread notion of continuity needs qualification. In an evolutionary process of gradual change, especially in the years after the Second World War, German social policy has been substantially transformed. What started as social insurance for limited groups of workers and with low benefits, gradually grew into a comprehensive, quasi-universalist network of social services for the entire population. Only after 1949 did Germany become a fully mixed society, representing a third way between economic liberalism and a residual welfare state on the one hand, and a socialist or communist system of totalitarian and authoritarian provision of goods by the state on the other. When Germans prefer the term 'social state', as entwined in the postwar Constitution, to the term 'welfare state', they want to draw a dividing line between social policy that respects the freedom of the individual and the market as a general principle ('social state'), and a hypertrophied system of state provision and control ('welfare state').

Nevertheless the West German welfare state has expanded considerably during the postwar decades, with social spending almost doubling its share in gross net product to around one-third (see Figure 9.1). In 1950 the FRG started with the highest level of social spending among Western countries although in later decades some countries spent even more. At the same time, the numbers of social services clients as well as of staff providing and delivering services have increased drastically. Currently, more than a third of the population derive most of their income from the welfare state, either as clients or as staff. Social law has expanded equally, with more complex legal regulations than in most other welfare states.

Continuity still remains a key feature of German social policy development. It can be seen, first, in the survival of the principle of social insurance which in Germany has the specific meaning of a 'pay-as-you-go' system financed not primarily by taxes but by contributions of employers and employees and run by semi-autonomous non-state bodies administered by employers and employees; second, in the deeply-entrenched federal structure of government with each of the three levels – central government, states (Länder) and municipalities – having their own domains of social policy; and third, in the informal great welfare state coalition that has shaped social policy since 1948. Both big parties alternately leading the federal government – the CDP and the SDP – have been welfare state parties throughout, equally fostering the expansion of the welfare state and joining forces in all major social policy

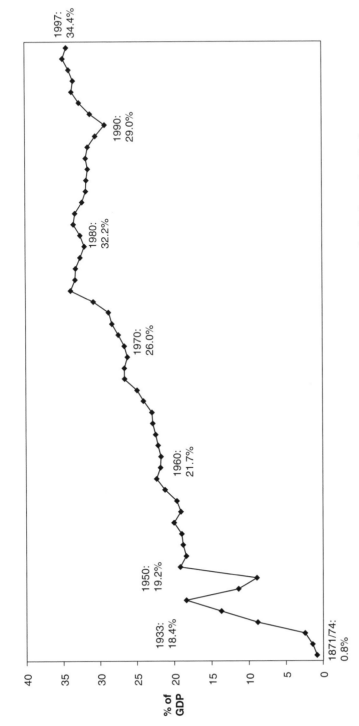

Figure 9.1 Social spending as a per cent of GDP, 1871–1997 (excluding education)

Note: Before 1933 the figures are for years 1871/74, 1885/89, 1900/04, 1925/29, 1930/32. The 1933 peak is due to a low GNP at the depression.

Source: Compiled from Lampert (1998, p. 293) Schmidt (1998, p. 154) and the Federal Ministry of Labour and Social Affairs (1998, p. 278).

reforms in postwar Germany. Since the mid-1990s, some of these principles are being questioned. Are we nearing the end of a model of social policy that started almost 120 years ago?

Consensus

German political culture is oriented towards consensus and compromise; compared to other countries there has been little confrontation either in politics or industrial relations. The expansion of state social policy could draw on relatively homogenous pro-welfare state beliefs and values backed by all political parties. Policy-making was dominated by a centre/centre-right party (the CDP) which led the government during two-thirds of the FRG's first half century, mostly supported in an informal sociopolitical coalition by the non-socialist SDP, itself open to compromise in postwar reconstruction. In this sense the FRG has been a 'centrist' welfare state (Schmidt, 1998, p. 220).

Economic liberalism among the Christian Democrats has been tempered by a pronounced conservatism with regard to family and social relationships, the social element being tangible in the strong and well-organised labour wing of the party. The Social Democrats, even whilst upholding the flag of socialism in the 1950s, supported legislation that restored the ingrained fabric of the welfare state. The small liberal party, the Free Democratic Party (FDP), in government for most of the postwar years alternating between coalitions with the Christian Democrats and the Social Democrats, was generally more critical of the welfare state but joined the general consensus in practical politics. The Green Party, founded in 1980 and, since 1998, in a government coalition with the Social Democrats, is an innovative, less dogmatic, pro-welfare-state party. Radical liberal critics of the welfare state have always had a voice in the debate but only from the mid-1990s did their views gain weight.

The relationship between labour and capital is equally geared to social integration and consensus. Their cooperation as 'industrial partners' (*Tarifpartner*) is also based on compromise, reflected in the very low level of industrial conflict. The German model of industrial democracy, enacted in 1951 and 1976, with a strong representation of trade unions on the executive boards of private companies (*Mitbestimmung*), has received attention worldwide. Social insurance as the core of the German welfare state expresses a normative compromise and consensus between collective and individualist values, through compulsory membership and earnings-related benefits.

Ludwig Erhard and the 'Social Market Economy'

The term 'Social Market Economy', coined in 1946 and explicitly designed as a 'third' or middle way, has been the hallmark of West German democratic welfare capitalism since the Second World War. The concept originated from the German school of economics called ordo-liberalism, developed in the 1930s and 1940s against both unfettered liberalism and the experience of totalitarian rule and a command economy under fascism and Stalinism. Although 'social state' also became a key term of the political language in Germany, it was not a founding formula of postwar Germany; as noted earlier, the late 1940s/early 1950s witnessed a restoration of the Bismarckian tradition rather than innovation as in Britain.

'Social Market Economy', with its promise of regaining wealth and welfare in a free society, won the CDP the first (1949) election. Its main protagonist, Ludwig Erhard, Minister for Economic Affairs 1949–63, became the 'father of the economic miracle' in postwar Germany. Erhard had a narrow conception of Social Market Economy, a kind of people's capitalism (Abelshauser, 1996), geared to increases in wages, consumption and property for all strata of society, rather than substantial social services provided by the state. He advocated measures like anti-inflation, currency and anti-trust policies to strengthen, not contain, the operation of the market. It was not a variety of, but an antidote to, the welfare state. Erhard saw the 'welfare state' – a negative term in his view – as a 'modern paranoia'.

The great 1957 old-age pensions reforms which Chancellor Adenauer had to fight through against Erhard, were the first political defeat for Erhard's perspective and a major step towards interpreting the 'social market economy' in a pro-, not anti-welfare-state way. By the early 1960s, it had become the widespread term signifying consensus and social peace in the middle ground. On the occasion of a (small) economic recession in 1967, elements of Keynesianism were officially adopted by policy-makers, thereby broadening the role of economic policy in welfare provision.

Intermediate Agencies and Corporatism

Dating back to the absolutist, militarist Prussian tradition and idealistic Hegelian social philosophy, a strong belief in the 'state' – an essentialist term preferred to the more pragmatic Anglo-Saxon term 'government' – is deeply entrenched in German social thought although the German politico-administrative system, especially in respect of social policy, is less centralised, less 'statist' than many other welfare states. This is reflected in the social budget, the budget not of any government agency or body but a sum of elements from a variety of scattered budgets of mainly non-governmental institutions. Most is spent in the five branches of social insurance, by para-state bodies, mainly funded and administered by its members and employers, the two largest branches, health and old-age pensions, accounting for half. However, social insurance, like other non-state bodies, is subject to legal regulation, to some financial support and to political control by the state. Old-Age Pensions Insurance receives an annual state subsidy of some DM100 billion.

The corporatist structure, the variegated web of semi-autonomous actors, groups and institutions, has been typical of German social policy since its inception. Social welfare is produced by a broad range of intermediate agencies which are neither purely governmental (such as a national health service) nor entirely independent (such as occupational pensions and private insurance).These agencies have been granted privileged status as providers or coordinators of welfare services, adding up to a tightly regulated structure of society. Liberal critics claim this accounts for much of Germany's inflexibility in adapting to the new global economy. The key elements of German corporatism are:

- The five branches of social insurance (see below): these systems are differentiated by occupational groups. For example, for many years members of the white-collar branch of old-age pensions enjoyed better conditions than members of the blue-collar branch.
- Social professions, above all medical doctors: they have higher socio-legal status and incomes than doctors in most other countries. From 1955, doctors who have signed in with Health Insurance have a monopoly. Treatment by private doctors is not reimbursed by Health Insurance so that they have remained marginal in the health sector. Contractual doctors are paid on a fee-for-service fixed price basis.
- 'Social partners': associations of employers and trade unions in industrial relations.
- Systems of coordination, negotiation and bargaining between corporate actors: between the 'social partners' – their autonomy being guaranteed by the Constitution – and between the sickness funds and the associations of medical doctors.
- Voluntary welfare organisations, which need to be described in more detail since they occupy a central position in the organisation of personal social services.

Subsidiarity, a key principle of the German welfare mix, laid down in the Social Assistance Act and in the Children and Youth Welfare Act, means that small units have priority over larger units, especially over the state, whenever appropriate. Help by bureaucratic organisations is subsidiary to support relationships within the family, and state aid is second to aid by voluntary welfare associations. This principle pertains to the entire range of personal social services directed to age groups (youth and elderly), to families and to 'problem groups' (the poor, people with disabilities). The welfare associations employ over one million waged employees (1996) and large numbers of unpaid (voluntary) helpers.

Major umbrella organisations of voluntary welfare include Caritas (Roman Catholic) and Diakonie (Protestant), mirroring the bi-confessional structure of German Christianity; the Non-Denominational, Workers and Central Jewish Welfare Associations; and the Red Cross. These associations act as service providers in service centres, hospitals, residential homes and care for the elderly and people with disabilities, and sheltered employment. In addition, they are political actors – in the field of children and youth services they have a formal say in the administrative board. Besides their welfare associations, the churches also play a direct part, for example by running social work schools. After many years of privileged symbiosis with the state and a high degree of bureaucratisation, the associations now find themselves under pressure to improve efficiency to survive in competition with commercial providers in the social services market developing under the new Care Insurance. In social policy debates, they have subsequently moved from conformism with official policies to sustained criticism of benefit cuts and lobbying for the poor.

National and Local

The German political system has a three-tier structure, with each tier – central government, the states (*Länder*) and the municipalities – having distinct legislative, fiscal and administrative powers. Domains are demarcated in detail in the Constitution which also gives to the municipalities the right to self-governance (Article 28). Conflicts between the three levels often cut across party lines. Since the 1980s, for example, the federal government has repeatedly cut unemployment benefits to shift burdens to Social Assistance which is regulated by central law in a fairly standardised way but financed by the *Länder* and the municipalities. Even after the growth of national social spending had ended, social spending's share of municipalities' budgets still almost doubled from 12 per cent in 1980 to 22 per cent in 1996. Although social assistance funding and administration is less centralised than in Britain, provisions do not vary as much between regions and communes as in Italy.

The emphasis of local social policy is on personal social services and social work: social planning for youth, elderly and the poor, arranging a local mix of voluntary and municipal welfare agencies, and securing quality of services. Health activities are limited because the centralised system of sickness funds and contractual doctors has tended to absorb the entire health service. In their predominant field, education, the states have not, however, lived up to the expectation to raise quality through competition, and their role in financing and planning hospitals has been a major obstacle in the reform of Health Insurance.

The Welfare Mix – Public and Private

As in other countries the welfare state is only one segment of the social production of welfare. There is a mix of public and private services and, even within the comprehensive German version of this mix, a pronounced mix within the public welfare domain. As noted, most of the institutions of the German welfare state are not 'state' proper, but 'intermediate' agencies.

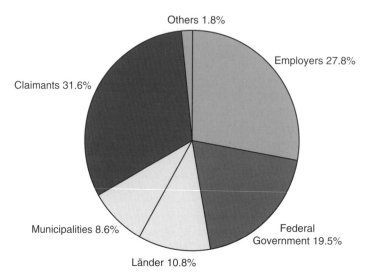

Figure 9.2   Financing the welfare state, 1997 (excluding education)

Note: 'Employees' includes non-waged members of social insurance such as the elderly members of Health Insurance and some self-employed persons.

Source: Federal Ministry of Labour and Social Affairs (1998, p. 295).

This is reflected in the financing of the social budget: Figure 9.2 clearly shows the three levels of government and also the massive share of social insurance contributions paid by employers and employees who also administer the scheme.

Thus, even in the comprehensive German welfare state, there has always been a mix of provision:

● Security in old age rests on the 'three pillars model' of state pensions, occupational pensions and private pensions, with, however, a strong emphasis on the state pillar.

● In the field of health insurance, the long-standing 'peace boundary' between public and private insurance – the income threshold where compulsory membership of public health insurance ends – has remained undisputed to the present day. Due to the high quality of public services, the publicly-insured are not driven to take up a (more than supplementary) private insurance. For civil servants (*Beamte*), there is a special state-run (non-insurance) scheme which covers half of medical bills, leaving the other half to private insurance.

● The complex institutional arrangement of health insurance includes links to semi-markets: to pharmaceutical industries and producers of medical technology, and to the doctors who are not employees of the state or of any sickness fund but business-like monopolistic providers with special privileged contractual relationships with Health Insurance. This corporatist welfare mix is, however, regulated by government.

- The German 'Dual System' of vocational training for youth, which is considered a model by other countries, combines state schooling during part of the week with company-based work and practical qualification. This system has led to higher qualification levels and less youth unemployment than in many other countries.
- German 'social housing' involves a public–private partnership. Private landlords get state subsidies for building flats if they agree to let them to low income people at a modest rent fixed by government.

The macro-welfare mix is mirrored in the micro-welfare mix that each citizen makes up for him- or herself. Most people derive their income and personal social services from more than one source; for example they top up a state pension by occupational and private pensions. However, in most cases there is a source of income that dominates the individual income package. Table 9.1 shows changes in the dominant source during the last four decades. The state's share in social welfare production has not only increased on the aggregate level (see Figure 9.1), but also on the individual level. Compared to market wages and income derived from one's family (including transfers from earners to their spouses and children) the social wage has gained weight. The data also shows that this pertains mainly to young and old people, that is to age groups. We can also see that the growth of state provisions is not a zero-sum game: the extension of higher education has simultaneously prolonged the time young people are cared for by their families. The figure also indicates that female labour market participation is increasing, though still on a lower scale than in many other countries.

Table 9.1 Main sources of income in the population, 1961 and 1998, as a percentage for the respective age group (female population in brackets)

Main income source	Age group							Total Population
	< 15	*15–20*	*20–25*	*25–55*	*55–60*	*60–65*	*65+*	
Market								
1961	1	58	80 (69)	65 (39)	55	39	9 (5)	44 (29)
1998 West	0	19	59 (54)	68 (58)	51	18	1 (1)	40 (31)
1998 East	0	30	62 (56)	74 (69)	48	7	0 (0)	41 (35)
Welfare state								
1961	1	2	2 (1)	6 (8)	19	37	76 (71)	15 (17)
1998 West	4	5	11 (10)	10 (9)	26	68	90 (86)	27 (27)
1998 East	2	6	24 (36)	23 (26)	47	92	100 (100)	38 (43)
Family								
1961	98	40	19 (29)	29 (53)	26	24	15 (25)	42 (54)
1998 West	96	75	31 (36)	18 (35)	21	19	8 (13)	33 (42)
1998 East	98	64	14 (17)	3 (5)	5	1	0 (0)	21 (22)

Note: Figures refer to individual income, not to household income, including intra-household transfers. *Market*, denotes income from own paid work (wage/salary); *Family*, denotes money transferred from spouse or parents; *Welfare state*, denotes income from cash benefits and some other sources.

Source: Calculations based on micro census data (Federal Statistical Office, 1964, 1999).

Social Insurance – the Road to Quasi-Universalism

Given the variety of intermediate and corporatist agencies, the picture of a highly-fragmented system emerges. Social insurance, in particular, is fragmented by occupational groups, with three main branches of old-age insurance, and 475 sickness funds, and with schemes for occupational groups outside social insurance, primarily for civil servants, farmers and some professional groups. However, changes since the 1950s have gradually transformed the system. The social insurance state has been increasingly integrated and extended. With regard to benefits, funding and institutional structure, this 'fragmented' system has given way to a tightly interwoven quasi-universalism:

- *Integration*: the difference between the white-collar and the blue-collar branch of Old-Age Pension Insurance has been steadily removed. Sickness funds nowadays offer virtually identical services to their members and a system of financial compensation established to account for different distributions of risks among the clientele, especially between West and East German funds.
- *Extension of coverage and benefits*: non-waged groups, for example self-employed, students, housewives and artists, were admitted to insurance. Aspects of family policy were introduced, especially in 1985 and 1997, thus acknowledging family work, i.e. raising a child as an independent source of entitlement to benefits in addition to paid work ('natural contribution'). Under the 1997 Act raising one child equals three years of paying contributions. In Health Insurance, non-waged (house)wives and children of an employed father have always been entitled to full services without paying contributions.
- *Extension of bargaining systems* ('corporatisation'): hospitals and, to some degree, the pharmaceutical industry, have been included in corporatist bargaining and planning, originally confined to medical doctors who run private surgeries outside the hospital system.

The system is thus nearing universality. More than 90 per cent of the population are currently covered by social insurance for old age and health. By contrast, truly universal citizenship-based schemes are rare in the German system. The most important universal scheme is Child Benefit, repeatedly reformed since the foundation of the FRG. In the 1990s there has been a strong pressure from all parties to raise it. There is also a substantial range of selective benefits, particularly Social Assistance (SA). Due to the strength of social insurance schemes, the number of SA recipients is much lower than in many other countries, although unemployment, growing numbers of lone mothers and immigration have led to the number of SA recipients (basic income support, not special needs support) more than quadrupling since 1970 to 5 per cent. Non-take up amounts to approximately 50 per cent of those entitled. However, most claims are short (see Figure 9.3) and German

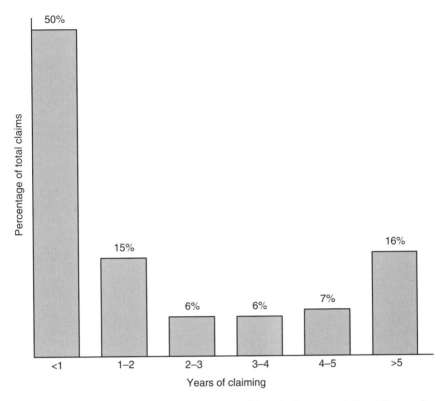

Figure 9.3 Duration of social assistance claims in Germany (city of Bremen)

Source: Leisering, Leibfried and Dahrendorf, *Time and Poverty in Western Welfare States: United Germany in Perspective* 1999, p. 63, Reproduced with the permission of Cambridge University Press; life take estimates, 10 per cent sample (922 case records) of all new Social Assitance claims made in the city of Bremen in 1989, observed till 1994.

social assistance is more 'universal' than related schemes in many other countries. Everybody below a certain income level, including wage-earners and foreigners, are entitled to benefits. Unemployment Assistance, the lower echelon of Unemployment Benefit, is half-way between means-testing and social insurance.

Security First, Equality Second

Although people often associate the concept of the welfare state with egalitarian values, many welfare states and Germany's in particular are geared more to achieving security than equality. Security is an objective of social policy in two ways:

- Some transfers and services aim to guarantee basic or minimum incomes and minimum provisions. The 1961 Social Assistance Act introduced

the right to assistance, establishing a sociocultural (not just physical) minimum, including full coverage by health services.
- Security can also mean safeguarding a status attained earlier in life. This is
  mainly achieved by social insurance. Pensions, industrial-injury insurance
  and unemployment benefit are earnings-related. The bulk of the German
  welfare state, therefore, is not directed to the poor but to the broad middle mass. This is redistribution over the individual life course, not between
  rich and poor.

However, the system also has egalitarian components:

- Health insurance and (long-term) care insurance not only redistribute
  between the sick and the non-sick, but also between rich and poor, since
  services are not earnings-related whilst contributions are.
- In addition, there is massive redistribution in favour of married couples
  and families with children because they pay the same contributions as sin-
  gles unless the spouse is in full-time employment.
- Survivors' pensions for old age create entitlements for people who have
  not paid contributions, thereby enhancing equality.
- There is a strong commitment to equality between age groups.
- Health insurance does not ration services for the elderly.
- Higher education is free.

By and large, social security policies have been effective. Poverty rates are
below the European average, and numbers of recipients even in East
Germany are surprisingly low and not growing fast (although the stigma of
social assistance is higher there). One reason is the enormous amount
of money paid for labour-market measures such as job-creation schemes.
Another reason is the extension of the West German system of old-age
pensions to the east which turned the East German elderly into unification
'winners'. Despite unprecedented social upheaval, therefore, the east has not,
as some predicted, become a German 'Mezzogiorno' (Leisering and
Leibfried, 1999).

The German welfare state and German society at large are more gender-
biased than other countries; the insurance system is geared to the male breadwinner based on contributions paid out of wages. The welfare state sets
strong incentives to stay in the family and stay out of the labour market
(Allmendinger, 1994). Labour-market participation among women, especially among married women, is rising but still low. One of the reasons,
besides the conservative ideology of the CDP, is the scarcity of social services
allowing women to delegate housework and child care and, at the same time,
the creation of job opportunities for women. Only from 1996 was there
a (formal) guarantee of a place in a nursery school for each child from the age
of three. Germany thus generally lags behind in the move towards a service
society. There are relatively few service jobs and few part-time jobs.

Germany – a Conservative Welfare Regime?

In Esping-Andersen's (1990) analysis, Germany is seen as the epitome of the conservative welfare-state regime: achieving a medium degree of decommod-ification (of enabling people to live independently of the market), grading benefits and entitlements by occupation and social status, and upholding a conservative concept of society emphasising family, traditional gender roles and intermediate social bodies such as churches, voluntary welfare associa-tions and occupational status groups. Esping-Andersen rightly depicts Germany as a middle-ground welfare regime, but the label 'conservative' oversimplifies and overemphasises differences from other countries, with regard to both institutional structure and ideological background.

First, the German welfare state is more egalitarian and universalist than it looks. Apart from civil servants, social insurance coverage has become quasi-universal in all its branches. In old-age pensions, differentiation by occupa-tional groups has effectively become irrelevant. The health system, although formally based on insurance, is strongly egalitarian and near-universal – a point obscured by Esping-Andersen's focus only on cash benefits.

Secondly, politically, the German regime is 'centrist' rather than conserva-tive (Schmidt, 1998, p. 220), shaped by a reformist centre/centre-right party in conjunction with a pragmatic, strong social democratic party (though mostly in opposition). Re-analysing Esping-Andersen's data, Obinger and Wagschal (1998) found that his conservative type actually falls into two types, a 'centrist European social insurance state' (including Germany) and a type which really meets Esping-Andersen's criteria of conservativism (found in France, Italy and Austria).The Kohl government (1982–98) further tem-pered the conservative outlook of German social policy.

Groping in the Dark: At the Threshold to a New Welfare State? (1995–2000)

Between the mid-1970s and the mid-1990s, the welfare state was under con-siderable pressure, both economically and politically; there was much talk about crisis, about dismantling the welfare state and, when Chancellor Kohl took office in 1982, a call for a moral change in social policy and society at large. However, the ingrained structure of social security systems survived and even took up the historical challenge of German unification in 1990, an event somewhat obscuring Kohl's lack of strategic vision. But from the mid-1990s, crisis has become more real. Several changes point to a transfor-mation of the postwar welfare state.

For a start, political consensus among the major parties and the social partners (the trade unions and the employers' associations) characterising the postwar period has become brittle. The SDP now acknowledges that the welfare state not only solves but creates problems. It has adopted the view that unemployment is partially caused by excessive rates of contributions, raising the price of labour.

Globalisation also exerts particular pressures on the competitiveness of the German economy, the world's second biggest export economy. Financing social benefits mostly by contributions rather than taxes makes the German benefit systems particularly vulnerable to the crisis in employment – and to competition by low-wage countries – because half of the contributions are paid by the employers as part of labour costs. Similarly, the design of social insurance as pay-as-you-go-systems rather than capital funding, in conjunction with high replacement rates, makes the system more vulnerable to the effects of the ageing of the population, especially in the context of one of the world's lowest birth rates.

There are further problems unique to Germany. Since the Second World War, German society has been more homogeneous than other societies, as revealed by data on beliefs and attitudes; the quest for social harmony between social groups was overwhelming. The 1990s, however, have confronted the Germans with a new – or newly perceived – world of social heterogeneity and social cleavage. Firstly, there is the East/West divide since national unification in 1990. Many of the support measures for East Germans were financed from social insurance funds (rather than general taxes), thus adding to pressures on social insurance. Unemployment in the east is still very high (*c.* 20 per cent), and economic growth too slow, only slightly above western rates; 'eastern' tax revenues continue to be low; and high transfers from the west will be needed for many years to come. Nine years after unification, there remains divisive resentment between east and west.

Secondly, there is a problem of immigration and ethnic conflict. Germany has one of the highest proportions of foreigners in Europe (8.5 per cent in 1993), and politicians have been slow in facing this fact. Between 1988 and 1996, 2.3 million settlers and *c.* 2 million asylum seekers came to Germany. Poverty rates among foreigners are twice that of native citizens; some of the settlers are becoming marginalised.

The changing composition of the social budget indicates some of the new challenges of the welfare state (Figure 9.4). Health insurance is a cost factor as can be seen from its growing share in the budget; the ageing of the population is not reflected in the figure because its peak lies ahead. All in all, the share of social insurance has grown from below to well above half social spending (including the 'labour market' item which largely flows from unemployment insurance). At the same time, social assistance and local personal services expenditures have more than doubled, indicating the increase in social risks not covered by the standard systems of social insurance.

The main features of welfare provision in Germany are summarised at the end of the chapter.

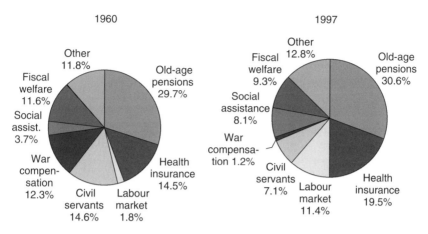

Figure 9.4   The social budget, 1960 and 1997 (excluding education)

Notes: Social assistance includes housing benefit, youth welfare and other local personal services. War compensation covers the war-disabled, war widows and civil compensation case.

Source: Compiled from Federal Ministry of Labour and Social Affairs (1998, p. 289).

Conclusion: Evolutionary Change

Despite the new challenges, and a weakening of political support for welfare, there is no sign of a fundamental break with the ingrained institutions of the welfare state. Most reform does not aim at new institutions or at privatising social services, as is evident in neoliberal regimes. It is rather a reform from within, especially a mobilisation of the existing intermediate institutions – non-state and non-market institutions like social insurance – so characteristic of German social policy. Moreover, there are few instances of straightforward privatisation – shifting provisions to market and family – but rather new links between public and private. Changing the welfare mix need not be a zero-sum game – more private, less public – but extending private welfare production may require increased state regulatory control, just as a more active role of the (non-state) social insurance agencies requires more government regulation.

One example is the changing role of intermediate agencies: social insurance (in the specific German meaning of a non-state and employment-based way of organising social security), corporate actors in the health sector (sickness funds and monopolistic doctors' associations) and local governments are revitalised as social policy agents, especially in health and social assistance. Another is the new links to private provisions and agencies (rather than mere 'privatisation'), especially in the field of long-term care, old-age pensions and again social assistance. Comparing welfare states we therefore have to bear in mind that in some countries change may be smoother and less visible but not necessarily smaller than in countries where visible institutional breaks are more common and where a rhetoric of change prevails. As described earlier, health insurance has been thoroughly transformed over the years to near universality while it formally still is 'social insurance'. More recently, old-age pension insurance, though particularly vulnerable to the ageing of the population, is being successfully adapted to demographic change.

All in all, true to its tradition of evolutionary adaptation to social change, the German welfare state in the 1990s is undergoing considerable change within the framework of old institutions and without the rhetoric of grand reform. Old and new, continuity and discontinuity, are intertwined. In a new situation – the return of political conflict, economic and demographic challenges, the decline of social harmony – old institutions are reformed from within: they change substantially but retain basic characteristics and continue to be viewed as the same institutions.

By the time the SDP won the 1998 election, Germany had come to be considered a laggard in adapting to the new exigencies of a globalising economy. Politicians pointed to the Netherlands, to Denmark, to Britain or the USA as models of reducing unemployment, of deregulating the economy and of successfully restructuring welfare. German unemployment rose, whilst it fell elsewhere. The German political system makes it truly difficult to induce changes, and political immobility seemed to prevail. Germany is highly fragmented with many 'veto players' (Schmidt, 1998): the Constitutional Court interferes massively with social policy; in the second chamber of the federal parliament, the Bundesrat, where the states are represented, the government party is often in a minority; and the states and the municipalities have a say in finance, taxation and hospital planning.

The new Chancellor, Gerhard Schröder, took up the challenge of improving Germany's competitiveness, in particular through reforms of taxation, old-age insurance and health insurance, and, above all, the fight against unemployment. In the fields of education and ethnic conflict, more far-reaching changes may be necessary; here there is much rhetoric and little determined action, despite some departures in higher education.

It remains to be seen if social cleavages will challenge the German model of social integration; if there will be a shift from the 'transfer state' to a 'social investment state' with more emphasis on education and employment, and less on paying for time off employment; and if there will be revolutionary breaks or, as before, a smooth and evolutionary adaptation. It is also an open question as to whether ongoing administrative modernisation will successfully transform the welfare state from within (and from below, by reform of local government). The future of the German welfare state is more uncertain than for many years although Germany's history suggests that the end of the welfare state is not near. In 1999, Schröder and Blair collaborated in a programmatic paper on the 'Third Way'. In principle, this is what the German 'social state' has always been about.

Key Features of Welfare Provision

Social Insurance: five branches

Financed equally by contributions from employers and employees, administered by both (accident insurance: only employers), supplemented from general taxation (mainly in old-age-insurance). Compulsory for most employees

Old-Age Pensions Insurance – 30 per cent of social budget, pay-as-you-go funding

- Retirement pensions – earnings-related, no minimum pension; from age 65 or earlier.
- Incapacity pension – for permanently incapacitated.
- Survivors' pensions – for widow(er)s and orphans.
- Rehabilitation – medical treatment, regeneration, retraining.
- Pension entitlements on grounds of child raising or caring.

Health Insurance – 20 per cent of social budget

- Prevention, treatment, rehabilitation.
- Free access for non-waged dependents.
- Corporatist administration by sickness funds, doctors' associations and the state.
- Contractual private providers – doctors, hospitals (municipal, voluntary/ NGOs), pharmaceutical industries
- Sickness Benefit – for 18 months sickness (after first 6 weeks of sick pay).

Unemployment Insurance

- Unemployment Benefit – earnings-related, for one year of unemployment (longer for older workers).
- Unemployment Aid – lower benefits, earnings-related and means-tested, unlimited duration.
- Job-creation schemes, vocational training, rehabilitation.
- Labour exchange and career advisory services.
- Labour-market monitoring.

Accident Insurance

- Industrial injury (including survivors') pensions.
- Prevention – regulations, inspectors.
- Rehabilitation.

Care Insurance

- Lump-sum payments for long-term care – graded by need; home and residential care.
- Free access for non-waged dependents.
- Contractual private and voluntary providers.

(Continued)

Need-based (Means-tested) Benefits

- Social Assistance (Basic Income Support) – cash benefits for all those in need, including working poor (excluding refugees).
- Asylum Seekers Benefit – reduced social assistance for refugees.
- Social Assistance (Special-needs Support) – cash and kind for the disabled, people in residential care and other groups.
- Housing Benefit – help with rent or maintenance of own home .
- Educational Benefit – for carers of children up to age of 2.
- Legal Aid – cost of lawyer and court.
- Students' grants – to secure subsistence; 50 per cent loan.

Universal Benefits

- Child Benefit – to all carers of children.
- Child-raising pension entitlements.

Merit-based ('Categorical') Benefits

- Provisions for tenured civil servants (*Beamte*) – old-age pensions, survivors' pensions, subsidy of private health care cost, special benefits.
- War Victims Benefits (war compensation) – old-age pensions, survivors' pensions.

Fiscal Welfare – *c.* 10 per cent of social budget

- Child allowances.
- Lower taxation for married couples.
- Savings allowances.

Private Market Benefits

- Sick pay – for first 6 weeks of sickness, earnings-related, paid by employer.
- Occupational pensions – limited coverage.
- Personal pensions – increasing coverage.
- Private health insurance – supplementing or (less widespread) replacing statutory insurance.
- Private care insurance – compulsory for non-members of statutory Care Insurance.

Social Services

- Under Social Insurance: rehabilitation, nursing, prevention, special treatment (under Health Insurance, Old-Age Pensions Insurance, Accident Insurance).
- Local provision: wide range of services for age groups (children, youth, elderly), families and people with social problems – provided by a mix of municipal authorities (Social Assistance Authority, Youth Welfare Authority and other authorities, varying by municipality), regional institutions (state/ Länder), voluntary welfare associations and private providers.

(Continued)

General Education

- State schools (mostly municipal) – private schools marginal.
- 6–15 years – compulsory primary (6–9) and secondary (10–15) education; curriculum varies by state (Land), examinations by school.
- 16–18 years – optional further secondary education in schools or vocational colleges, leading to final examination (*Abitur*).
- 18+ years – optional higher education at universities (4½ years required, empirical average 6 years) or colleges (3½ years), with means-tested grant (50 per cent loan) for few students; entry requirement: *Abitur*, selection only in some subjects; no fees; few part-time students.
- Graded structure of secondary education (10–18 years): separate schools for three levels of performance (correlated with class origin of pupils) (*Hauptschule, Realschule, Gymnasium*), only comprehensive schools in some States; plus special schools differentiated by type of disability.

Vocational Schooling

German 'Dual System', combining apprenticeship in a private company with vocational teaching in state schools (e.g. 2 days per week); attended by majority of youth leaving secondary schooling at age 15/16.

Housing

- 39 per cent of dwellings (26 per cent in East Germany) owner-occupied, remainder rented.
- Dwellings bought for cash price in open market (or from housing association under 'right to buy'), mostly financed by a savings contract with a building society.
- Private renting: tenants pay rent to a private landlord according to market price; rents subsidised by means-tested housing benefit.
- Social Housing: private landlords or housing associations receive state subsidies to build flats, conditional on charging state-regulated low rents to low-income tenants.

References

Abelshauser, W. (1996) 'Erhard oder Bismarck? Die Richtungsentscheidung der deutschen Sozialpolitik am Beispiel der Reform der Sozialversicherung in den Fünfziger Jahren', in *Geschichte und Gesellschaft. Zeitschrift für Historische Sozialwissenschaft*, 22(3), pp. 376–92.

Allmendinger, J. (1994) *Lebensverlauf und Sozialpolitik*, Campus.

Esping-Andersen, G. (1990) *The Three Worlds of Welfare Capitalism*, Polity Press.

Federal Ministry of Labour and Social Affairs (Bundesministerium für Arbeit und Sozialordnung, BMA) (1998) *Sozialbericht 1997*.

Federal Statistical Office (Statistisches Bundesamt) (1964) *Statistisches Jahrbuch*, Kohlhammer.

Federal Statistical Office (1999) *Fachserie 1*, Reihe 4.1.1, Kohlhammer.

Lampert, H. (1998) *Lehrbuch der Sozialpolitik*, 5th edn, Spriner. [The best overview
of the current institutional structure of the German welfare state, plus a history of
German social policy since the nineteenth century.]

Leisering, L. and Leibfried, S. (1999) *Time and Poverty in Western Welfare States:
United Germany in Perspective*, Cambridge University Press.

Obinger, H. and Wagschal, U. (1998) 'Drei Welten des Wohlfahrtsstaats? Das
Stratifizierungskonzept in der clusteranalytischen Überprüfung', in S. Lessenich,
and I. Ostner (eds), *Welten des Wohlfahrtskapitalismus*, Campus.

Schmidt, M. G. (1998) *Sozialpolitik in Deutschland. Historische Entwicklung und
internationaler Vergleich*, 2nd edn, Leske & Budrich.

[See Schmidt 1998 for the authoritative, most comprehensive and up-to-date analysis
of German social policy, including history, theory and cross-national comparison,
from the point of view of political science.]

CHAPTER 10

Italy: Moving from the Southern Model

VALERIA FARGION

Italian Society

In social and economic terms, at least, Italy is really two countries in one. While northern regions display a very dynamic economy that is well-integrated into the global market, southern regions are still in search of a route to economic development and to social and political modernisation. One of the most important consequences of this divergence is that the unemployment rate is close to 22 per cent in the south, whereas industrial firms in the north-eastern regions are in fact experiencing labour shortages.

The origins of the north–south divide can be traced far back into the history of the country, and the unification of Italy in 1861 did little to change the situation. Indeed it perpetuated the division through a compromise between the landed aristocracy of the *Mezzogiorno* and emerging industrial entrepreneurs in the northern regions. Nor was this settlement challenged by the fascist regime which came into power in 1922 and ruled the country until the end of the Second World War. As a result, throughout the twentieth century southern regions have lingered in a backward condition, far more similar to Greece and Portugal than to their northern Italian counterparts.

The postwar governments actually attempted to redress the territorial imbalance by promoting state-assisted industrialisation. This was done by setting up huge industrial and petrochemical plants – popularly labelled as 'desert cathedrals' – but the strategy proved a complete failure and ended with the closing of most state-owned firms over the course of the 1980s. Quite clearly, the massive dismissals connected to this downturn further complicated an already quite dramatic situation. Consequently southern Italian regions are very distant from European averages. The territorial dimension is therefore an essential feature of the Italian welfare state, especially so as Italy – as well as most other continental European countries – experienced a wide decentralisation process over the course of the 1990s. In particular, regional governments have been entrusted with further responsibilities in a number of policy areas that are increasingly crucial for the content of social citizenship in the different parts of the country.

In addition to this internal dimension, it is also useful to set the Italian case in a comparative perspective within leading welfare state typologies. Given the importance of income maintenance programmes (in particular pensions) in Italy, this country appears as a transfer-centred model. Accordingly, Esping-Andersen classifies Italy as a conservative regime along with the main continental European countries. On the other hand, there are a number of features which differentiate Italy from the rest of the countries falling into this category, particularly France and Germany. For instance, the Italian welfare state encompasses a national health system granting universal access on the basis of citizenship. This openly clashes with the occupational principles underpinning conservative regimes, although, as Esping-Andersen (1999, p. 92) himself suggests, 'in the final analysis it all comes down to the choice of indicators and measurement'.

Yet, if the main thrust of recent efforts devoted to welfare-state classification is to identify some underlying connecting logic of movement (Esping-Andersen, 1999, p. 73), recent works by Leibfried, Castles and Ferrera provide new light on the Italian case. All three authors point to some kind of communality among Mediterranean countries, albeit differently interpreted. To capture the inner logic of social protection in Italy we must trace the privileges and inequities within the system, which resemble those of Spain, Portugal and Greece. For instance:

- overprotection of core sectors of the labour force and underprotection of the periphery, the long-term unemployed and outsiders;
- generous coverage for certain risks (old age) and neglect of others (unemployment, family needs);
- misuse – if not the overt abuse – of a number of schemes, such as invalidity pensions (where this worked to the advantage of individual beneficiaries willing and able to enter clientelistic exchanges) and health care (where perverse incentives geared the system to the interests of service providers rather than patients).

This configuration is often labelled 'welfare all'Italiana' (after the title of a well-known book, Ascoli, 1984), and, despite the occupational thrust, is quite distant from either the German or the French model. It is a product of a complex mix of low administrative capacity and weak state legitimation, a largely uncivic political culture and entrenched distributive politics in the decision-making arena. However, over the 1990s most of the particularistic mechanisms embedded in the social protection system have been severely undermined, and the privileges and inequities mentioned earlier are starting to crumble, as we return to discuss later.

The Development of Italian Welfare

The Origins of the Italian Model

Considering that the first compulsory social insurance was introduced in 1898, the Italian welfare state is just over a century old. The programme was actually very limited and covered industrial injuries for only a small number of workers employed in dangerous plants. Although Bismarck's model of social insurance represented the reference point, Italy proceeded at a much slower pace in its development: the insurance on work accidents remained the only compulsory programme until 1919. Indeed, up to the First World War charitable institutions were the only response to the needs of the poor, apart from the friendly societies set up by the working class and operating almost exclusively in industrialised areas. The power of the Church and the strong Catholic tradition gave rise to a greater number of charities than was common in other European countries. Further, their widespread diffusion made it possible for liberal ruling élites to avoid financial commitment by the state.

It was only at the end of the First World War that the country experienced a sudden acceleration in social legislation, turning Italy from a laggard into a forerunner. In 1919 a far-reaching insurance programme was introduced providing coverage not only for old age but also for unemployment, a risk that most neighbouring countries started taking into consideration only much later. The programme was financed through social contributions by employers and employees and granted contributory benefits. Moreover, the beneficiaries included agricultural workers instead of just industrial workers – as was normally the case in other European countries. Unfortunately, with the support of large landowners and industrialists, right-wing armed bands managed to organise throughout the country against the 'red threat', and in 1922 the liberal state collapsed giving way to the fascist regime.

Social Protection under the Fascist Regime

One of the first measures introduced by Mussolini was a repeal of the extension of social insurance benefits to the agricultural sector. However, it would be misleading to downplay fascist intervention in the social field. The regime extended social protection to include certain risks that were especially relevant for its ideology, such as compulsory insurance for tuberculosis; establishment of maternity insurance and a single-purpose national agency to protect maternity and childhood; and promotion of occupational health funds by employers' associations to complement corporatist labour agreements. In line with the Latin motto *divide et impera*, fascist social legislation constantly emphasised differentiation in the types of benefits and services available to various categories. Special privileges were granted to groups such as judges, journalists, railway or telephone company workers which were crucial to the regime; and the extreme fragmentation lamented in the literature on the postwar Italian welfare state was essentially a fascist legacy.

With regard to the institutional design and organisation of social protection, Fascism consolidated the management of a variety of different programmes into two major funds. Insurance programmes covering work accidents were merged into a single fund which is still responsible for this policy field (Italian National Work Accident Programme, INAIL), and in 1935 a major restructuring of the private employees' pension fund was launched giving birth to what is nowadays the giant of the Italian welfare state, the Italian National Pension Scheme (INPS). Apart from running the pension scheme for private employees and separate schemes for particular groups of workers, the agency was entrusted with responsibility for insurance programmes covering unemployment, maternity, family allowances and tuberculosis.

The mergers offered the opportunity to manipulate huge amounts of resources, and added to the fascist strategy of obtaining direct political control over all public agencies. This is particularly relevant in a long-term perspective – the political colonisation of social security organisations, which thrived during postwar governments, was a continuation of the fascist practice rather than a deviation inaugurated by Italian Christian Democracy.

Postwar Social Policy

Despite the collapse of the fascist regime, the downturn of the monarchy by popular referendum and the establishment of a Republic in its place, there was no postwar 'revolution' in the Italian welfare state. Actually, during the immediate postwar period, the coalition government formed by socialists, communists and Christian Democrats, originally endorsed the idea of recasting social protection along the lines of the Beveridge Report. As a result, the new republican Constitution reflected a broad conception of social rights. However, no structural reforms were effectively introduced and the shift in 1947 from a cooperative climate to cold-war confrontation put an end to any such attempts.

The elections of 1948 opened a new phase; Christian Democracy gained the absolute majority of the vote in an outright clash against the Socialist and the Communist Party. As a result, the former acquired a pivotal position which remained unchallenged for almost 45 years. Indeed, despite changes in coalition partners the Christian Democratic Party (DC) was never out of office up until the early 1990s, when the whole Italian party system collapsed and DC itself disappeared into two splinter parties.

Throughout this period the major opposition party was the Communist Party – the largest in Western Europe, but nevertheless with no hope of gaining office. This situation resulted in both irresponsible government and irresponsible opposition. On the one hand, thriving on permanent incumbency the DC had the opportunity to expand the public sector and penetrate state administration to a degree unparalleled elsewhere. On the other hand, knowing it would not have to keep its promises, the opposition could easily make unrealistic claims and raise people's expectations. However, the demands put forward by left-wing parties – which accounted for at least one third of the electorate – could not be totally ignored. Hence, a sort of trade-off developed between government exclusion and parliamentary inclusion, a process usually referred to as 'negative integration' of the Communist Party. The latter in fact often supported legislation passed by Parliament. It is exactly on these grounds that Italy is associated to the Netherlands and described as a 'consociational' democracy – an attempt to accommodate quite diverse interests and political cultures by extensively developing distributive policies, notably in the field of social protection, while concealing the cost of these.

The Extension of Social Coverage to the Self-employed

The centre coalitions running the country from 1948 to the early 1960s focused on economic and industrial development. These years correspond to the Italian 'economic miracle' with massive migrations from the economically deprived regions in the south to the northern part of the country. From a political point of view the rhetoric and ideological confrontation typical of the early cold-war period dominated the scene with left-wing parties and workers' unions experiencing severe membership losses. In particular, the links between the Christian Democratic Party and the associations representing the self-employed, meant that social policy-making largely ignored industrial workers. Social coverage was substantially increased, but primarily benefiting the self-employed, with a range of privileges granted to small farmers, artisans and shopkeepers rather than to wage-earners.

More specifically, separate schemes were progressively set up providing health insurance as well as old-age and invalidity pensions to these groups. But social contributions were set at a much lower level compared to private sector employees, and included a costly 'first generation gift'. As a result, for instance, within just a few years relevant contributions only covered 10 per cent of the pension benefits going to small farmers and share-croppers. However, since the three pension schemes for the self-employed were consolidated into INPS, other schemes running a surplus helped to balance their deficits, thereby masking the real picture. However, in the following decades these surpluses disappeared leading to a need for state financial support. At the same time a number of occupational categories, such as journalists, top managers and professionals, were allowed to maintain their own pension funds independent from INPS, which de facto exempted them from supporting the pensions funds for the self-employed.

The financial conditions of pension schemes deteriorated even further due to the widespread misuse of disability pensions in Italy. By the mid-1970s the number of people receiving disability pensions reached 5.3 million, greatly outnumbering old-age pensions. Disability benefits were paid after just a five-year contributory requirement, and local commissions had considerable discretionary power in processing relevant applications. As a result, disability pensions became the object of clientelistic exchanges thriving especially in the agricultural sector and in the most impoverished southern areas. Apart from building on patronage ties especially rooted in southern civil society, this kind of outcome was also enhanced by the inadequate coverage offered by unemployment compensation. Indeed, some have suggested that disability pensions functioned as a substitute for unemployment benefit.

Looking more broadly at the distribution of social expenditure among the various income-maintenance programmes, at the beginning of the 1950s pension expenditure represented 45 per cent of total outlays, equal to spending for family allowances. But over the next three decades pension spending increased to the point that by 1980 it accounted for 80 per cent, while spending on family allowances decreased to about 10 per cent, and sickness, work injuries and unemployment insurance made up the remaining 10 per cent (Ferrera, 1984). According to Eurostat data, in 1995 Italy ranked first for pension expenditure among all EU member states, allocating 62 per cent of expenditure to pensions compared to a European average of 42 per cent, and leading to considerable inter-generational inequity in Italian social protection.

The 'Hot Autumn': Social Mobilisation and 'Catching up' by Blue-Collar Workers

In contrast with the 1950s, during the following decade the balance of power between capital and labour gradually shifted in favour of the latter culminating in the widespread mobilisation and social upheaval of 1968–69. Workers' trade unions regained strength within and outside the firm, and organised a rising number of strikes aiming not only at salary increases but also at improved working conditions, housing, pension benefits, health and public services in general. At the same time the Socialist Party entered the first centre-left cabinet in 1963. However, the zeal of this first centre-left coalition produced very few broad-ranging reforms and soon gave way to a prosaic bargaining approach, more in tune with the well-entrenched practice of clientelistic exchange and distributive policy-making.

The pension reforms of the late 1960s and early 1970s were conceived within this context and reflected the mounting pressure exerted by the strikes and street demonstrations of what is popularly labelled the 'hot autumn' of 1969. Workers' trade unions were interested in guaranteeing that retired workers maintain a standard of living close to that in the firm. And policymakers were willing to accommodate this so long as it did not entail selecting among alternative allocations and cutting other programmes. As a result, between 1968 and 1975 Parliament approved reforms which substantially changed the basis of the pension system, and allowed for an unprecedented improvement in the average pension level. These included:

- a shift from contributory to earnings-related pension benefits with pensions linked tightly to the salary earned by private employees during the last three years of their working lives;
- indexation of pensions to the cost of living; and
- progressive upgrading of maximum pension benefits in 1969 from 65 per cent to 74 per cent of the last three years' salary, raised in 1975 to 80 per cent.

In short, within just a few years, old-age protection for private employees became very generous compared to most European countries – with significant financial implications. Policy-makers assumed that the industrial expansion experienced during the previous two decades would substantially continue with large enough numbers of workers paying for social contributions, and so postponed the problem to future generations. Tactically this may have seemed a wise move. But, unfortunately, in the following two decades the combined effect of demographic and occupational trends brought about a quite different situation.

Ageing of the population has become a particularly acute problem in Italy, as a result of a comparatively higher life expectancy and a sharp drop in fertility rates, which nowadays places Italy in the lowest ranked position in Europe. The image of a 'demographic time bomb' – suggested by EU documents – appears particularly accurate for Italy. On the other hand, after the first oil shock in 1973 or earlier, Italian economic development entered a new phase characterised by slow growth and limited job creation. For instance, in 1970 workers contributing to the private employees fund totalled 10.85 million while pensions recipients stood at 6.2 million, but by 1990 the figures were 11.3 million and 9.5 million respectively. Under these circumstances there was no way that the pension system could maintain any sort of financial viability.

Key Features of Italian Welfare Provision

Deviating from the Occupational Model: The Introduction of Universal Health Care

The pension measures passed during the 1970s appeared to be in line with the original furrow of the Italian welfare model, even further enhancing differences in treatment among occupational categories. This sharply contrasts with what happened instead in the health sector. In 1978 a National Health Service was established emphasising universality, equality, uniformity and access. Prior to the 1978 reform, health care was offered by several sickness funds. Coverage varied widely across occupational groups, and regional dis-parities were superimposed on disparities among social groups; and the wealthier northern and central areas were better endowed with hospitals and physicians than were the poorer cities of southern Italy and the rural areas.

The system came under attack in the late 1960s and early 1970s. However, in this particular case the result was not a mere rationalisation but a radical change. Three factors account for this unusual outcome of Italian social policy-making:

- sickness funds had accumulated enormous debts with respect to hospitals, and state rescue appeared as the only possible alternative;
- the creation of the Regions in 1970 provided the institutional foundation for the devolution of health responsibilities; and
- the Communist Party considered the establishment of a universal health service as a 'pay-off' for supporting the first 'national solidarity' government.

Thus the political circumstances underpinning the passing of the health reform were exceptional within the postwar period. Most notably, the nati-onal solidarity's short-lived coalition emerged against the backdrop of the Red Brigades' kidnapping and murder of the DC national leader Aldo Moro. This helps explain why in the midst of an almost exclusively incremental and micro-sector legislation, the health reform is one of the very few wide-ranging reforms approved until the 1990s.

The passing of the health reform produced an injection of universal princi-ples into the Italian welfare state and the extension of coverage to 3.5 million citizens. There was also a new organisational design with a three-tier system involving the central government, the Regions and the Local Health Units (USL). Although the British NHS represented the alleged model, the Italian Reform Law attempted to combine central budgeting and planning with local control – a unique and contradictory mix. And, from the outset, this resulted in widespread central/local conflict. The national government was responsi-ble for raising the money and distributing it to the Regions. Pay-roll taxes from employers, employees and the self-employed made up the bulk of fund-ing with general revenues contributing for about 35 per cent of the total. The Regions in turn were supposed to allocate resources to Local Health Units. However, the system allowed for decentralised decision – making with respect to the level and delivery of services, in line with left-wing parties' ideals of democratic participation and accountability. As a corollary, lay management committees reflecting the power balance among local parties were responsible for running Local Health Units.

Considering how easy it was to shift the blame, the separation of funding and spending responsibilities did not enhance cooperative intergovernmental relations. After 1978 the central government deliberately underfunded health care, and set tight budgetary ceilings at the beginning of each fiscal year.

Failure by the Regions to respect these ceilings would regularly result in extensive financial borrowing on the part of Regional governments and in Local Health Units running chronic deficits. The central government generally ended up by footing the bill but the overall uncertainty on funding levels tended to create a siege mentality oriented towards crisis management with little time for questions of economy and efficiency or medium-term planning.

Thus over the 1980s opinion polls showed Italians expressing increasing discontent with respect to NHS performance and lamenting the poor quality of services provided along with the red tape which entangled the whole system – causing all sorts of inequities and inefficiencies. Local management committees came under the strongest criticism; however, responsibilities were so intermingled that in fact management committees had no discretionary power over a very large share of the local budget. For instance, the national government set the wages for hospital doctors, and all NHS personnel; it signed the relevant agreements with general practitioners for primary care, and decided what medications were free of charge. On top of this, regional governments were responsible for deciding investment plans within their jurisdiction and for assigning personnel to the local units establishing well-defined ceilings for each category.

Finally, the legislation endorsed a perverse public–private mix. Public hospital doctors were allowed to operate freely in both the public and the private sector, and since their pay-check was totally unrelated to performance and much lower than what they earned if they practised privately, this arrangement provided a formidable indirect incentive for maintaining public inefficiency. Be it for diagnostic tests, specialist or hospital care, doctors could use their public position as a spring-board to increase the stock of private clients. Keeping performance standards low in the public sphere would in fact divert increasing numbers of patients to private facilities that the doctors themselves often owned or where they might work on a part-time basis.

Notwithstanding this long list of problems, legislation on the NHS focused only on cost-containment instead of providing guidelines to improve service standards. Priority was given to introducing co-payments for medications, diagnostic tests and specialist care. However, public health spending in the 1980s was not spiralling out of control, but was growing at roughly the same rate as GDP – although Italians got far less for their money than did the citizens of other European countries. However, given the political context of the 1980s and the powerful interests behind the health system (and for that matter also the pension system), any attempt to introduce substantial changes was politically impossible.

Unemployment: A Mismatch between Needs and Policy Responses

Unemployment policies have always played a marginal role within the Italian system of social protection, and this continued into the 1980s when the jobless total started to soar to double-digit figures. Throughout that decade expenditure for passive labour policies never exceeded 1 per cent of GDP, constantly placing Italy at the bottom of European rankings. Such an outcome is less surprising, however, if we consider the labour-market regime within which the Italian system of shock absorbers is embedded, for it is based on a high level of labour-market regulation. In a nutshell, labour legislation since the 1960s strengthened workers' rights and entitlements at employers' expense. The strategy pursued by the trade unions and formally sanctioned in the Workers Code of 1970 aimed at reinforcing workers representation in the workplace and strictly limiting employers' freedom to hire and fire. From a different perspective this also meant erecting high barriers around those who already had regular permanent jobs, to the disadvantage of growing numbers of outsiders, consolidating a dual labour market, with highly negative implications from economic, social, political and fiscal points of view. Not surprisingly such a dual market reflects the north/south cleavage: according to current estimates, non-regular work represents some 34 per cent of total employment in the south as against 18 per cent in the north.

Turning to specific protections for the unemployed, only minor adjustments were introduced to unemployment benefit throughout the postwar period. The benefit was and remains payable for a maximum of 180 days and consisted (until 1988) of a ridiculously low daily flat rate. From 1988 to 1994 the level of the benefit was upgraded and set first at 28 per cent and then at 30 per cent of the previous wage. These conditions are largely responsible for spurring on the clientelistic misuse of invalidity pensions mentioned above, a situation which only changed in the mid-1980s when legislative restrictions were eventually introduced in order to curb the disproportionate growth of these benefits.

In sharp contrast, temporary unemployment attracted a good deal of attention. INPS was entrusted with the management of the programme and a specific fund therein was set up for this purpose. During the 1970s and 1980s the profile of the fund increased to the point that, in the eyes of the public, the *Cassa Integrazione Guadagni* (Wage Compensation Fund) almost became synonymous for unemployment policies altogether. Short-term compensation was first introduced in 1968 and soon absorbed most of unemployment expenditure in Italy – a situation unmatched in other western countries. The trade unions successfully pressed for the extension of the original programme in order to avoid massive layoffs during the economic downturn and industrial readjustments triggered by the first oil shock. The measure was extremely generous, offering a replacement rate of 80 per cent of previous earnings and protecting redundant workers from job-loss. Eligibility was subject to negotiation between trade unions and employers and, up until 1988, the programme was entirely financed by the state.

The programme was very palatable to both unions and employers because it allowed for a freezing of firings whilst allowing firms to externalise the financial and the social costs of industrial restructuring. Highly-unionised large firms were also in a better position to take advantage of the discretionary procedures involved in the operation of special short-term unemployment compensation. The result was such that this type of benefit entirely lost its temporary nature. Irrespective of whether or not the restructuring process would eventually create new working opportunities within the firm, coverage renewals, especially in large industrial plants, were granted for up to as many as ten years. Early retirement measures further reinforced the allocative distortion typical of Italian shock absorbers. Along with France, Italy is the country that has most extensively used this measure. During the 1980s, early retirement schemes involved on average 32,000 workers a year, again largely confined to core sectors of the labour force.

Despite the high level of protection guaranteed by these measures, Italian unemployment protection offers no public assistance for workers whose ordinary unemployment benefits have expired or who do not even qualify for such 'second-class' measures. Indeed, the lack of any social protection coverage for a young unemployed person in search of first employment has been identified by Ferrera (1996) as an indicator of a distinct southern model of welfare, where the absence of a basic safety net and the unevenness of coverage among workers distinguish Mediterranean countries from the rest of Western Europe.

The coverage offered by the various programmes operating in Southern Europe remained low throughout the 1980s and continues to be the lowest in the European Union. According to Eurostat data, in 1993 only around a third of unemployed men 25 years of age and over received a benefit in Greece, Italy and Portugal in contrast to virtually all men in Belgium, Denmark, Germany, Ireland and the UK. Not surprisingly, in the same three countries the proportion drops even more for men under age 25, falling below 20 per cent. The absence of a universal public assistance scheme in Italy also means that the vast majority of the unemployed have to resort to the discretionary benefits granted by municipalities. However, whereas regional governments in central and northern Italy have passed legislation promoting the establishment of minimum income programmes by local authorities, quite the opposite holds true for the south (Fargion, 1996, 1997). Unfortunately, this is exactly where the bulk of unemployment is concentrated and where two-thirds of Italian people living below the poverty line are located.

The 1990s: The Italian Welfare State in Transition

The 1990s mark a definite turning point in the development of postwar Italy, which in domestic debates is often referred to as the transition from the First to the Second Republics. The collapse of the old party system reflected a deep change in the style and content of policy-making. The change was most clearly visible in macroeconomic and financial policies, but could also be seen in social policy reforms where there were open attempts to redress the major distortions of the Italian welfare model. While most European countries were already striving with fiscal restraint and austerity over the 1980s, in the case of Italy it is during this period that public expenditure spiralled out of control. Over the ten-year period from 1980 to 1990, total public expenditure rose from 42 to 53 per cent of GNP, and, although fiscal pressures increased this was by no means sufficient to cover rising outflows. Thus the gap between public expenditure and revenue rose to double the European average. In short, distributive games and easy spending dominated the political scene throughout the decade with public debt skyrocketing from 54 to 104 per cent of GNP and the annual budget deficit reaching a 1989 high of 11 per cent.

In the 1990s, policy was reversed with Italy's public finances turning at last from a vicious into a virtuous circle. Over the period the budgetary gap between revenues and expenditure narrowed to the point that Italy managed to meet the Maastricht criteria for entering the European Monetary Union – largely unexpected until a year earlier. In 1997 the country reached the required threshold of a 3 per cent annual deficit, and in the next two years consolidated the downward trend even further; in addition, inflation was curbed and debt service substantially reduced. These 'radical' achievements, together with the passing of a number of long-needed social policy reforms, were the product of significant changes in the political system.

Exogenous variables played a crucial role here. In particular, the fall of the Berlin wall made it impossible for the Christian Democratic Party to uphold its popular image as a bulwark against communism; and what remained instead was a 40-year record of corrupt and inefficient state administration combined with an astonishing lack of problem-solving capacity. The 'clean hands' investigations launched by the judiciary in the early 1990s undermined the legitimacy of the old leadership and many Parliamentary members from government parties were charged with corruption and fraudulent behaviour. Thus the core parties of the First Republic which made up the *Pentapartito* coalition (the Christian Democrats, the Socialists, the Social-Democrats, the Republicans and the Liberals) almost vanished after the 1994 election. While the old parties were crumbling, two new political actors emerged: the *Lega Nord* which vociferously campaigned against state centralisation advocating a federal system, and '*Forza Italia*', the conservative political movement led by Berlusconi, which won the elections in 1994.

In the midst of such political turmoil the executive substantially strengthened its position with respect to Parliament, and consequently acquired increasing autonomy in policy-making. The technocratic cabinets of Amato, Ciampi and Dini thus looked for the support of organised interests in order to counterbalance their political isolation and sought to pursue their policy objectives through extensive negotiations with workers' trade unions and employers. This resulted in a resurgence of neo-corporatist arrangements, for instance, the 1995 pension reform which represented a major turning point in the structure of the Italian welfare state.

Pension Reform

Over the 1980s, pension expenditure had spiralled totally out of control, although the benefits of these increases were not evenly distributed. Spending levels for the private employees' fund went up by 20 per cent, whereas pension expenditure in the public sector increased by 84 per cent. The pension system therefore increasingly came under attack as being highly inequitable and for granting an intricate maze of privileges, primarily within the public sector – most blatantly 'Baby Pensions', under which civil servants of any age with only 20 years service were entitled to 'seniority' benefits, which for some female employees could be reduced to 12 years.

There was much parliamentary debate about pension reform but no legislation was passed until 1992 when the problem was finally approached by a measure raising the retirement age from 60 to 65 for men and from 55 to 60 for women. Three years later the Dini government was able to pass a comprehensive reform of the pension system on the basis of extensive consultation with workers' trade unions and employers. This replaced the old earnings-related formula with a new contribution-related formula to be phased in by 2013, with calculation of the benefit linked to life expectancy at retirement age. The standardisation of rules for all public and private employees would lead to greater inter- and intra-generational equity, insuring that yield rates would be the same regardless of occupational category. However, the rules for workers already in the system created an artificial barrier between younger and older workers, completely exempting individuals with more than 18 years of work experience. This was a product of the negotiation with the trade unions within which retired workers were gaining increasing political weight. From the mid-1980s to the mid-1990s the three major unions acquired over 2.4 million retired members whilst losing 685,000 active workers.

Altogether, the 1992 and 1995 reforms aimed to limit public pension spending from increasing beyond 16 per cent of GDP by 2030, a reduction of 7 per cent from the estimates projected under the old rules. Current expenditure on public pensions still dominates Italian welfare spending at the rate of 14 per cent of GDP (see Table 10.1).

Unemployment Policies

In the 1990s, unemployment policies were also set on a new track. In 1991 legislation to deal with the misuse of short-term earnings compensation was introduced, and at the same time workers were formally required to attend training programmes or to engage in 'socially useful' jobs, introducing elements of conditionality and obligation in return for the benefit, comparable to the 'workfare' ideologies of Anglo-Saxon and other European countries. In the second half of the decade, reform and reorganisation accelerated further, in particular under the Prodi government of June 1996, and the active

Table 10.1 Expenditures for social protection (billions of lira), Italy, 1998

Category	Expenditure
Health	103.235
Social Insurance	329.258
Pensions	293.524
Severance pay	11.559
Sickness; occupational injuries; maternity	5.607
Regular unemployment benefits	6.812
Short-term unemployment compensation	1.547
Family allowances	7.957
Other	2.252
Public Assistance	29.651
Non-contributory pensions	3.576
Veterans benefits	2.448
Disability benefits	14.244
Blindness benefits	1.466
Assistance for deaf/mute	241
Other assistance	1.888
Social assistance	5.788
Total Social Protection	462.144

Source: *Relazione sulla situazione economica del paese*, 1999.

stance taken by Labour and Social Security Minister, Tiziano Treu, a leading Italian scholar in labour law and industrial relations. The 'Treu package', as it was labelled, was a comprehensive law on a wide range of issues including:

- new types of work (fixed-term contracts, temporary work, part-time),
- working time and over-time work, and
- vocational training.

The government was also entrusted with responsibility for drafting a special employment plan for the *Mezzogiorno* and devising a set of incentives promoting the transition of firms from the irregular to the formal sector of the economy.

There was also decentralisation, however, following a new phase in the development of active labour policies, which ended the confusion and overlap between the regional and the central levels of government. Under this, regions emerged as the pivotal points of the newly-designed system, with responsibility for job placement transferred from the national Ministry of Labour.

Finally the Prodi government set up a 'Special Commission on the Reform of the Italian Welfare State', known as the Onofri Commission after its President. This provided a sharp analysis of the sins and ills of Italian unemployment policies and proposed a three-tier system of social shock-absorbers, including:

- short-term compensation with extended coverage and standardised eligibility criteria,

- ordinary unemployment benefit upgraded to 60 per cent of previous earnings, and
- a public assistance safety net to comply with EU recommendations.

Although the proposals were not implemented, they set the pace for all subsequent policy developments. For example an experimental minimum income programme was established in 39 Italian municipalities, and is expected to be extended nationwide by 2001. Parliament also mandated that the Onofri Commission's guidelines be put into place by the executive government by April 2000.

Personal Social Services

The personal social services are another policy area that has recently attracted increasing political attention. Here too the north–south divide is important in consideration of the extent to which care needs are met in the country. The Constitution entrusted the Regions with legislative power in the field of public assistance and social services, but the required national guidelines were never introduced – leading to significant regional differentiation after 1970. The system inherited by the Regions was essentially geared to the poor and dominated by institutional care, with religious bodies and charities acting as the main providers of institutional care for the elderly as well as for children and the disabled. After 1970, the southern regions largely continued along this path, but the northern and central regions moved to expansion of a wide range of community services. This was particularly true of the regions run by leftist majorities, which aimed at establishing comprehensive networks of public social care services directly managed by local authorities.

However, the regions could only provide extremely limited funding for the new services, and this left the financial burden with local authorities, who were in no better positions to meet new legislative requirements. Municipalities almost exclusively relied on state transfers, and, from the 1980s in particular, were limited by central government actions to curtail funding and impose a hiring freeze on personnel. Municipalities, especially in urban areas, were increasingly 'squeezed' between mounting social care demands (legitimated by regional legislation) and growing inability to provide services. Under these circumstances, local authorities increasingly turned to non-statutory suppliers, including the stimulation of new types of not-for- profit organisations – particularly cooperatives, which could provide a wide range of services including home help while also addressing the increasingly dramatic issue of youth unemployment. The outcome of this was an intricate web of public–private arrangements even in leftist regions which had originally attempted to create an Italian version of the Scandinavian model. Over the 1980s, even Communist-led regions gradually endorsed a pluralist welfare model shifting from a publicly-centred approach to the mixed economy of welfare.

Ranci has suggested that this relationship can best be described as 'mutual adjustment' rather than privatisation. Local political élites developed clientelistic ties and partisan links with the third sector, thus reinforcing sheltered markets rather than prompting open competition. However, the 1990s led to a change here too. Starting in 1991, Parliament began to issue comprehensive regulations on voluntary associations and cooperatives, and on the sensitive issue of tax concessions to not-for-profit organisations. And, although southern Italy continued to lag behind, the new provisions stimulated local authorities to redefine their relations with the third sector, including service specifications, staff skills, monitoring and performance requirements, tendering procedures and, more generally, a degree of openness and competition among suppliers. However, the Italian third sector remains almost entirely reliant on public funding by local authorities, and the room for manoeuvre by sub-national authorities experiencing a sharp drop in state transfers is severely limited here.

Housing

Housing policies have never represented a major social policy priority in Italy. At the end of the 1980s the public stock of rented housing was among the least developed within Europe, whilst the level of home ownership considerably exceeded the OECD average. This situation is largely similar to the one prevailing in the other Southern welfare states, as Ferrera and Castles (1996, pp. 172–3) suggest,

> saving rates have always been quite high in the countries of this area, with the extended family acting as the natural unit for the pooling of both resources and needs ... the propensity to invest in housing has continued to be very strong ... The use of personal capital for the acquisition of housing property has been further encouraged by the scarcity of alternative investment opportunities, given the underdevelopment of the stock market and the inefficiency of the banking sector.

Government policies, while reinforcing this popular inclination did not adequately address the needs of those citizens who could not afford to purchase a house. State intervention consisted primarily in the establishment of rigid systems of rent control, which ended up by creating major market distortions to the disadvantage of the young and the worse off. For instance, the introduction in 1978 of a 'just rent' scheme produced perverse unintended consequences: a shrinkage of the housing stock available and an unofficial market of virtually unaffordable rents. In metropolitan areas especially, therefore, there are acute housing problems with long and almost blocked waiting lists for the very limited stock of public dwellings.

In the mid-1990s, the Prodi government opened up new avenues to redress intergenerational inequities stemming from the current distribution of housing resources and improve available accommodation opportunities especially for the younger generations. A variety of financial benefits have been introduced to support rented accommodation, and also to facilitate house purchase by young couples and the restoration of old buildings. Further, in line with the devolution of powers taking place in many other policy fields, the regional agencies currently responsible for public housing were dismantled and their property handed down to municipalities. In contrast with the fragmentation of the past, local authorities are in the future supposed to be fully in charge of public housing policies, and to coordinate their activities through joint agreements.

Education

In Italy in the 1990s, practically all aspects of social policy were subject to reform and revision. This is especially the case in pensions – and in education. Until the period 1997–99, the school system was completely locked into immobility, operating on the basis of the 1923 legislation of the fascist minister, Gentile – apart from the extension of compulsory education to 14 years of age and the reorganisation of junior high schools (*scuola media*) in 1962. The performance of the system was also extremely poor in most respects. Educational attainment in Italy was among the lowest in the Western world, and the country only provided for eight years of compulsory schooling, up to the age of 14 – extended in 1999 to 15. And, although enrolment in the *scuola secondaria superiore* (which covers the age group 14–18) has been increasing enormously – from a rate around 20 per cent in the early 1960s to 50 per cent in the mid-1970s, 60 per cent a decade later and 78 per cent at the end of the 1990s – only 50 per cent of these completed, with many leaving school after the first year of post-compulsory education.

How can we explain such a poor record? Part may be due to the quality of teaching, which has attracted much criticism. Teachers' salaries in Italy are the lowest in Western Europe, with few financial incentives or opportunities for career development. However, the number of teachers has been rising and the teacher to pupil ratio is currently the lowest in Europe; and it would be unfair to put all the blame on teachers. The school system has suffered from over-centralisation, with national regulation of practically all crucial matters. Central administration decides on the allocation of resources to individual schools and defines in detail the curricula for all levels, with local authorities responsible for school buildings and for providing maintenance services, school transport and meals.

In 1997, legislation was passed aimed at substantially increasing both teaching and organisational autonomy at the school level. After September 1999 schools were experimenting in budgetary control over activities, and enjoyed some scope for teaching innovation and management flexibility – with more comprehensive reform planned for the following year. The aim of these reforms is to bring the Italian education system into line with European standards, although debate continues on a number of issues, including state funding of private schools, where a stalemate exists between left and right strands within the Parliament.

Health

The dramatic financial crisis of September 1992 opened up the political opportunity for the Amato government to push through what has been called 'the reform of the reform'. A decree passed in December 1992 was followed by further change initiated by Prime Minister Ciampi. The aims were to introduce managerial criteria in the health sector, and to alter the centre–local balance of powers – progressively increasing regional responsibilities, particularly on the revenue side.

The original 659 Local Health Units were transformed into 199 Local Health Enterprises (ASL) with more operating autonomy, commercial accounting procedures and performance auditing; and a General Manager appointed by the region on the basis of a private contract replaced the old Management Committees. Following British experiences elements of managed competition were also introduced into the system, although they resulted in quite different outcomes. In particular, hospitals were allowed to set up independent bodies which could sell their services to the Local Health Enterprises on a tariff basis. However, it was left to the Regions to decide how far they wanted to pursue the separation between purchasers (the ASL) and providers (the Hospital Enterprises). As a result, while Lombardy enhanced the formation of autonomous Hospital Enterprises, most of the other Regions opted for an integrated model which kept the majority of hospitals under the jurisdiction of Local Health Enterprises (Maino, 1999).

In short, the reforms of the early 1990s paved the way for the creation of distinct if not divergent regional health-care models. This trend was further reinforced by the third reform wave, under then Health Minister Bindi, to bolster regional financial autonomy, which culminated in the 1999 law on 'fiscal federalism'. This replaced compulsory heath contributions and abolished earmarked state funding for the health sector, with regions participating in revenue-sharing balanced by an equalisation fund to address fiscal disparities between them. The perverse mix between the doctors' private and public interests was also addressed by a requirement that medical personnel either work full-time for the health service or opt out of the public system.

Future Prospects

The previous sections show the extent to which Italian social policies have departed from their original path over the last decade. The 1990s witnessed considerable legislative innovation aimed at eliminating the distortions and inequities embedded in the Italian welfare model; and major social policy reforms were the result of extensive negotiations between the executive and workers' trade unions. The literature documents how the 'resurgence of neo-corporatist arrangements' triggered a virtuous circle, especially with respect to macroeconomic planning and social policy (Ferrera and Gualmini, 1999; Regini and Regalia, 1997).

However, recent events suggest tripartite agreements might have exhausted their potential for innovation. It only takes a quick look at the distribution of social expenditure in Table 10.1 to see that much remains to be done to shift resources from the old to the new priorities and to adequately address emerging needs, with pensions still currently dominating expenditure commitments. The scope for further action is still considerable, particularly with respect to the dramatic rates of unemployment and child poverty in southern Italy. Furthermore, although over the second half of the 1990s concertation was progressively institutionalised through the 1996 Social Pact and the 1998 'Christmas Pact', policy-making in the social field then came to a slowdown – if not a deadlock. The trade unions repeatedly refused confrontation with the government on the pension system prior to the deadline envisaged by the Dini reform. In 1999 the executive was mandated by Parliament to provide within six months a comprehensive reform of social shock absorbers but only passed two measures delaying reforms to December 2000, and then to December 2001. And the health reforms envisaged in 1999 have been postponed by the new Health Minister.

Over the 1990s, Italian policy-makers did carry through most of the 'puzzling' needed to recast provision along more equitable lines. Yet, if the new principles and goals are to produce the intended results, the reform process needs to be consolidated further – a prospect which cannot now be taken for granted. On the one hand, the trade unions can hardly be expected to play a proactive role in redressing current social spending imbalances, especially given the increasing proportion of retired workers within their members; and, on the other, future developments of current neo-corporate arrangements along with other political priorities, the scope for redistribution and the ideological underpinnings of social policies are bound to vary considerably as electoral fortunes fluctuate.

References

Ascoli, U. (ed.) (1984) *Welfare State all' Italiana*, Latesza.

Castellino, O. (1976) *Il Labirinto delle pensioni*, Il Mulino.

Castles, F. and Ferrera M. (1996) 'Home Ownership and the Welfare State: Is Southern Europe Different?', *South European Society and Politics*, 1(2), pp. 163–85.

Esping-Andersen G. (1999) *Social Foundations of Post-Industrial Economies*, Oxford University Press.

Fargion, V. (1996) 'Social Assistance and the North–South Cleavage in Italy', *South European Society and Politics*, 1(3), pp. 135–54.

Fargion, V. (1997) *Geografia della cittadinanza sociale in Italia*, Il Mulino.

Ferrera, M. (1984) *Il welfare state in Italia. Sviluppo e crisi in prospettiva comparata*, Il Mulino.

Ferrera, M. (1996) 'The "Southern Model" of Welfare in Social Europe', *Journal of European Social Policy*, 6(1), pp. 17–37.

Ferrera, M. and Gualmini E. (1999) *Salvati dall' Europa? Welfare e lavoro in Italia*, Il Mulino.

Gualmini, E. (1998) *La politica del lavoro*, Il Mulino.

Guillén, A. (1999) 'Improving Efficiency and Containing Costs: Health Care Reform in Southern Europe', European University Institute, Florence, Conference Paper WS/31.

Maino, F. (1999) 'La regionalizzazione della sanita italiana negli anni novanti', *Il Polititco*, 64(4), pp. 583–21.

Maioni, A. and Maino F. (1999) 'Fiscal Federalism and Health Care Reform in Canada and Italy', European University Institute, Florence, Conference Paper WS/93.

Ranci, C. (1999) *Oltre il Welfare State. Terzo settore, nuove solidarietà e trasformazioni del welfare*, Il Mulino.

Regini, M. and Regalia, I. (1997) 'Employers, Unions and the State: The Resurgence of Concertation in Italy?', *West European Politics*, 20(1), pp. 210–30.

Saraceno, C. (1998) *Mutamenti della famiglia e politiche sociali in Italia*, Il Mulino.

Trifiletti, R. (1999) 'Southern European Welfare Regimes and the Worsening Position of Women', *Journal of European Social Policy*, 9(4), pp. 63–78.

Ventura, S. (1998) *La Politica scolastica*, Il Mulino.

CHAPTER 11

Russia: Revolution or Evolution?

NICK MANNING AND NADIA DAVIDOVA

Social Issues and Social Policy since 1917

The Soviet Union was a large, diverse empire founded in 1917, which not only created a distinct pattern of social policy amongst the 15 republics within it, but imposed this pattern on other Central European countries. Within this vast area there was great cultural, linguistic, industrial and natural variation. Even within the USSR, Russians comprised little more than 50 per cent of the population. The USSR disappeared in 1991, the 'Eastern bloc' separating into 27 separate states. Over this period the development of social policy broadly followed six periods: utopian, urban, industrial, welfare, productivity and transition (George and Manning, 1980). This chapter briefly summarises developments in each of these periods and then focuses in more depth on key issues underpinning social policy since 1991. This is followed by a short summary of provision in the major policy areas and some discussion of the future prospects for policy development in Russia.

Utopian: 1917–21

In the first period, social issues were seen to be the result of social disorganisation brought about by war and capitalism. Although this was a time of wide debate about the future of social policy, the main priorities were clear: about 50 per cent of the population was illiterate, and epidemics such as typhus were rife and growing. Mass campaigns were mobilised to deal with these threats, but other changes were slow. Income support and medical care were only extended to wage-earners, excluding most rural dwellers; and there was forced redistribution of housing in urban areas from rich to poor.

With the 1918 civil war, however, nationalisation was imposed on a wide scale. Income support and education were extended in principle to the whole population, and family policy was liberalised to remove all legal constraint over marital, parental and sexual relationships. Celebrated by the left as revolutionary gains, these utopian promises could not in fact be implemented.

Urban: 1921–27

Greater debate now developed about the nature and existence of social issues, and the kind of solutions to be adopted. But there was a clear shift from an assumption of value consensus, to a struggle over value conflict; from a struggle with objective conditions (civil war) to a struggle to label problem groups (farmers). This change paved the way for Stalin's 'Urals-Siberian method' for procuring grain. Problem groups justified the use of violence, since a more familiar method, education, was unlikely to produce desired changes quickly enough. Conflicts about this policy in the party illustrate graphically both the decay of consensus and the process – the isolation of opponents – adopted for reestablishing it.

The main government programme was the New Economic Policy. Industrial and agricultural production increased, housing construction recovered, and social policy returned to a more realistic programme. Parental and family responsibilities were reimposed, health care was targeted on key industrial workers and children before agricultural workers, and progressive educational ideas returned to the control of the relatively conservative teaching profession.

Industrial: 1927–53

During the years of Stalin's power, the main concern was with industrialisation, both as a means of defending 'socialism in one country', and to rebuild the country after the widespread destruction caused by the Second World War. The supply and discipline of labour was a perennial concern, and anything that obstructed this objective was liable to be seen as deviant. Rules defining rights at work, social security entitlements, security of tenure and sickness absence were all progressively tightened during the 1930s; their infraction came to be seen as an individual failing. Wage inequality, selection in education, and a tougher family code, especially restrictions on the right to abortion, were all pursued, but the most significant social policy was the abolition of unemployment benefit in 1930, followed in 1937 with the right to employment – illustrating the mix of conservative and progressive elements within Stalin's Russia.

Welfare: 1953–64

After his death Stalin's policies were openly debated and criticised by the new leadership. There was also more intensive debate about the future direction of economic and social policy – stimulating new debate in the West about the real nature of soviet society. However, the shift in the 1920s from social issues as objective conditions to the identification of problem groups was repeated. The new middle classes, made up by industrial managers, senior intellectuals and party careerists were targeted. This can be seen in Khrushchev's education reforms, prioritising workers at the expense of more privileged groups precisely in the most important site for the reproduction of inequalities. Agricultural workers, excluded since 1921 from the social security system, were brought into the scheme in 1964.

Productivity: 1964–83

The years after Krushchev's demise presented a marked contrast in the way social issues were perceived. Stability rather than change was paramount with a return to consensus about the problems facing soviet society. 'Developed socialism' was to be built slowly and methodically with no 'great leaps forward'. Social issues therefore became departures from a common norm of steady progress; and, rather than a struggle to identify and label problem groups, perceptions shifted, as in the 1930s and 1940s, to rooting out deviant individuals. Whilst this never matched Stalinist paranoia, the pursuit of dissidents through psychiatry – reflecting a belief in dissent as a form of madness – indicated the absence of legitimate debate. In a sense there were no 1970s 'social problems'. Although social conditions changed (divorce rose, the population aged, the economy slowed and life expectancy faltered), increasingly unreal assurances were given of 'business as usual'.

Basic indicators such as numbers of teachers, doctors and nurses, supplies of clothing, flats, food and televisions, and employment for all, reflected growing levels of essential service delivery. Their quality was low, but for millions of Russian workers – and for the 50 per cent non-Russian population, especially in central Asia – this was a period of security and rising living standards. Inequalities in inter-republic provision of such basics as income, housing and health care steadily declined. Many Russians outside the major cities now look back fondly on the 1970s and 1980s.

Transition: 1983–91

The origins of the desire in the Soviet Union for far-reaching changes lay in three problems.

- First, and paramount, was the slowdown in economic growth during the 1970s. This was a product in part of the peculiar incentives for waste and poor quality (Kornai, 1980), and the 'partial ignorance' (Ellman, 1989) that comes with highly-centralised planning but poor data processing in a complex economy.
- Second was the erosion of the popular legitimacy of the state, revealed in the activities of dissidents of various persuasions, and compounded by the growth of government corruption.

- Third was the fear of decay in family and community life, characterised by rising infant and adult mortality, and growth in such classic social problems as divorce, crime, drug misuse, and particularly alcoholism.

The outcomes of this were the *perestroika* (restructuring) and *glasnost* (openness) of the Gorbachev era. They originated in the notorious 'Novosibirsk Manifesto', presented by Academician Tatyana Zaslavskaya (President of the Soviet Sociological Association) to a closed official seminar in 1983, which argued that the main obstacle to improved economic performance was the economic system itself. Zaslavskaya and others were arguing for decentralisation and quasi-markets; but the real innovation in the report was in its social analysis which argued that economic and educational levels had reached the point at which the social characteristics of workers had outstripped those required by strategic and technical mechanisms unchanged since the 1930s command economy. There were widespread frustrated aspirations which undermined motivation at work. Moreover, she contended that sharply-felt contradictory social interests had developed between different groups. Without an adequate understanding of these interests, and their support or opposition to change, she argued, little could be done to solve pressing social and economic problems.

Within two years, long-dormant social and political forces began to appear, and independent political clubs, demonstrations, new social movements and popular fronts were formed. After the collapse of the 1991 coup and Gorbachev's resignation from the Communist Party, a new phase of authoritarian populism began, marked by the search for a positive alternative to communist ideology, political and economic structures. The new leader, Yeltsin, also decreed an immediate widespread price liberalisation from 1992.

These momentous changes inevitably had social policy consequences. The 1991 Employment Law ended the right/duty to work by imposing a 1 per cent payroll levy to generate funds to finance unemployment benefit, retraining, public community work and career guidance. Homelessness and begging increased, whilst older problems of housing access, quality and infrastructure remained. Health problems, already in decline, began to escalate with further declines in life-expectancy and increases in infant mortality developing from the late 1970s (Mezentseva and Rimachevskaya, 1990), occasioning the suspension of publication of mortality statistics from 1972 to 1986. Alcohol abuse became a major public policy concern.

Social Change and Social Policy

Russian social policy has thus been in turmoil in the 1990s. However, there is still considerable continuity from the state socialist era. What, therefore, was the soviet era about? There have been two dominant – though changing – views, drawing largely on either cold war, or Marxist sympathies:

- First, the totalitarian model in which soviet society was assumed to be a dictatorship, in which a single party ruled through a non-democratic monopoly of force and centrally-planned industrialisation. This monolithic structure arose from the personal drive of strong personalities, particularly Lenin and Stalin, and the military requirements of defending a revolutionary government.
- Second, the Marxist model based on a social material analysis, traditionally centred on economic development as integral to explanations of political change

By the 1980s, however, these models were seen as less informative of the real developments in soviet economic and social development and were strongly criticised. Political scientists replaced them with middle-range theories focused on various social actors and institutions such as interest groups, corporatism, industrialism and a functionalist use of systems theory, all of which tried to identify alternative explanations for the basic patterns of soviet social change, and to analyse ways in which political actions appeared to be independent of economic constraints. Neither of these approaches had much to say about social policy issues, however. The question therefore remains of how the USSR, now Russia, can be characterised in its social-policy approach. In Esping-Andersen's (1990) terminology, there has been little analysis of the Russian welfare regimes as these have emerged. Rather, debate has focused upon stability and change and the ways in which social issues have been differently conceived and responded to in policy-planning.

Social issues have been theorised in a number of ways with a basic split between an analysis emphasising social conditions as objectively detrimental to human well-being, and a focus on the public perception of, and political reaction to, social threats, whatever their underlying cause. While the latter view is in the ascendant, for example in the analysis of 'moral panics' about public disorder and the changing fortunes of the ideological battle over welfare, it is clear that many social scientists still argue that social conditions have objective effects.

Where objective social conditions are acknowledged to exist which offend against a widely-shared value consensus, individual victims of those conditions are often blamed for their situation. This typically leads to research and policies based on the presumption that the individual victim must be changed in some respect. However, where the existence of social conditions is the subject of wide disagreement, or where their significance is in dispute, a more openly political debate is common. Key actors enter this debate vigorously, often with the aim of securing their preferred interpretation of the causes and solutions to the problem. This analysis provides a useful alternative to older cold war and Marxist models in the analysis of soviet social policy development.

Table 11.1   A cycle of consensus and conflict over social issues

	Value consensus	Victims blamed	Groups blamed
1920s	No (New Economic Policy)	No	Yes (farmers)
1930/40s	Yes (Stalinism)	Yes (party members)	No
1950s	No (Khrushchev's 'debates')	No	Yes (industrialists)
1960/70s	Yes (Brezhnev – 'developed socialism')	Yes (dissidents)	No
1980s	No (perestroika)	No	Yes (system structure)
1990s	Yes (market capitalism)	Yes (inflexible workers; corrupt élites)	No

A particular difficulty with these was their inability to analyse or even acknowledge change, whereas a close examination of social policy reveals regular oscillations in the Russian analysis of social and policy issues between value consensus and value conflict, as shown in Table 11.1.

The Post-Transition Welfare State, 1991–99

The Soviet welfare state had been characterised by a universal guarantee of employment, low controlled prices, and state social and pension provision, although the role of employers in ensuring the welfare of Soviet citizens was also significant. When the state socialist system, with its centralised distribution of social guarantees through social consumption funds, collapsed, Russia faced the serious matter of choosing a new social paradigm. Russian economic reforms initially proceeded from the liberal model of efficiency, which sees the social sphere acting as an impediment to development. At the same time it was proposed that existing social policy resources should provide funding for radical reforms. Zaslavskaya's view is that Russia's economic reforms simply did not incorporate a well-thought-out social policy.

Policy options were stark. In the short run, a total absence of social support might enable the quickest restructuring of the economy, but it could only be possible with either Draconian suppression of social unrest (hardly now possible), or where the economy was ready for 'take off' (as for example in the Czech Republic). The alternative was to take a slower path to economic change and target help as sharply as possible in the short term, with the longer-term goal of a Western mix of social insurance and private provision.

Russia appears to have opted for the latter, although benefits are still closely tied to enterprises and poorly-targeted. However, repeated declarations of social policy reforms, for example in 1993 prior to the new constitution and in 1997 arising out of the 1996 presidential election campaign, are not being effectively implemented, particularly seen from regional perspectives. In legal and administrative terms, the most significant development has been the new constitution adopted at the end of 1993. Social policy issues are covered in a variety of proposals, but there are omissions. And the constitution is heavily weighted towards presidential powers; while ministers take responsibility for managing various parts of domestic policy programmes (for example in ministries for labour, social protection, or health), Presidential decrees continue to lead policy initiatives.

In 1993, Yeltsin published a review of policy goals which hinted at intended social policy plans, including minimum social guarantees, income maintenance and minimum wages and pensions (*Current Digest of Post-Soviet Press*, 1993, 45, 44, p. 4). This proclamation of a policy direction towards a 'social state', was followed in 1995–96 by a raft of basic social legislation on the eve of campaigns for the State Parliament and Russian Presidential elections. In many ways this took on the populist stamp of the day, adopted out of immediate political interest, and frequently in violation of the legislative process.

More particularly none of these proclaimed social goals were possible without the necessary finance. The initial solution, to print money or to allow extended credit to central and local government and to enterprises, has – through inflation – enabled a rapid and cruel income restructuring. Pensioners and public sector workers have been unable to maintain their incomes, whilst others have advanced theirs. Both the beneficiaries and providers of welfare services have suffered. Monthly inflation slowed considerably towards 1996 and it was felt to be under control: around 4–5 per cent compared with 25 per cent in 1993 and 40 per cent in early 1992. But after August 1998 when Russia found itself near to financial default, inflation began to rise steeply.

As in many Western countries, social policy is the most expensive section of public expenditure, and is particularly sensitive to two factors: the rate of unemployment, and the level of pensions, both vigorously debated in Russia. The official rate of unemployment as measured by registration with the Federal Employment Service is about 3 per cent. Labour force surveys indicate that for 1997 it is nearer 9 per cent, with a further 11 per cent on involuntary leave and short time (Chetvernina, 1997, pp. 227–9). By early 1999, surveyed unemployment in Russia was at a record high, totalling 12.4 per cent of the economically active population. Although much larger than official figures, this is still lower than many have expected. However, with unemployment benefit at around 10 per cent of the average wage, and average pensions about a third of the average wage, pensions take the lion's share of expenditure, driving the social budget.

A further feature of contemporary Russian social protection is the splitting of sources of funding, now subdivided between four federal extra-budgetary Funds, technically outside the state budget: employment, social insurance, pension and medical insurance. Generated since 1991 by a 39 per cent payroll tax, in 1994 they amounted to 17 per cent of GDP. The separation of funding not only demarcates liability, but also markedly fragments social policy. Lack of balance in implementing this system, reinforced by economic instability, contributes to the financial and organisational incapacity of the state to meet ambitious social commitments.

The Social Reform Programme for 1996–2000 states realistically that, in the medium term, significant rises in the social spending share of GDP should not be expected. However, periodical suggestions coming from the Ministry of Labour and Social Development to lower social insurance rates have been voted down by the state Duma (Parliament), despite an argument that raising employees' legal wages would increase total amounts contributed for social welfare. By 1997, the government was forced to announce that it would make social reform an urgent priority, since – from the time when the reforms began – it had not managed to accomplish deep structural transformations. Periodic attempts at financial stabilisation and budget deficit reduction undertaken by the Russian government had led to a fall in state expenditure of about 10 per cent of GDP, cutting spending on social goals in real terms. Social policy thus remained ineffective, although, as before, social spending represented over half of all consolidated budget expenditures and extra-budgetary Funds.

Permanent Crisis?

The reasons for the crisis in the social sphere lie in labour-market processes driving up unemployment, in the growth of long-term wage arrears, in the Pension Fund crisis and in the appearance of deficits on all extra-budgetary social Funds. In 1997–98, strikes occurred in the education and health-care sectors because of systematic non-payment of salaries. The crisis was intensified by a complete muddle in relation to social benefits and subsidies, and it became apparent that social issues could not be resolved by simple increases in funding allocations without a change in mechanisms and a reallocation of money expenditure for various purposes.

Following the 1996 presidential elections policy-making took a new turn. The government suspended laws for the implementation of which there were no appropriations in the budget, especially in the social sphere. The Duma maintained the 'golden rule' that 'laws must be backed up by money'; and there was a moratorium on the adoption of new legislative acts establishing such benefits. Instead, abolishing entitlement benefits and gradually replacing them with a few targeted, means-tested benefits became elevated as the key solution to the ineffective formal system of social protection. The reason for reexamining the concept was that Russia had more than 150 types of benefits and allowances, given to more than 100 million Russians. Groups with the highest incomes (upper deciles 8–10) received 42 per cent of social benefits expenditure, while those with the lowest incomes (deciles 1–3) received only 27 per cent (Dmytriev, 1997). The poorest people were not entitled to some kinds of state social support at all, including transport and medicines. Thus at the beginning of 1998 Yeltsin argued that the only way to change the social situation for the better was through targeted social assistance.

The main Russian social goals now are to:

- provide monetary benefits only to those living below minimum living standards;
- adopt a package of draft laws on targeted social support and establish a common database on social benefit recipients;
- stabilise the financial situation of the Pension Fund and gradually move the whole system towards the savings/investment scheme proposed by the World Bank;
- concentrate health-care funding on institutions whose services are in high demand;
- step up the collection of taxes from wealthy citizens; and
- continue the practice of concluding general agreements between employers, unions and the government, not only at federal but also at regional level.

However, the 1998 currency crisis undermined the fragile economic stability developed in 1997, making the implementation of this new social policy package highly problematic. Russia was faced with the complex task of finding a sensible compromise between the demands of economic growth and social protection. Objective social needs exist which cannot be neglected if social stability is not to be threatened. Conceptually, reform of the social sphere has been fairly clearly formulated; but this has not yet meant real reforms. Realisation of these depends on the existence of political will and effective cooperation between authorities at different levels; and even after the replacement of Yeltsin with Putin it was still not clear that these could be developed and delivered.

Aspects of Regional Inequality

Regional inequalities, policies and provision are central to understanding Russian social policy. The former USSR was an allied state made up of 15 Soviet socialist republics. Although considered formally independent, each was an inalienable part of the 'family of nations' – a geographically vast totalitarian empire. Even after the collapse of the USSR, Russia remains the largest European state, occupying a huge territory with notable ethnic, cultural and social diversity. During the period of transformation, former Soviet republics have acquired real sovereign status. As a result, the Russian population has fallen, although it still numbers almost 150 million. At present, there are 89 members of the Russian Federation, divided between 11 large economic/territorial zones: Moscow, St Petersburg and the Kaliningrad enclave each have a special status.

Yeltsin's task of achieving an 'upswing' in Russia in the late 1990s was dependent on the development of local self-government for the promotion of regional reforms. The constitution retains policy for health, education and social security at the federal level, leaving only housing to the various republics, territories, regions and federal cities. However, recent government initiatives propose that local authorities should be in direct charge not only of housing, but also of other social policies such as social assistance, education and health care. Since budgetary provision for these services has moved away from the federal level, local finance (taxes, charges, insurance, mortgages, charities, and so on) has assumed increasing importance. Growing regional inequities are likely to result because the Russian regions are moving towards market economies at different speeds, their economic resources are not equal in value and political preferences of their local élites can be diametrically opposed. Unlike education and health care, where local budgets are still relatively protected, social assistance for poorer people and families is suffering especially badly, because it has become completely dependent on the local financial situation. Further decentralisation of social policy would require the creation of efficient mechanisms for federal redistribution of incomes from more successful to relatively poor regions. Such federal mechanisms remain extremely vague and of little apparent priority.

Yet regional disparities are great, and growing. In Moscow, nominal monetary incomes, at 3,600 roubles and 660 per cent of regional subsistence levels, are now over three times the average Russian figures of 1020 roubles and 224 per cent. The corresponding figures for St Petersburg are 1020 (219 per cent), for the North Caucasus 500 (153 per cent) and for Eastern Siberia 710 (140 per cent). Even if incomes are adjusted for official subsistence levels and local prices, Moscow is far ahead of the Western Siberian export giants, let alone other regions. Since the official subsistence minimum poverty line in 1997 was over 400 roubles, it is unlikely there are many prosperous groups in most big Russian territories; and ten depressed regions (mostly territories and republics with ethnic minorities) have average per capita incomes below local minimum living standards.

Differing Social Policy Areas

The Social Role of Enterprises

In the past, the role of enterprises in making social provision for their staff was fairly significant: one-third of all the Soviet state's social infrastructure belonged to enterprises. In a market economy, oriented towards efficiency, enterprises have been unable to maintain social objectives and have no financial interest in doing so. Proposals were therefore made for restructuring these functions and handing them over to the municipalities. This reform had two aims: to replace the previous system in which public access to social goods depended on a person's status at work and particular branch of industry; and to improve enterprises' financial position, freeing them from social functions atypical for businesses operating in market conditions. By the end of the 1990s, 60 per cent of Russian enterprises were transferring their social establishments onto the books of local authorities. The role of enterprises in social provision for both their staff and the general public, however, is still fairly high, continuing to cover up to half their expenditure on maintaining social infrastructure. However, enterprise managers no longer have the slightest pretensions to play a leading social role.

In the course of the reform, the enterprises' recreational, sporting and medical establishments were found to be most commercially promising, and therefore attractive to the municipalities. Housing has proved to be the stumbling block: enterprises want to offload it as soon as possible, while local authorities simply refuse to accept it. This situation has arisen because relevant legislation was insufficiently worked out at the regional level, leaving it open for financially-pressed municipal authorities to hinder the transfer process by administrative delay. Enterprise directors are increasingly calling for stricter federal regulation of transfer to the municipalities, and this can lead to local conflicts.

Employment

In starting to move towards a market economy Russian reformers made allowances for social effects, as these applied to employment issues, in a very particular way (Manning, 1998). On the macroeconomic level, they consciously chose to support inefficient producers, to prevent mass redundancies and consequent unemployment. This also meant that the government's intentions to put bankruptcy measures into operation became purely rhetorical. This strategy resulted in high levels of hidden unemployment, whereby workers remained technically employed (their labour books were held by an employer), but on permanent leave. No other country in economic transformation has experienced this scale of hidden unemployment; but it comes at a cost in terms of perverse incentives for employers and employees. Thus, during 1993–94 only 40 per cent of Russia's workers were fully paid on time.

In the longer term this employment policy may only be delaying job changes, but is consistent with the slow pace and relative inefficiency of other Russian socio-economic reforms. However, this picture is complicated by the scale of the 'shadow economy' in Russia. In Western countries the proportion of GDP represented by the 'informal' (that is, illegal) sector varies between

5 and 10 per cent; by the end of the 1990s in Russia actual GDP was perhaps as much as 60 per cent higher than official GDP. One of the primary causes of this situation has been destabilisation created in the course of implementing the Russian model of economic reform – forced privatisation, overnight price liberalisation, imperfect tax legislation, restrictive credit and monetary policy. It has been estimated that at least 10 million people (about 15 per cent of the economically-active population) engage in such activities, generating overall, according to official figures, a minimum of 25 per cent of people's income.

Poverty

Price liberalisation in the early 1990s not only provoked gigantic price rises but also devalued most of the population's savings – bringing about, in effect, a large-scale redistribution of wealth. Thus, the main outcome of the price liberalisation process was not that people benefited from the flooding of the market with consumer goods, but suffered a fall in real incomes, with a substantial polarisation of society and a growth in poverty. Between 6 and 10 per cent of Russian families have taken control of over 50 per cent of income and own 70 to 80 per cent of the country's national wealth. Manning and Davidova (1998) show that over the reform years, the very structure of poverty has changed: it is now linked not only with a particular set of demographic characteristics (above all, with the presence of children in the family), but also with unemployment and insecure employment – where working people fall into poverty.

   The issue of poverty is also connected with the question of the minimum wage and its relationship to the subsistence minimum (Pirogov and Pronin, 1999). At the start of the reforms, the minimum wage was one-and-a-half times the subsistence minimum, but by 1992 this relationship had begun to change. By the end of the 1990s it was five times lower than the official Ministry of Labour subsistence minimum, and the minimum wage had effectively lost its role as a major social guarantee. It had not changed since 1997, and the salaries of many workers in budget-funded sectors have not changed since 1995. However, government refused to implement proposals to increase the monthly minimum wage from 83 to 110 roubles (at a time when inflation changed its nominal value from US$15 in 1997 to US$4–5 in 1999), in part because so many other social payments are tied to it.

Health Care and Education

Health care and education reforms have become inevitable in Russia, since the fact that they rely on residual budget funding has made it impossible for them to continue to function as before. In essence, reform amounts to ending the former state monopoly and replacing it with either a new state or private system, although taking a purely economic approach to health and education would put access to the most important public services beyond much of the population.

In health care, Russia has pursued the insurance option, replacing the budget-funding mechanism by a system of compulsory medical insurance (OMS) – seen as a compromise between a monopoly, which limits choice, and privatisation, which limits access. In practice, OMS has not yet shown its real advantages in comparison with the old system. It is essentially fiscal in nature, allowing expenditures to be taken into account and liabilities to be spread. The plan is to bring the proportion of medical care funded by insurance to 70 per cent of total national spending on health care, but, as yet, less than 50 per cent of the prescribed cash requirement for the programme has been redistributed from the state to OMS.

Russia is now spending significantly fewer resources on health care than her economic potential would potentially allow – on the basis of percentage share of GDP the country is 98th in the world. And ill-health is effectively the price that the nation is paying for reform. A process of population decline has begun, with perceptible increases in socially-dangerous diseases such as tuberculosis, venereal diseases, drug addiction and alcoholism. Deaths from alcohol abuse have increased by 2.3 times during the reform years. Birth rates and life expectancy (especially for men) have fallen substantially, and maternal and infant mortality rates have risen.

In contrast, education reform is increasingly shaped by market principles. The new approach presupposes that both higher and primary/secondary schools have the right to engage in independent economic activities. The government sequestered part of the education funding, cutting the education budget by a full 25 per cent, yet the Minister of Education categorically denied the accusation that Russia was building an educational system funded by individual families. In practice, the reforms mean cuts in the numbers employed in the budget-funded sector, the reorganisation of educational institutions funded from the federal budget, and their gradual transfer to the jurisdiction of regions.

Market-oriented education should give a person the possibility of taking out a loan in order to get an education. However, this goal is undermined by the high level of corruption and the lack of a stable financial system. There is a real danger that the country is moving towards a hierarchy of 'élite' and 'cheap' educational establishments where the chance of receiving specialist or higher education varies dramatically for members of different social groups – with only nine-years' basic general education remaining accessible to the mass of people.

Pensions

The accumulation of huge pension arrears since the mid-1990s shows that the Russian distributive pension system is in long-term crisis. The burden on working people is growing, especially as, in general, businesses operating in the informal economy rarely deduct taxes for extra-budgetary Funds. This may be explained by the very high level of Pension Fund contributions, at 29 per cent of the wages fund. In addition, the ratio of payers to recipients is gradually falling: in 1991 employed people exceeded pensioners in a ratio of 2.1:1, but by 1997 the ratio was 1.7:1 (Bureau of Economic Analysis, 1998); and the growth of a rapidly-ageing Russian population, resulting from marked falls in the birth rate, will substantially aggravate this problem. However, achieving political consensus on the reform of pension provision has proved to be extraordinarily difficult, as in Russia pensioners are the most active section of the electorate.

Thus reforms of the existing distributive system are proposed to introduce elements of compulsory-funded pension financing. The foundation of this reform is a so-called 'mixed model' with three levels of provision:

1   The chief component of the system is 'pay-as-you-go' state pension insurance using current Pension Fund receipts;
2   Supplementary pension insurance under funded schemes conditional on receiving investment income;
3   State pension provision out of federal budget funds for certain categories of citizen, such as senior civil servants, armed forces personnel, and people who have not acquired the right to a state insurance pension.

Under this compromise model, by the year 2007 the overall rate of pension contributions will be 27 per cent, out of which still only 7 per cent will be going into the funded system. And even if further reform is finally implemented, as approved by government, but postponed indefinitely because many of its operational mechanisms are vague (despite its role as a World Bank condition for granting Russia a multimillion dollar loan in 1998), its real results will not become apparent for some time.

Housing

Housing was a major source of frustration under the Soviet system. Waiting lists were very long, except for members of privileged groups such as senior military and party officials. From 1991, government reform of housing and municipal services envisaged the transfer of housing either to private ownership, or to municipal control where it was owned by enterprises. In addition there were plans for utility payments to be shouldered entirely by Russian citizens by 2003. Since 1998, utility rates have been gradually rising. Ordinary people will not be alone in contributing more to housing costs; local government will have to pay more too, to receive matching federal monies.

Housing privatisation began swiftly in the early 1990s, but has since stalled at less than 50 per cent overall as a result of public uncertainty about the costs of repairs and fears that private owners might have to pay disproportionately more for services. At the end of 1997, citizens paid, on average, only 38 per cent of the cost of electricity, water, housing services and repairs. The rest was covered by local budgets. The decision to have the population pay half the real cost of housing and utilities in 1998 was made as part of housing and municipal services reform. Government resolutions only 'recommend' the regions to collect 50 per cent of the costs from the population; the final decision is still, as in the past, in the hands of local authorities.

Women

During the reforms of the 1990s women were steadily forced out of the most important sectors of society, most particularly from the sphere of government – before perestroika they made up 30 per cent of the membership of elective bodies whereas in the 1989 USSR Supreme Soviet they accounted for 15 per cent and in the state Duma for 11 per cent. In the labour market, too, women's position has been declining. Between 60–90 per cent of the unemployed are women, Russia has a list of more than 400 occupations closed to women, and the system of maternity benefits discourages businesses from hiring women (Pascall and Manning, 1999). Women have also been squeezed out of higher education; and now that people have to pay for tuition, the majority of students at prestigious higher schools are male.

Conclusion: Which Way for the Russian Welfare State?

In summary, the key elements of current Russian social policy are as follows:

- a move from state budget to payroll finance funding;
- decentralised institutional ownership and control;
- privatisation of housing, and parts of health care and education;
- slow growth of unemployment, but with labour market flexibility;
- continuity of enterprise welfare functions;
- rapid growth of regional inequality;
- more informed debate and realism in social policy;
- continued uncertainty over health and education policy;
- very low guaranteed income minima;
- deep poverty for certain families, especially with children; and
- worsening health and demographic patterns.

Barr (1994, pp. 26–7) has observed the distinction between short-term, sometimes emergency, social policy measures forced by events developing in the early transition phase (for example the rate of inflation in 1992/3), and the medium-term reconstruction of social policy. There were two clear points at which President Yeltsin attempted to give overall shape to the development of the Russian welfare state. The first, in the run-up to the 1993 referendum, focused on the basic rights and expectations that Russian citizens could have of social policies. For example, it was proclaimed that a system of minimum social guarantees, including living standards, wages and pensions, would provide for those without sufficient means, and that social protection would be targeted on 'the right people'.

These decrees have not been fulfilled. There is widespread and very deep poverty, however measured, for many Russians. The targeting of social support is also regressive, in that those on higher incomes get more than those on lower incomes. This is a result of continued support coming through enterprises, but particularly through more successful enterprises, and to better-paid staff in them. There is thus a growing majority of citizens calling for the state to secure basic social support, and some members of the government who recognise that the market may not be the solution to social policy development, particularly in view of the difficult 1996–97 year when wages arrears grew rapidly. More recently, in 1998, there was a further pronouncement on the '12 Main Tasks in the Area of Social and Economic Policy'. These exhibit a mixture of political expediency and realism that the current arrangements are muddled. For example, the aim to ensure that wages and pensions are paid on time reflects the widespread public discontent over arrears in the last year or two, and the emergence of renewed strike action amongst politically active groups such as miners, which might spread. Similarly the offer to finance housing for the military direct from the Ministry of Finance addresses both the pressing issue of returning servicemen from abroad, but more significantly is designed to appease a still-significantly powerful group in Russian society.

Other items are more organisational. The recognition that with limited resources the government will inevitably have to target them on the poorest if they are to be of any use, is a notable break from the 1993 declarations. This will entail challenging monopolies in the system, political or economic, and the development of a clear understanding of the way the finance and organisation of social policy has developed in the 1990s. It is significant that there is planned to be an inventory drawn up of budget-financed organisations, starting with education and health. The chaos and *de facto* decentralisation of finance and organisation that has developed since 1991 appears to have left the government ignorant of even the most basic knowledge of how social policy currently works.

These tasks are some advance on those of 1993. They are certainly more realistic in the sense that they have been formulated against a far more accurate assessment of the difficult circumstances for social policy, and an admission that the organisation and implementation of social policies has been perverse – the pretence that universal social guarantees could be maintained has in effect resulted in guarantees for the better-off, and dire poverty for others. But realism does not mean that the implied massive shift in priorities towards the poor can actually be achieved. The barriers to this shift are those that distorted social policy in the first place. The continued delivery of social policies through the enterprise as 'occupational welfare' means that enterprises are a major multiplier of disadvantage, since they channel social support to the relatively better-off. Just as the retention of surplus labour in these very large organisations has kept unemployment under control, and, importantly, suppressed the potential for political disaffection, it has also contributed to the sharp rise in inequality in Russia in recent years.

Continuities in enterprise welfare activities can be contrasted to the rapid changes evident in a second barrier to changing social policy priorities on the ground, the *de facto* regionalisation that developed surprisingly quickly in the 1990s. Regional inequality has arisen out of the differential effects of rapid inflation, and the adjustment in economic restructuring that has been possible in some areas but not others. This has been compounded for some regions by local political élites which have tried hard to resist the economic changes, for example by blocking development of new small and medium-sized private enterprises. Regional differences are now so large that there would have to be an enormous recentralisation of government services to even them out – hardly possible now. It is difficult to see how the federal government will be able to slow down, let alone halt or reverse these regional inequalities which have had such a marked impact on social policy.

References

Barr, N. (ed.) (1994) *Labor Markets and Social Policy in Central and Eastern Europe, the Transition and Beyond*, Oxford University Press.

Bureau of Economic Analysis (1998) *Survey on Economic Policy in Russia in 1997*, Bureau of Economic Analysis.

Chetvernina, T. (1997) 'Forms and Main Features of Hidden Unemployment in Russia', in T. Zaslavskaya (ed.), *Kuda Idet Rossia*, Intertsentr.

Dmytriev, A. (1997) unpublished Report for Annual International Symposium, Moscow Inter-Disciplinary Centre for Social Science, 17–19 January.

Ellman, M. (1989) *Socialist Planning*, 2nd edn, Cambridge University Press.

Esping-Andersen, G. (1990) *The Three Worlds of Welfare Capitalism*, Polity Press.

George, V. and Manning, N. (1980) *Socialism, Social Welfare and the Soviet Union*, Routledge & Kegan Paul.

Kornai, J. (1980) *Economics of Shortage*, North-Holland.

Manning, N. and Davidova, N. (1998) 'Townsend, Poverty and the New Russia: Unemployed Households and Poverty in Moscow, St. Petersburg and Voronezh', Paper to the Seebohm Rowntree Centenary Conference, University of York, 18–20 March.

Manning, N. (1998) 'Social Policy, Labour Markets, Unemployment, and Household Strategies in Russia', *International Journal of Manpower*, 19(1–2), pp. 48–67.

Mezentseva, E. and Rimachevskaya, N. (1990) 'The Soviet Country Profile: Health of the USSR Population in the 70s and 80s – an approach to a Comprehensive Analysis', *Social Science and Medicine*, 31(8), pp. 867–77.

Pascall, J. and Manning, N. (1999) 'Background Paper' in preparation for UNICEF, *Women in Transition*, Regional Monitoring Report, no. 6.

Pirogov, G. and Pronin, S. (1999) 'The Russian Case: Social Policy Concerns', in Y. Atal (ed.), *Poverty in Transition and Transition in Poverty*, Berghhahn Books/UNESCO.

[See also *The Regions of Russia: Collected Statistics*, Vol. 2, 1998, Goskomstat Rossi.]

CHAPTER 12

South Africa: Transition Under Pressure

FRANCIE LUND

Introduction

South Africa's transition from apartheid to democracy in 1994 was accompanied by significant changes in all social policies. South African social policy during the twentieth century was so closely related to the political economy of apartheid that it cannot easily be classified according to any of the conventional welfare regimes. Nevertheless, even as a 'special case', it has much of interest in the comparative study of welfare systems.

The urgency of getting rid of the racially discriminatory policies of the former regime has meant that key elements and stages of the policy process have been telescoped into a short period. Thus, during the 1990s, policy formulation and then its translation into legislation, budgetary reallocations, the reorientation of staff and the development of new or different administrative capacities, and the adjustment of information and communication systems, all happened rapidly. Tensions always inherent in the policy process were forced to the surface, and are more visible than they would be in societies where the pace of change is slower. And it is possible to see how even in a country so eager to shed its past, policy changes are constrained by history.

The country is characterised by pervasive inequality, and extremes of wealth and poverty. Some citizens have access to all the services and technology of very modern societies; others live without basic services such as water, electricity and access to transport. There is thus a juxtaposition of 'first and third worlds', or development and underdevelopment, within one country. One of the effects of this is that the student can see how the scope of social policy – what sectors qualify for inclusion under this term – is related to how far basic needs have been met.

Two examples illustrate this point. In industrialised countries the provision of water and electricity to households and communities would not normally fall within the scope of social policies regarding health and education. Yet in a country like South Africa, the improvement of health status through the provision of primary health care services will fail unless it is accompanied by a supply of clean potable water within easy reach of households. The impact of improvements to the school system will be diluted if learners are not able to study at home because there is no affordable lighting.

The chapter starts with a brief history of social policy development in South Africa during the twentieth century, and then describes present patterns of poverty and inequality which post-apartheid social policies have to address. Three main areas of reform are then outlined – the development of new policies, shifts in resource allocation and reform of the institutional frameworks. These are discussed with reference mainly to education, health, social security and social services. The chapter then considers the mixed economy of provision, and the theme of universality and selectivity. It concludes with a consideration of the main lessons for social policy which can be derived from this transitional period in South Africa, and an assessment of future prospects.

Phases of Social Policy Development

The foundations of apartheid were laid well before the Nationalist Party came to power in 1948. The Dutch were the first colonial settlers, and were followed by the British. Both colonial powers dealt with the indigenous and non-white immigrant people as inferior races. By the close of the nineteenth century, labour policies had been developed which sowed the seeds for the formal policy of apartheid which was to follow. Gold mines, white-owned farms and the new cities needed workers, and the migrant labour policy drew men away from rural areas while strictly regulating their presence in urban areas. Under apartheid all citizens were classified into one of four so-called 'race groups': African, coloured, Indian and white. The term 'black' is commonly used to refer collectively to the three groups who were not white, who were disenfranchised. Because the allocation of resources and opportunities was fundamentally determined by official racial classification, the terms need to continue to be used, as racial classification remains the primary explanatory variable for patterns of poverty and inequality, which are central to social policy. Over the first half of the twentieth century, policies were introduced which stripped Africans, and then coloured and Indian people, of property rights, of free labour mobility, and of the right to live where they pleased.

Industrial social legislation developed early in the twentieth century. Compensation for industrial disease and accidents was regulated in 1914, and an unemployment insurance fund was started in 1937. Benefit levels were racially differentiated, and lower-paid workers and women were disadvantaged. Through this industrial welfare, some black people got access to social benefits as workers, but not as citizens. In the 1930s and 1940s, a number of initiatives reflected an awareness of the importance of collective provision of social services. Public works programmes were established to provide temporary employment to impoverished white people, and the state ran nutrition schemes in white schools. The Gluckman Commission on Health, in the

1940s, was years ahead of its time in recommending free health care for all citizens through a system of primary health care centres. The Cape Town Poverty Survey in the late 1930s modelled itself on Rowntree's surveys of York in England, and empirically showed the extent of poverty, especially among the coloured population. The Survey findings were influential in the work of two commissions which found for the establishment of a comprehensive social security scheme.

When the Nationalist Party government came to power in 1948, aspects of the citizenship-based aspects of welfare state thinking survived – but for whites only. There were elements of the model of family life found in Beveridge's thinking: a two-generational nuclear family, with a father in formal employment, and a mother doing the reproductive work at home. These Beveridge-like elements were underpinned with a deeply conservative Calvinist religiosity as far as white family life was concerned. African, coloured and Indian people, on the other hand, were largely expected to take care of themselves.

The 1950s and 1960s saw the consolidation and implementation of apartheid or separate development, a key characteristic of which was the role of a strong, central and authoritarian state. The government created the 'bantustans' (mainly undeveloped rural areas which had been traditionally settled by Africans), into which millions of additional Africans were now exported and given a token form of 'self-government'. Local authorities had no role in the control or delivery of education, and very little in health or social services, and this is still the case today. Later we will see how large a problem this is for the consolidation of the new democracy.

Across all fields of social policy, patterns of provision emerged which were skewed towards the protection of white interests. The social security system was initially set up to cover white elderly people and white people with disabilities; a bundle of grants and other policy measures provided for the protection of white family life. Gradually basic state assistance was expanded in scope and coverage, first to urban-based Indian and coloured people, then to African people in rural areas. Finally, all South Africans were covered with the exception of African people in the bantustans, who never became eligible for some benefits. Racially-differentiated amounts of benefits (the formula in the 1970s was a ratio of 10:5:1 for white: Indian/Coloured: African beneficiaries) finally disappeared only in 1993.

Social services developed as a partnership between government and a network of voluntary organisations. The state used a combination of its own subsidies and legislation controlling fund-raising to force all welfare organisations to apply racial discrimination in services. Virtually no attention was paid to the development of the voluntary welfare sector where the poorest people lived, in the bantustans. Education policy was deeply inequitable. The wealthy white population had access to free education, though they could opt to pay for élite private schools as well. The Indian community developed a very good network of community-based schools which preserved cultural traditions; these were broken down by the state, and the state curriculum was imposed. The African population was given 'Bantu education', which was based on the idea that black people were naturally inferior, and should only be taught sufficiently to serve the needs of the white élites and capitalist industry. A few religious and mission schools offered a private and better-quality education to people who were not white. Most of these, as well as mission hospitals, were eventually absorbed by the state.

In similar vein, apartheid housing policy broke up existing neighbourhoods, displacing people either to the bantustans, or to controlled township developments far from city centres. The government disallowed or severely restricted private-sector involvement in housing for the poor, relaxing this only as late as the mid-1980s. There was a free market in housing for white people and to a lesser extent for Indian and coloured people, with high rates of home ownership as opposed to rented housing. A series of strikes led by black unions in 1973 marked the beginnings of the breakdown of the old regime. The strikes were followed by the 1976 student uprisings, and the threat of ungovernability coincided with a downturn in the economy. By the early 1980s, the government embarked on what has been described as the twin strategies of reform and repression. It started paying attention to the provision of some basic infra-structural development in black townships (like water and electricity), and to address racial discrepancies in social spending, while ruthlessly repressing political protest activity.

By the end of the 1980s, policy work for 'after the struggle' was firmly on the agenda. Sectoral policy forums were set up which included a broad range of stakeholders – representatives of political parties, the mass democratic movement, professional associations, civic organisations, academics and trade unions, among others. The forums were intended to start formulating new policies, and also to stop the then government from unilaterally restructuring social sectors in the interregnum. By the time of the democratic elections in 1994, therefore, significant policy work had been done, and people from opposite sides of the political fence had started learning how to work together.

Selected Characteristics of South African Society

A few characteristics of South African society have been selected to demonstrate the kinds of policy challenges which now have to be faced. The population of some 40 million lives in an area about ten times the size of England. The population is relatively young, with half being younger than 20 years old. The proportion of the population age 65 years and older is just less than 5 per cent. This is much lower than the figure in northern industrial countries, and has markedly different implications for social policy regarding retirement provision and health services for elderly people. South Africa has one of the highest rates of measured inequality in the world. It is classified as an upper-middle-income country, but (roughly speaking) the poorest 40 per cent of households comprise 50 per cent of the population and get 11 per cent of overall income, while the richest 10 per cent of households comprise 7 per cent of the population and get 40 per cent of the income (May, Woolard and Klasen, 2000, p. 27).

Unsurprisingly, the patterns of poverty and inequality in South Africa largely take a racial form. Being born into one of the four classified racial groups determined one's life chances and opportunities. Africans constitute 77 per cent of the population, and 60 per cent of Africans are classified as poor. Whites constitute 11 per cent of the population, with only 1 per cent being classified poor. Indicators of human development for white people, and to a lesser extent for Indian people, compare with the best of the upper-income countries; those for the African population are as bad as, and often worse than, those for countries with lower wealth levels than South Africa. There is increasingly steep inequality within the African population, with the growth of an as yet small but very wealthy élite.

The urbanisation rate is now just over 50 per cent, and millions of poor people also live in peri-urban informal settlements where life is hazardous, services are poor and environmental controls are few. Rural areas, especially former bantustan areas, experience the highest rates and shares of poverty.

The infant mortality rate in the early 1990s was more than 11 times higher for Africans than for whites. The health status of the poor is obviously the result of material poverty, but is also an outcome of the lack of state attention to public health and preventive measures (immunisation against measles, for example, and the control of tuberculosis), as well as to hazardous working conditions.

In common with other countries, female-headed households in South Africa are poorer and more vulnerable than male-headed households. Women have less access to employment opportunities than men, and when they are employed they are more likely to earn less than men. Yet households headed by younger women, in urban areas, perform better on nearly every important indicator than do households overall. If one were designing a policy measure to target people in poor households, this example shows that it would be important to consider the combination of the variables of gender, rural/urban location, and the stage in the household's life-cycle at the same time, rather than just one indicator such as gender of the household head.

In all countries, social policies regarding income maintenance, social services, education and housing are based, implicitly or explicitly, on some construct of family life. South Africa has a rich diversity of cultures, with cultural forms and practices which have survived both industrialisation and apartheid policies. However, the migrant labour system and the forced movement of people smashed stable family life for millions of citizens. Labour policies also led to the phenomenon of 'double-rootedness', where many men have a household in town and a separate one in the rural area, with little or no overlap between the two. This may or may not be formalised in polygamous marriages, which are still common in some parts of the country (Republic of South Africa, 1996, pp. 15–18).

Finally, South Africa has an exceptionally high unemployment rate of around 30 per cent (Klasen and Woolard, 1999). Unemployment is highest for African people, and in rural areas, and amongst women – with African women in rural areas being triply disadvantaged. It also particularly affects young people. Two-thirds of the unemployed have never had a job; the average age of entry to the labour market for young African people is 27 years. Increasingly, the unemployment rate is determined by factors external to South Africa. Globalisation, and South Africa's particular history, have led to a rapid recent growth of the informal economy and an increase in the proportion of people working in the informal economy, rather than in formal employment. It is obvious that growing numbers of people, therefore, will not get access to social welfare benefits through the workplace.

Social Policy Reform: from Racial Ideology to Meeting Basic Needs

Post-apartheid social policy developments take as their starting point the new South African Constitution. This document enshrines the idea of national unity, and a society in which individual rights and cultural diversity are protected. The Constitution guarantees certain socioeconomic rights, including access to health, social security, education and housing. In South Africa's march back to international legitimacy, it signed many international conventions regarding *inter alia* human rights, gender equality and the protection of children. South Africa has thus come to have a complex mixture of commitments and obligations. The Constitution is more progressive than many Northern countries in terms of respecting different sexual orientations. The same Constitution, however, protects 'cultural diversity', and cultural attitudes (regardless of racial group) in South Africa are deeply patriarchal, and distinctly homophobic.

The Constitution is committed to the 'progressive realisation' of a broad range of socioeconomic rights. In 1994 the newly-elected African National Congress announced that the primary mechanism for addressing the apartheid legacy of inequality was the Reconstruction and Development Programme (RDP), which was strongly redistributive in intent, with a central role for government. Two short years later, a new and conservative macroeconomic policy, called Growth, Employment and Redistribution (GEAR) was introduced. It withdraws in substantial ways from the RDP's commitment to redistribution, and emphasises fiscal austerity. Many fear that this will act as a brake on the pace of the 'progressive realisation' of socioeconomic rights.

There are common themes in the policy direction for all of the social sectors: moving away from racial discrimination, and from urban services serving the needs of a privileged few, towards accessible services for the majority of

South Africans who are poor and mostly African. Rural areas are especially identified, as well as vulnerable groups, particularly women, children and people with disabilities. All of the policies express commitment to citizen participation.

Education

New policy gives all people the right to a basic education, and provides the framework for a single non-racial school system. The move is towards universal free compulsory schooling for nine years, with two types of school, public and independent. There will be one national curriculum at primary and secondary school levels, with a national system of accreditation, rather than the fragmented systems of the past. There is a commitment towards overcoming provincial inequalities in educational resource allocation.

Most middle- and lower-income countries have steep gender inequality in access to all levels of schooling, with lower enrolment and completion rates for girl children. South Africa is unusual in this respect, with equitable enrolment rates for boys and girls at primary and secondary school levels. On the other hand, there are extremely high rates of teenage pregnancy and many girls interrupt their schooling to have a child. However, again unlike in other developing countries, in South Africa young mothers have been able to return to school to attempt to complete their secondary schooling.

The new government is concerned about the number of over-aged young people – both young men and young women – who are still at school because of the very high repetition rates. It plans to introduce a new system of age-grade norms, which will force exit from the school system at a certain age. If this is implemented too rapidly, it will work against the interests of young women. Already very vulnerable in terms of employment possibilities, they will be more so if they are unable to get the school leaving certificate which is needed to be considered for even low-skilled work.

There is a stated commitment to shifting state resource allocation away from tertiary educational institutions, so that the shift towards compulsory basic education can take place. Tertiary fees have risen sharply, making access difficult for those from poorer households. For the first time, private universities are being established. Proportionately more students are now enrolling at technical colleges, which are more vocationally-oriented, than at universities.

Health

There were and still are parallel public and private systems. In the past, rural people had little access to either (though having access to privately-practising traditional healers), while at the same time the private health sector accounted for nearly 60 per cent of total health-care spending, yet served only one-quarter of the population. The private sector would dump onto the public sector those people whose private insurance benefits were exhausted.

The new health policy will seek to continue the tax-financed public health system, orienting towards primary health care and delivered through a new district health system. Free health care is available for certain categories of people such as pregnant women, and mothers of young children. User fees will be paid by those who can afford them. Medical aids schemes will now have to provide a minimum set of health care benefits, and will have to discontinue the practice of setting up fragmented and separate schemes for the young and healthy – to stop 'cream-skimming'. In a parallel initiative the government seeks to establish a national social health insurance scheme, which would see that all people in formal employment, and their dependants, are insured for public hospital treatment. This would go along with the decentralisation of public hospital management, giving managers more incentive to perform better by being able to retain the revenue that they do bring in.

Significant progress has been made in vitally important areas. Abortion has been legalised. Legislation has been introduced which will outlaw smoking in public spaces, and tobacco advertising will be banned outright. A generic drugs policy has been introduced which will make drugs cheaper for the public, while cutting the profits of the drug firms. The ability of the international tobacco and pharmaceutical industries to contest these policy measures as they come online should not, however, be underestimated.

Two key problems remain. The fiscal formula that has been devised to overcome inter-provincial inequities in health-resource allocation appears to be less than successful. McIntyre *et al.* (1999, p. 51) hold that a key factor has been the constrained public-sector resource environment:

> Resource redistribution is considerably more difficult to achieve in the face of a declining real budget. In addition…there is a fundamental conflict between provincial level decision making about the allocation of resources between sectors (i.e. fiscal federalism) and the goal of achieving equity in the distribution of resources within a particular sector.

Secondly, the ANC government has been unable, in the six years since the elections, to develop a timely, coherent and consistent policy on HIV/AIDS. This will no doubt be judged its greatest policy failure across the health, social, political and economic domains.

Income Maintenance

South Africa has mixed private and public provision for contingencies such as disability, support in old age, and for the protection of family life (Ardington and Lund, 1995; Lund, 1997; van der Berg, 1997). The basic policy position is that people should care for themselves where possible, and use government support as a last resort.

People who are employed in the formal economy have access to social insurance for retirement provision, for occupational disability, for maternity benefits and for unemployment. Coverage is relatively good for those who have work, and the insurance industry for retirement is a significant pillar of the South African economy. However, there is gender discrimination in aspects of all pillars. Furthermore, the unemployment coverage is not underpinned by any form of retraining or skills development. With regard to industrial injuries, large numbers of lower-level workers are unaware of their rights to compensation for injuries at work; and an unacceptably large proportion of the compensation payments go to professional fees of lawyers and doctors, rather than to the beneficiaries themselves.

There are formal and informal private savings schemes in South Africa. Individuals invest in formal financial institutions, for example in provident funds, and informal rotating credit associations. Many African people also contribute to burial societies, speaking to the deep importance attached to a dignified burial.

An important pillar of the overall social security system is state social assistance, extended to elderly people, people with disabilities, and to women and children. Cash benefits are non-contributory (that is, not insurance-based), means-tested, and in 1998 were awarded to just less than three million direct beneficiaries, and millions more indirect beneficiaries. The redistributive mechanism in the Old Age Pension, and to a lesser extent the Disability Grant, lies in the fact that the grant is claimed by an elderly person, or a person with a disability, but gets pooled as a household resource (Ardington and Lund, 1995; Lund, 1997). This is unlike the case in industrialised countries where the benefit is claimed by an individual largely for his or her own consumption.

In South Africa, poor elderly and disabled people commonly live in three-generational households, and a disproportionate number of poor young children live in households where elderly pension-receiving people are present. Because the pension money goes to the household purse, and because it is delivered deep into rural areas, it has unusual distributive features. It is well-targeted towards lower income groups; it is gender sensitive towards women (women draw it earlier, and live longer), and towards children. Significant flows of wealth go from older to younger generations, rather than in the more usual opposite direction, where younger people support elderly people. Also, for many older African people who were excluded from formal employment, or were erratically employed, the pension income is the largest and most reliable income they have ever received. Offsetting these positive features are the enormous administrative inefficiencies in the system, which can make it very difficult for elderly people and people with disabilities to access.

In the field of support for child and family care, there are procedures for the formal fostering and adoption of children, with limited financial support

for foster parents, and none for adoptive parents. There is a judicial procedure for getting financial support from fathers; it works poorly, and is being
reformed. A means-tested State Maintenance Grant, for women and children
who could not get private financial support, reached about 400,000 women
and children, but was effectively inaccessible for most poor African women. It
is being replaced by a new benefit, the Child Support Grant, where the aim is
to reach three million poor children, but at a much lower rate than the old
State Maintenance Grant (Republic of South Africa, 1996).

Visitors to South Africa with an interest in social policy and development
studies are surprised by the state social assistance system. Those familiar with
social security in developing countries, and especially with neighbouring
Southern African countries, are amazed at the extent of the system, and many
disapprove of the state's taking so much responsibility. On the other hand,
those familiar with, for example, European systems are shocked by how inadequate a safety net it is. If you are poor and young, and have never been in
employment, there is no assistance for you at all. If you are in your fifties, and
have been retrenched, and your unemployment benefits run out after six
months, there is nothing to cushion you until, as a woman at 60, and a man
at 65, you become eligible for the pension for elderly people.

There are gaps between the private and the public pillars in social security,
and the government has called for an investigation of how to establish a comprehensive social security system. How far the ideal of a comprehensive system will be able to be reconciled with fiscal constraints imposed by
macroeconomic policy will be one of the key social policy questions of the
early twenty-first century.

Social Services

Social services in South Africa have historically been delivered in a partnership
between the state and voluntary-sector organisations. The usual apartheid
pattern prevailed: institutional care and personal social service delivery was
skewed towards the white population, and within that towards the elderly
white population. There was little encouragement of the development of
the voluntary sector in black areas. The welfare White Paper signals a shift
away from curative welfare services towards 'developmental social welfare' (the
concept was developed in South Africa by Patel, 1992, who drew significantly
from Midgeley's work on social development). The value base of the developmental shift is good in human terms, with its emphasis on independence and
self-help.

However, in a time of slow economic growth, with fiscal constraints being
imposed on the social services and in the face of new demands which will be
made for care of people affected by HIV/AIDS (including hundreds of thousands of children orphaned by HIV/AIDS), it may unintentionally make social
services very vulnerable. Studies of welfare and community-based organisations

attempting to cope with children affected by AIDS show that the poor communities, who are worst affected by the epidemic, are prepared to care, but need assistance to do so (Harber, 1999). And social workers in the subsidised voluntary welfare sector continue to do a great deal of time-consuming statutory work for government, for example in foster-care placements and in overseeing offenders on parole. They have little spare capacity to initiate 'developmental' services.

Redistribution: Changing the Trends in Resource Allocation

For redistributive policies to have an impact, they clearly have to be accompanied or followed by shifts in resource allocation. Figure 12.1 shows in a very graphic way how political changes in South Africa have shifted social spending patterns. The rapid decrease in the defence budget is remarkable. There had been times when defence was the largest single item of government expenditure, being used to support the former regime. Much of the decrease was diverted towards increasing the budget for education. It can also be seen that health received a real increase of 30 per cent between 1990/91 and 1996/97. Since then, however, free health care has been introduced with only limited additional budget allocation. Figure 12.1 reflects the small role played by government in housing, relative to other social sectors. Finally, the 130 per cent increase in the social security and welfare budget was largely driven by the need to overcome the racial disparities in state social assistance. That growth has now levelled off.

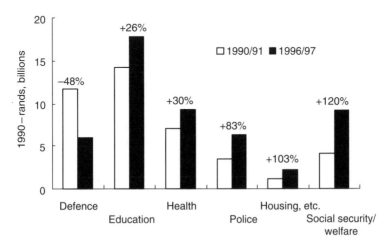

Figure 12.1 Change in general government expenditure on some functions, fiscal years 1990/91 to 1996/97, 1990 rands

Source: Republic of South Africa (1996).

How much is spent on social services as a proportion of all government expenditure, and how much as a proportion of GDP, is, quite literally, impossible to calculate for trends going back before 1990 due to the complex and fragmented administrative systems devised by the apartheid government (which included 'exporting' 8 million citizens to the bantustan areas). As to the present, Mokate (1999, pp. 66–8) calculates that in the 1997/98 allocations, welfare accounted for nearly half (47 per cent) of national and provincial expenditures. Total expenditures constituted 30.6 per cent of GDP, with health (3.3 per cent), education (6.5 per cent) and social security (3 per cent) accounting for nearly 13 per cent of GDP between them.

As in all countries, the different sectors compete with each other for a larger share of the expenditure. However, it is becoming clear in South Africa that attention must be paid to outputs as well – the outcomes of spending on, for example, health and education. There is widespread agreement within education policy circles by now that the problems in education will not be solved with more money. Education received 22 per cent of the total government budget in 1997/98, and 7 per cent of GDP. However, there is little relationship between what is spent and educational outcomes. Better management of schools is needed; the curriculum needs to be restructured to align it better with the real world of work; an agreement needs to be reached with the teacher unions to solve the problem whereby more than 90 per cent of the educational budget is locked into teacher salaries, leaving little over for the building of new schools in rural areas.

Some of the work in policy development, and experiments in the delivery of new services, have benefited from technical and financial assistance from governments and non-governmental organisations in other countries. Great Britain's Department for International Development (formerly the Overseas Development Administration), for example, has supported the development of reproductive health policy and services, and has played an active role in supporting the ambitious programme of land reform.

Reforming the Institutional Framework

The new South African government inherited a set of racially-separated administrations of immense complexity. There were 14 first-tier (central state) departments of health and of education, for example, and 17 for welfare. There was little commitment to public service, no reasonable demographic information on which to base social policies and planning, and outmoded information systems. An urgent task has been to amalgamate these former administrations, integrating them into nine new provinces, with each provincial department (say of health or of education) reporting directly to only one national department.

The government committed itself to two contradictory goals: to reduce or contain the size of the civil service, and to make it more representative of the population – that is, to encourage white bureaucrats to leave by offering generous severance packages, which would open up spaces for black people. In education, the government itself acknowledges that this has rapidly had disastrous consequences. Many of the best teachers, white and black, have left for the growing private sector, or for other careers altogether.

The implications of policy changes on personnel are clearly seen in the health field. The removal of geographical inequities in health, and the development of district health systems, mean that more human resources are needed at lower levels of the professional hierarchy, and at local level and in rural areas – the move that is required is 'downwards and outwards'. Yet professional élites everywhere want to move in the opposite direction – upwards in the status hierarchy, and inwards to the urban centres. At the apex of the professional pyramid are the doctors, who in South Africa are well-trained. Many feel ill at ease with aspects of the new health policy (for example, no new private psychiatric hospitals or clinics can be built) and with other aspects of 'the new South Africa', and find it easy to emigrate. Their university training has been heavily subsidised by the former and present government, which is thus effectively paying for skills development for other more developed countries.

A counter-flow to the emigration has been a scheme involving the temporary employment in South Africa of numbers of Cuban doctors. There is an oversupply of doctors in Cuba, and their training in primary health care is appropriate to the new health policy in South Africa. Many are placed in the rural areas where other doctors will not go. It is hoped that the new compulsory one year of community placements for newly-graduating doctors will fill rural posts in the short term, and encourage more young graduates to take up the challenges posed by rural health care.

A Mixed Economy of Welfare

During the liberation struggle, most people assumed that in future the state would play a strong, if not sole, role in social provision. Each sector eyed the bloated defence budget as its own potential future resource base for extending free health, education, social security or housing to all. Overall, however, there has been a move towards, or entrenchment of, a mixed economy in social provision.

Some think that the present state commitment to social spending is too great. There are others who would sympathise with an active role for the state, but who question the capacity of the national or provincial governments to deliver anything effectively and efficiently over the short to middle term, and at least until stronger local government is developed. However, the bantustan policy led to severe market distortions in the poorest areas, and many hold the view that at least up until the middle term, the state is the only agency with the resources and the ability to penetrate to where poverty is greatest.

A linked issue is whether the state has the capacity to manage or regulate the relationship in the emerging private–public partnerships. The delivery of state social assistance pensions and grants, for example, has been outsourced to the private sector. Advanced technical knowledge is needed to write tender specifications about this, and to adjudicate tender awards, and the state has been short on this capacity. It is clear that private firms have taken advantage of this, and some are profiting handsomely through delivering state cash transfers to the poorest households.

As in other countries, much of the work of health and welfare in South Africa is done through the unpaid, or low-paid, work of mostly women. The HIV/AIDS epidemic will place increasing strains on health and welfare budgets, and on society as a whole. New calls for 'community care' are already being made, but community care policies will erode many of the gender gains that have been made in the last ten years, if they are not underpinned by state assistance. In this regard, South Africa has been at the forefront of the growing international movement to undertake gendered analyses of state spending. The Women's Budget Initiative (Budlender, 1996) is a collaborative exercise between government and non-governmental organisations, and each year has sought to do an analysis of a selection of budget votes as well as a gendered analysis of taxation systems, for example, and the public sector. This is published and tabled at the same time as the annual Budget Speech. This can be used to raise awareness about the hidden work that underpins formal health and welfare services.

Universal and Selective Social Provision

The South African Freedom Charter, formulated in the 1950s, expressed the universal terms in which the struggle for liberation was fought: 'There shall be health, education, land, and security for all'. It will be clear by now that, faced with an economic growth rate which is less than population growth rate, and a large national debt, there has been a retreat towards more selective provision.

The introduction of the Child Support Grant, described earlier, provides an interesting example of the tensions in contemporary policy work. The Grant (the intention had been to call this a Benefit; state legal advisers won the battle and insisted on the term Grant) is intended to be a modest income supplement to poor children. The pattern of income distribution is such that the majority of people (including children) are very poor, and a few people are very rich indeed. This would suggest that the most effective way of reaching poor children would be through a universal grant to all children. This would give the important signal that all children are important. The tax system could then be used to claw back from wealthier households, and wealthier parents and/or care-givers would simply not bother to apply for the Grant. There was some political opposition to a universal grant: how could the new government rationalise introducing a welfare measure which included white people? Fiscal constraints then forced the administration of a means test on the Grant, designed to exclude about 50 per cent of children.

Even a sophisticated state would be hard-pressed to devise and administer a means test which can finely discriminate income and asset levels in households on either side of the 50 per cent line – the income distribution curve is very flat at that point. Much administrative effort is now being spent on finding ways of keeping some children out, rather than bringing all in. This goes against the rhetoric, which pervades all of the social policies, of the inclusion of previously marginalised groups (see Chisholm and Fuller, 1996, for an account of narrowing of policies in education).

Lessons and Future Prospects

What can be learned about social policy in this decade of rapid transition in South Africa? It is clearly too early to make any assessment of the effects of these policies on patterns of poverty and inequality. Early results from different policy domains suggest that while the racial discrimination of the past is being addressed in many areas, little has yet been achieved in addressing poverty. It is possible, though, to reflect on the policy process and draw out the main lessons learned to date. South Africans have learned how important good censuses and national surveys are for planning, implementation and monitoring. These would be taken for granted in more developed countries, but are quite new in South Africa. A recent book (May, 1999) summarises the results of key studies since 1993, which have enabled a much clearer understanding of where the poor are, the economic position of women, the movement of children between households, and the (lack of) relationship between educational inputs and learning outcomes, for example.

Those involved in policy-making underestimated three important things. The first concerns time. There was an underestimation of how long it takes to formulate policy, especially when there is a high commitment to public participation, and then to get from policy through legislation to implementation. The parliamentary cycle, the legislative cycle, and the budgetary and planning cycles may as well be set in stone, so rigidly are the calendar dates fixed. These procedures are important for orderly governance, but there is a trade-off with rapid service delivery and with promoting opportunities for citizen participation in policy-making.

Second, there was an underestimation of the power of the old guard inside the various former administrations to undermine attempts at change. They were familiar with the rules of the bureaucracy, and many have played procedural games with the new politicians and administrators. The new governors by definition could not have had the inside knowledge of how the institutions and procedures worked, because they were excluded altogether from governing. This is quite unlike the case where a country simply has a change in the ruling party. In addition, the governing institutions are deeply wired by apartheid characteristics of authoritarianism and lack of accountability to the public. The new government has taken express steps to address and change this mode of governance, but this will take a long time to change.

Third, in health and in social services there was an underestimation of the 'double-hump budget effect' which happens when moving from a curative model of provision to a preventive one. Preventive health services will in the longer term reduce health costs, but until their impact is felt one needs to budget for both ongoing curative services as well as the preventive ones. This must be especially the case in a society such as South Africa which is highly politically and psychologically traumatised, has one of the world's highest crime rates, high levels of domestic violence and abuse, high incidence of traffic accidents, and high rates of diseases which now include HIV/AIDS. One cannot easily, or in the short term, reduce the demand for curative care and counselling.

On the other hand, it is also being realised that in some services it is not the lack of money which is the key problem, but the of lack of financial and human-resource management. Many would now agree that it would have been better to have proceeded more cautiously, piloted new reforms in small areas, and gradually built the capacity to go to scale nationally (de Bruyn *et al.*, 1998). However, this probably could not have been managed politically. There was strong national consensus about the need for redistribution. Also, the prospect of the second national election in 1999 clearly concentrated the mind of the African National Congress, even though its winning the election was assured.

South Africa has learned important lessons about public participation in the policy process. There is greater discernment about the conditions under which participation can enhance policy relevance, as well as the management of implementation and the quality of services rendered. There is a greater awareness that asking for participation under conditions of unequal power between stakeholders (between a health specialist and a community health committee; between water engineers and a rural water committee; between the headmaster and the new parent bodies of schools) can disempower, rather than empower, the beneficiaries of services.

At the same time, however, participation in local-level delivery is critically important in the fledgling democracy. The local level is a key site for the practice and consolidation of democracy, where citizens can engage in civic activity. In many rural areas, there is either no effective democratically elected local government yet, or areas are under the control of the traditional (tribal) authorities, who have a tendency to be authoritarian élites who can easily co-opt the control and benefits of services. Most of them are deeply patriarchal, and limit the participation of women in any meaningful way.

Those concerned with social policy must concentrate on the particular ways in which the global economic and political order is affecting South Africa. In the economic realm, the casualisation of labour, combined with the high formal unemployment rate, means that increasing numbers of people will not get access to formal social protection through their work. There will almost inevitably be a conflict of interests between the organised labour movement in the formal economy, and the new entrants to the informal economy, regarding the social wage.

In the political realm, there will be an issue about citizenship and access to welfare. A characteristic of globalisation is the greater movement of people between countries, seeking work, and formation of regional economic blocs. South Africa is the economic giant of the Southern African Development Community (SADC), capturing three-quarters of the total GDP of the nine member countries. As deep and stark as poverty is within South Africa, it is the desired goal of many citizens of the SADC and other countries to work and trade in South Africa. The country has long and porous borders, which are difficult to patrol. Questions of citizenship, and of access to state social assistance, are forced sharply into focus when people from neighbouring countries can easily 'become' South African citizens. This is a very difficult moral issue of social policy when, on the one hand, there is a political commitment to repay countries in some measure for their support in the struggle, but on the other there is a commitment to controlling state spending, combined with intense xenophobia.

One major victim of the transition has been an early and coherent national policy response to HIV/AIDS, and South Africa will feel the effects of this for some 50 years into the twenty-first century, even if a vaccination or cure is found. There are exceptionally high prevalence rates, especially in the poorest provinces. Changes in schooling patterns are visible, as are increasing absentee rates in the workplace. Grandparents and children are having to do more of the informal caring work at home. The government has as yet failed to capitalise on the scientific knowledge, energy and skills in building local organisations in the non-governmental organisation sector. This is a bleak prospect indeed.

Finally, and on a more positive note, South Africa's political settlement has meant that it is able, now, to start building up a tradition of social-policy research and writing which simply could not exist before. Academics were isolated from the international debates, and there were no reliable internal databases in the public domain on which to base good planning. Social policy work will certainly continue to borrow eclectically from international experience, while trying to develop indigenous policies appropriate to the new democracy. Below follows a summary of South Africa's welfare provisions.

Annex: Key Features of Welfare Provision

Education

State Education and Training

- Move towards one national curriculum, and one system of accreditation (the National Qualifications Framework).
- Nine years of compulsory free education.

(Continued)

- Trend towards 'Model-C schools' – mix of public and private provision.
- State nutrition programme delivered through primary schools.
- Commitment to Adult Basic Education to address 30 per cent adult illiteracy rate, but few resources allocated.
- Commitment to more emphasis on early childhood development (pre-school level), but few resources allocated.

Private Primary and Secondary Education

- Fee-paying access to private primary and secondary education.

Tertiary Education

Joint state-subsidised and fee-paying technical, vocational and academic; some private universities twinned to (USA) universities.

Housing

Private Ownership

- Cash price on open market.
- Mortgage from bank or building society, repaid over 20 to 30 years.
- Interest rates over 20 per cent in last half of 1990s.
- In private sector, some housing perks through private firms for senior managers, and through link to provident funds for some union members.
- In the mining and other industries, extensive hostels for single men, now being converted to family living.
- In agriculture, tied housing for farm workers – being addressed through land reform legislation.
- In domestic work, decreasing numbers of live-in workers.

Local Authorities

- Deregulation of the limited housing provision.

Central State Provision

- In civil service, extensive housing subsidies (thus public subsidisation of private property ownership).
- New R15,000 subsidy for first-time buyers, in attempt to address the enormous backlog.

Social Security

Social Insurance

- No national insurance.
- Separate insurance-based schemes for unemployment, maternity, incapacity or death caused through the workplace (workers compensation), retirement provision (pension and provident funds), road accident victims.
- Domestic workers not covered for unemployment, maternity or workers compensation.

(Continued)

Social Assistance

- Income support for elderly people: women at 60, men at 65, non-contributory, means-tested. War-veterans pension for those who fought in certain wars.
- Income support for people with physical and mental disabilities: non-contributory, means-tested, from age 18.
- Income support for poor children through new Child Support Benefit, which replaces State Maintenance Grant for women and children.
- Income support for foster parents.
- No support for adoptive parents.
- Limited grant to carer of person with profound disability.

Social Relief

- Limited disaster relief for victims of floods and fires.

Social Services

State Provision

- Limited state-run institutions for people with drug dependency, and for people with profound mental disability.
- Direct social work services provided, especially in rural areas where no voluntary sector operates.

Formal Voluntary Sector Provision

- State-subsidised.
- Undertake statutory services for the state (children's court work, fostering process, probation services etc.).
- Most formal organisations linked to a national council for the field of service e.g. National Council for Child and Family Welfare, National Council for the Aged, etc.

Informal Voluntary Provision

- Networks of community-based groups; new legislation seeks to enable them to qualify for state subsidy.

Private Practice

- Very small body of privately practising social workers, and clinical psychologists.

Health

State Health

- Tax-based public health system.
- Free primary health care through district health services.
- Plans for Social Health Insurance, where those who can, will pay for service at public hospitals.

Private Health

- Parallel private health system, with extensive insurance coverage of those in formal employment, and with higher incomes.
- New legislation re-regulates the fragmented medical aids.
- User fees are paid to indigenous traditional healers.

References

Ardington, E. and Lund, F. (1995) 'Pensions and Development: Social Security as Complementary to Programmes of Reconstruction and Development', *Development Southern Africa*, 12(4).

Budlender, D. (ed.) (1996) *The Women's Budget*, Institute for Democracy in South Africa.

Chisholm, L. and Fuller, B. (1996) 'Remember People's Education? Shifting Alliances, State-building and South Africa's Narrowing Policy Agenda', *Journal of Education Policy*, 11(6), pp. 693–716.

De Bruyn, J., McIntyre, D., Mthethwa, N., Naidoo, K., Ntenga, K., Ntenga, L., Pillay, P. and Pintusewitz, C. (1998) *Public Expenditure on Basic Social Services in South Africa: An FFC Report for UNICEF and UNDP*, Financial and Fiscal Commission.

Harber, M. (1998) *Who will Care for the Children? Social Policy Implications for the Care and Welfare of Children Affected by HIV/ AIDS in KwaZulu-Natal*, School of Development Studies Research Report no. 17, University of Natal.

Klasen, S. and Woolard, I. (1999) 'Levels, Trends and Consistency of Employment and Unemployment Figures in South Africa', *Development Southern Africa*, 16(1).

Lund, F. J. (1997) 'Social Security for Disabled People in South Africa', in P. de Jong, and T. Marmor (eds), *Social policy and the labour market*, Ashgate.

May, J. (ed.) (2000) *Poverty and inequality in South Africa: Meeting the Challenge*, David Philip and Zed Books.

May, J., Woolard, I. and Klasen, S. (2000) 'The Nature and Measurement of Poverty and Inequality', in J. May (ed.), *op. cit.*

McIntyre, D., Thomas, S., Mbatsha, S. and Baba, L. (1999) 'Equity in Public Health Care Financing and Expenditure', in Health Systems Trust, *South African Health Review 1999*.

Mokate, R. (2000) 'Macro-Economic Context', in J. May (ed.), *op. cit.*

Patel, L. (1992) *Restructuring Social Welfare: Options for South Africa*, Ravan Press, Johannesburg.

Republic of South Africa (1996) *Report of the Lund Committee on Child and Family Support*, Government Printer.

Van der Berg, S. (1997) 'South African Social Security under Apartheid and Beyond', *Development Southern Africa*, 14(4).

CHAPTER 13

Hong Kong: Between State and Market

PAUL WILDING AND KA-HO MOK

Introduction

Hong Kong is portrayed by many commentators as the apotheosis of a capitalist society and a residual welfare regime (see for example McLaughlin, 1993). Public expenditure is low – below 20 per cent of gross domestic product, around half the norm for industrial societies. Rates of taxation are low with a maximum salaries tax of 15 per cent. There are no pensions, no unemployment benefit, no child benefit. There is much stress on the value and virtues of the free market.

The reality is rather more complex. Hong Kong is certainly not a welfare state; it does not claim to be and does not want to be, but it is far from being the archetypal residual welfare regime. As Catherine Jones put it 'the image of capitalist paradise – minimum government – Hong Kong bears precious little relation to reality' (Jones, 1990, p. 87). Castells *et al.* write of 'a non-interventionist ideology increasingly refuted in the practice of government' (Castells *et al.*, 1990, p. 138). In Nelson Chow's view 'there is hardly any reason to believe that residualism is still the most appropriate term to describe the social welfare system in Hong Kong' (Chow, 1998, p. 8). In spite of the famous characterisation of the philosophy of Hong Kong government as 'positive non-interventionism' (Haddon Cave, 1985, p. xv), what has developed in Hong Kong is a state actively intervening to provide and finance social and infrastructural programmes – though as many commentators have pointed out it is action without clearly articulated social goals (for example Tang, 1997, p. 451).

The Phases and Stages of Social Policy Development

It is useful, if not altogether accurate, to divide the development of social policy in Hong Kong into four periods.

1945–66

In a sense these years constitute the pre-history of modern Hong Kong. In 1945, when liberated from the Japanese, Hong Kong was in a state of devastation with a population of only 600,000 – less than one-tenth of what it is today. The social welfare office was established in 1948 as a sub-department of the Secretariat for Chinese Affairs with the task of liaising with voluntary agencies which remained the main providers of social services.

In 1965 the government produced its first White Paper on Social Welfare which set out the government's approach – individual self-reliance, reliance on the family and on voluntary effort with government providing a residual safety net. In a sense, things had begun to change a decade before 1965. On Christmas Eve 1953 a fire in a squatter settlement at Shek Kip Mei left 53,000 people homeless. At a meeting on Boxing Day morning at 6.00 a.m., the governor committed the government to a housing resettlement programme – the beginning of Hong Kong's massive investment in public housing. Within ten years the resettlement programme had rehoused 250,000 people and by 1971 the resettlement estates housed a third of Hong Kong's population – though at a minimal standard in terms of space and with communal cooking, toilet and washing facilities.

Apart from housing, these were years of non-development in welfare and growing popular dissatisfaction with government. A massive influx of refugees from mainland China in the 1960s put pressure on the economy and on housing. There were high levels of inequality as the economy began to take off. The government was slow to recruit local Hong Kong Chinese people to the civil service and resisted pressure to adopt Chinese as an official language. There was evidence of significant corruption among civil servants and the police. There seemed a gulf between people and government (Sing, 1997, p. 223).

1966–82

In 1966 and 1967 there were serious riots in Hong Kong, the product partly of local grievances and partly of events across the Chinese border. The judgment of Castells and his colleagues is that the riots 'shook the very foundations of the colony, to the point of calling into question its economic and institutional future' (Castells *et al.*, 1990, p. 122). All those who have written about the development of social policy in Hong Kong emphasise the riots as a watershed. Scott's view is that they 'showed conclusively that it was no longer possible for the government to be both unrepresentative and slow to improve living and working conditions' (Scott, 1989, pp. 81–2). There was argument about the contribution of social factors to the disturbances but there is no argument that they were a major element in the exciting developments in social policy in the colony in the 1970's.

Sir Murray MacLehose became governor and he initiated a radical and visionary programme of social development in his landmark Governor's Address in October 1972. In the years that followed, the government pushed forward labour and health reforms, launched a ten-year housing programme and a New Town building programme. In 1971 it introduced compulsory primary education – in Chan's view 'perhaps the first recognized social right to social services in Hong Kong enjoyed by both the rich and the poor' (Chan, 1996, p. 99). There was also the first scheme of cash assistance, a drive against corruption and massive developments in public transport.

MacLehose sought to give Hong Kong the pattern of public and social services appropriate to a rapidly growing industrial economy. All was not, however, plain sailing. In the early–mid-1970s the downturn in the international economy hit Hong Kong. There was also opposition from the Hong Kong bureaucracy which sought to fight off the challenge to its small-government, low-spending tradition. Some of MacLehose's plans failed to achieve their targets – in particular his plan to build one and a half million dwellings in ten years – but in 1982 Hong Kong was a very different place from what it had been ten years before.

1983–97

This period lacks the unity of either of the earlier periods. The early years were years of consolidation – or stagnation – depending on one's political stance. MacLehose was the only governor committed to social policy as an instrument of social development, and his two successors – Sir Edward Youde and Sir David Wilson – were preoccupied with the negotiations with China over the future of Hong Kong after July 1997. Nevertheless there were important developments. Hospital services were reorganised and a new Hospital Authority was created in 1987. A new Long-Term Housing Strategy was also launched along with plans to increase opportunities for home ownership. A massive expansion of higher education was launched in 1989. Social Policy developments in Hong Kong were also affected by the so-called 'crisis of the welfare state' which became part of economic and political discourse in the 1980s – that welfare states always need more resources than democratic governments can raise through taxation, and that 'burdens' imposed by state provision seriously weaken the economy. The themes of privatisation and residualisation also entered the Hong Kong debates.

In the 1990s development began again not in terms of changes in philosophy or new policy initiatives, but in terms of increased spending. In the five years 1991/2–1996/7 total expenditure on social services recorded an average annual growth of over 16 per cent – trends which provoked denunciation from Chinese commentators in Beijing.

July 1997 Onwards

In his first Policy Address, Tung Chee Hwa, the new Chief Executive, set out his vision for the development of the Special Administrative Regime (SAR). There were some important policy initiatives but the Address was, in effect, a restatement of the traditional Hong Kong approach to social policy. In education, he committed the government to raise the percentage of children in whole-day schooling from 40 per cent to 60 per cent by 2002, to develop an information-technology strategy, to provide training for kindergarten teachers and to extend mother-tongue teaching. In housing, he aimed to build at least 85,000 flats a year in the public and private sectors, to achieve a home ownership rate of 70 per cent by 2007 and to reduce the maximum waiting time for public rental housing to 3 years (see Mok and Lau, 1998). In health and social security, he announced comprehensive reviews of the two systems – both to take place in 1998.

Landmarks in the Development of Social Policy in Hong Kong

1948 Social Welfare Office established
1954 Mark 1 Resettlement Estates begun
1958 Social Welfare Department established
1964 White Paper on The Development of Medical Services in Hong Kong
1965 White Paper on Aims and Policy for Social Welfare in Hong Kong
1965 Housing Board established for overall planning of housing
1965 White Paper on Educational Policy
1971 Compulsory primary education established
1971 Public Assistance in cash begins
1972 Ten-Year Housing Plan
1973 White Paper on Social Welfare in Hong Kong: The Way Ahead
1973 Housing Authority established
1974 White Paper on The Further Development of Medical and Health Services in Hong Kong
1976 Home Ownership Scheme
1977 Green Paper on Social Security Development
1978 Three Years of Secondary Education for All
1979 White Paper on Social Welfare into the 1980s
1987 Long-Term Housing Strategy
1987 Housing Authority reformed with a broader brief
1988 Provisional Hospital Authority established
1991 White Paper on Social Welfare into the 1990s and Beyond
1995 Mandatory Provident Fund endorsed by Legislative Council
1998 White Paper on Homes for Hong Kong People into the 21st Century

The Pattern Today

Health

In health there is a very clear (if negative) principle frequently enunciated – that no-one in Hong Kong should be denied the health care she or he needs because of inability to afford it; and only 12 per cent of the population have private health insurance. In practice primary care is substantially privately provided. Although there are some government-funded clinics, 70 per cent of primary consultations take place in the private sector. Hospital care is tax funded and effectively free at the point of use apart from a small 'hotel charge' for in-patients. There are complaints about waiting lists for treatment and about overcrowding in public hospitals, but these are paralleled by complaints from private hospitals that improvements in the public sector threaten their future – public hospitals currently have 92 per cent of the inpatient workload.

Overall spending on health care in Hong Kong is low – probably around 4.5 per cent of GDP – but on a range of key health indices, for example infant mortality rates and expectation of life, Hong Kong emerges as one of the healthiest places in the world. The major charge against the health care system in Hong Kong (see for example Gauld, 1997, p. 35) is that there is no government health *policy*. Nowhere is health policy debated and decided. There is a *Hospital* Authority but no *Health* authority.

Housing

Almost half the population of Hong Kong live in public housing. However, since the 1970s there have been schemes to encourage the spread of home ownership with various subsidies. Hong Kong is now committed to selling off public rented housing at huge discounts and in 1998 tax relief on mortgage interest was introduced as a further spur to expand owner occupation.

Public housing in Hong Kong is highly sought after; it has no real stigma – as it does in the UK. The more recently built housing is of a high standard of amenity with more generous space standards compared to the older public housing which is far below acceptable standards in terms of size or amenities. The worst-off in housing terms in Hong Kong, apart from the street sleepers, are the cagemen – people whose housing consists of a bed space made secure by a wire mesh cage.

Education

Education in Hong Kong is basically free though most schools are still actually provided by voluntary bodies, and kindergarten provision and higher education is based on fee payment. To have moved, as Hong Kong has, in 25 years from the institution of compulsory primary education in 1971 to 18 per cent of the age group in higher education in the mid-1990s must be considered an immense achievement. Education now absorbs about 3 per cent of GDP.

The main concerns about education remain the slow speed of the move to whole-day education, the size of classes and the quality of the education provided. In higher education there has been concern about the impact of such rapid expansion and about the rising proportion of the cost which students now bear – and their less-assured employment opportunities.

Social Security

It is when we examine social security provision that the underdevelopment of social policy in Hong Kong is most obvious. The basis of provision is the Comprehensive Social Security Assistance Scheme (CSSA) – a tax-funded, means-tested system delivering benefits, which research has shown cannot sustain an acceptable level of living (MacPherson, 1994). The basic scheme of Assistance is complemented by demogrants for elderly people and those with severe disabilities. MacPherson's judgment in 1993 was that 'public assistance in Hong Kong is consciously and deliberately residual' (MacPherson, 1993, p. 50). Little has changed since then in terms of approach; what has changed dramatically is the size and cost of the scheme. The number of cases increased from 91,000 in 1993 to 227,000 in 1998, and the cost rose from HK$1.4 billion to HK$9.4 billion (Hong Kong Government, 1999).

More than 60 per cent of CSSA cases – 99,000 out of 167,000 in 1996–97 – were elderly people. In recent years there have been sharp increases in single-parent and unemployed cases though they still make up only a very small percentage of the total caseload. In general, the system has been under great pressure with the number of cases more than doubling in the years 1992–93 to 1996–97 and increasing by 20 per cent between 1996–97 and 1997–98.

Hong Kong is in the process of setting up a Mandatory Provident Fund Scheme to provide incomes in old age, and contributions are planned to begin in 2000. This will clearly improve the financial position of elderly people who have spent their lives in stable, continuous employment but nothing has been said about improving the financial position of elderly people in the long years till that happens.

Social Care

Most social care/personal social services for elderly people, children and people with disabilities are provided by voluntary bodies financed by government grants. The Hong Kong government has always preferred supporting non-governmental organisations to providing services itself. In all debates about social care, the government always stresses the central role of the family. There is a deep-seated anxiety that public provision of services will under-mine family responsibility, and these fears are used to justify a hands-off, minimalist stance.

A Hong Kong Model?

Hong Kong's approach to social policy has certain very clear and interlinking assumptions and elements.

- The health of the economy must be the government's primary welfare concern because economic growth is the best way of promoting welfare. Only a healthy economy can guarantee the full employment on which indi-vidual welfare depends. Only economic growth and full employment can provide the social stability which is basic to individual and social welfare.
- Work is and must be the basis of welfare. As Governor Patten put it in his 1995 address to the Legislative Council 'full employment should be the government's single most important welfare objective' (Hong Kong Government, 1995, para. 26). Work is the way most people secure income and independence and are bound into society. It is the means to increase individual and national incomes and so also welfare. With no retirement pension and no unemployment benefit in Hong Kong, work is the only route to security. Nothing must be done, therefore, to weaken or under-mine work incentives.
- Social and political stability are the basis of social well-being. Economic and social policy must therefore have stability as a primary goal. For peo-ple in Hong Kong stability has been more important than democracy – because instability is what many people in Hong Kong have fled from. According to Hong Kong wisdom, the health of the economy is the key element in social stability, not social services. It must, therefore, be given an appropriate priority.
- Increases in social expenditure must not exceed the trend rate of growth in the economy because improvements in social services are secondary to economic development in terms of their contribution to individual and social well-being, and because increases in public expenditure are seen as a threat to economic development. This principle was enunciated in 1987 and frequently reasserted.
- Social Policy in Hong Kong must be adapted to Hong Kong's situation, that is to the exposed and dependent position of the Hong Kong econ-omy, to Chinese culture and values, to Chinese attitudes to individual and social responsibility, to local attitudes to government and to the central role of the Chinese family. Hong Kong, the argument runs, is *different*. Western approaches to the promotion of individual and social welfare cannot simply be imposed on Hong Kong.

- The proper aim and role of social policy in Hong Kong is the provision of a safety net for those unable to provide for themselves. Patten summed it up in his final address to the Legislative Council in October 1996. Our welfare system, he insisted, and he was clearly thinking primarily of cash benefits, 'does not exist to iron out inequalities. It does not exist to redistribute income. Our welfare programmes have a different purpose. They exist because this community believes that we have a duty to protect the vulnerable and the disadvantaged members of society' (Hong Kong Government, 1996, para. 78).

In our view there is an approach to social development which could be described as a Hong Kong model. It sees economic growth and full employment as the main instruments in promoting welfare; it accepts a major role for the state in providing and funding housing, health, education and social care but it is pragmatic intervention without clear positive goals; it is essentially reactive, it talks much of the superiority of a free-market approach but in reality it intervenes vigorously in a wide range of areas.

Superficially this places Hong Kong into the 'liberal' group of welfare states, according to Esping-Andersen's (1990) typology, characterised by residualist, means-tested schemes of social assistance. But a closer study shows the limitations of Esping-Andersen's social-security-focused analysis when applied to Hong Hong and East Asia generally. In terms of social security, Hong Kong is clearly a residualist regime but if analysis is extended to housing, health and education the picture is rather different. In these areas, there are clear elements of universalism and of Esping-Andersen's social democratic regime. A focus on social security gives only a partial picture of Hong Kong's approach to the role of the state in welfare.

Levels of welfare spending in East Asia and Hong Kong are lower for a range of reasons – ideology, culture, and the fact that social security schemes have not yet matured because of different patterns of industrialisation. There is much debate as to whether there is an East Asian welfare model (Goodman *et al.*, 1998), but probably more is gained by comparing Hong Kong with other countries in East Asia than in trying to locate it in relation to a European-based regime theory. Different cultures, different histories, different patterns of economic development and different political systems generate different types of welfare regime.

What has Shaped the Hong Kong Approach?

Economic Factors

Economic and social policy in Hong Kong have been shaped by a strong sense of the fragility of the Hong Kong economy. It has been an enormously successful economy (though facing sharp problems after the 1997–98 Asian economic crisis) with the highest sustained rate of economic growth in the world in the 1960s and 1970s, but there is a sense of fragility generated by Hong Kong's dependence on the health of the international economy. Hong Kong has no natural resources except its people. It is even dependent on China for 70 per cent of its water. The success of Hong Kong's economy has made successive governors and their advisors unwilling to take the risk that policy changes 'might kill the goose that has laid such golden eggs' (Miners, 1995, pp. 50–1).

Dependence on international trade and investment means that Hong Kong has to be attractive to international capital, leading to policies of low taxation and keeping down labour costs, which is one element in the thirty-year-long opposition to a contributory social insurance scheme. It also gives business leaders power and influence; they are the people who supposedly know best how to maintain and improve the economy. Therefore they have the ear of government. It is important also to distinguish between the objective realities of Hong Kong's economic situation and dominant beliefs about that situation. The situation we have been sketching is, partly at least, a product of the way in which certain beliefs and ideologies have dominated economic policy-making in Hong Kong whatever the facts of the situation might be. There are the firm beliefs in the superiority of markets in most economic transaction, in the role of low taxation in attracting international capital, and in the socially destructive effects of high levels of social spending. 'Economy first' has been the philosophy, and, in its own terms, this policy has been immensely successful. Success gave it legitimacy – and also helped to perpetuate it by forestalling or weakening pressure for a change of policy (see Sing, 1997, p. 216).

Clearly the Hong Kong government's approach to the economy has constrained social policy development – most obviously in relation to social security but also in other areas, such as environmental policy. On the other hand, in some areas economic needs have helped social developments, for example the way in which public housing programmes were adopted to clear land for commercial and industrial development (Drakakis-Smith, 1979, p. 20). Whether the reduced pressure for wage increases resulting from the provision of subsidised housing was a motive for government involvement in housing or simply a happy result is a matter of debate, but there were clearly implications for labour costs and so for competitiveness. Equally, economic needs have contributed to educational developments. A motive in the introduction of compulsory primary education in 1971 was to satisfy international opinion that Hong Kong was not using child labour in its industries and to head off a threatened international boycott (Sweeting, 1992, p. 49). The rapid expansion of higher education in the 1990s was partly at least generated by the economic need to make good the loss of professional workers from emigration after the Tiananmen Square massacre in June 1989.

Political Factors

Key aspects of the political order in Hong Kong have been an important influence on the development – and non-development – of social policy. These include:

- *Absence of democracy* Democracy does not necessarily produce welfare states but it can generate demands and pressures for new initiatives and spending. In Hong Kong, there was no democracy of any kind until the 1980s. In 1985, elected members were added to the Legislative Council and in 1995 it was wholly elected for the first time. Chow sees democratisation as leading to 'a greater demand for universal social welfare services which would soon be perceived as rights of the people' (Chow, 1990, p. 438).

- *Rule by the civil service* In Hong Kong the civil servants have been the key policy-makers but their approach is reactive, *ad hoc* and incrementalist. Their role is aptly captured in two famous phrases: King's description of Hong Kong as 'the administrative absorption of politics' (King, 1981, p. 129) and Lau's characterisation of Hong Kong as 'a secluded bureaucratic policy' (Lau, 1993, p. 18) – secluded in the sense of insulation from political pressure.

- *The role of the governor* Miners describes the powers held by governors of Hong Kong as 'awesome' and akin to the powers enjoyed by medieval kings (Miners, 1995, p. 69). As long as they appointed members of the Legislative Council, governors could rely on a majority committed to their approach. In the postwar years only MacLehose could be described as socially radical. All the rest were profoundly conservative.

- *The power of the financial secretary* After the governor, the financial secretary is the key figure in the Hong Kong administration. This includes responsibility for the annual financial statement and thus a wide and decisive role in policy-making. Without exception, Hong Kong financial secretaries have been strong supporters of a free-market approach and opponents of major increases in government spending and responsibilities (Wilding, 1997).

- *The concern for stability* Stability has been a major concern as Hong Kong is a society of refugees. The aim of the people and of the government was to achieve economic, political and social stability (Lau, 1981, p. 207). It was this concern about stability which made the 1966–67 riots so significant and gave MacLehose the opportunity to launch a major new programme of restabilising social development. The same concern contributed to the 1989 plans to extend home ownership and expand higher education as anxiety increased about the destabilising effects of emigration after Tiananmen Square.

- *Political culture* A significant factor in the politics of Hong Kong has been the political attitudes of the Hong Kong Chinese population. Jones talks of 'ingrained political passivity' (1990, p. 68). Miners writes of 'the apathy of the people of Hong Kong and their passive acceptance of the decisions of the administration' (1995, p. 33). Scott thinks that pre-1984 'politically apathetic' was a reasonable characterisation of the Hong Kong people (1989, p. 8). The crucial question is whether these attitudes are cultural or simply an adaptation to the reality of powerlessness. There has certainly been a high level of satisfaction with the Hong Kong political system, and two things help explain these high levels of satisfaction. First, there is people's conception of democracy, only 28 per cent saw popular election as the defining criterion of democracy (Lau, 1992b, pp. 134–50). Second, people expected little of the government in the way of services. The family was the front-line service provider and this reduced both expectations of government and the politicisation of social needs.

- *The China factor* China 'exercises a persuasive influence over government policy making … merely by the fact that she is there and potentially capable of causing difficulties' (Miners, 1995, p. 230). That influence has been both conservative and radical. There was the supposition in Hong Kong that China would object to any extension of democratisation in the colony and this was a deterrent to change; and the fact that China exercised a conservative influence on development was by providing a negative reference point for Hong Kong people. Although just prior to the return to Chinese sovereignty the impending changes also stimulated middle-class political demands and provided a spur to social policy development (Leung, 1995, p. 378).
- *The search for legitimacy* All governments need legitimacy and this has been an especially important issue in Hong Kong. After the threats contained in the 1967 riots, the government chose to extend government-provided services to enhance its legitimacy; but it also set out to do this in other ways. The main strategy was the development of a network of advisory bodies. By the 1990s there were some 400 boards and committees set up to advise executive departments (Cheek Milby, 1995, p. 289), and these bodies successfully incorporated the Chinese élite into the political and social system. Legitimacy was also enhanced by establishing a relatively high level of civil liberties in Hong Kong compared, for example, to South Korea and Taiwan where harsh suppression of civil liberties eventually generated pressures for democratisation (Sing, 1997, p. 220), and by the successful 1970s drive against corruption in the civil service and the police to promote 'clean' government.

Social Factors

The transient population has always been a significant social factor underlying the Hong Kong approach to social policy. Until the 1970s, two arguments were frequently put forward against the development of social services in

Hong Kong. The first was that there was little point in providing services for a transient population which came briefly to work in Hong Kong and then returned to China or moved on elsewhere. The second argument was that providing generous social services would attract more immigrants from the mainland so increasing the pressure on employment, housing and other services.

The second major social factor has been the family and its role as a central institution in Chinese society and in Hong Kong. The family has remained a major source of welfare. Young people, for example, still expect to support their parents financially in their old age. In a 1985 survey, 77 per cent of respondents agreed or strongly agreed that the government should pass laws to punish children who failed to take care of their elderly parents (Lau and Kuan, 1991, p. 59). The government uses the strength of the family as a reason for not providing services – they are simply not necessary. It also argues that government provision would weaken family service provision – and the family as an institution. 'The capability of the familial groups to draw on their own resources to cater to their needs', says Lau, 'is instrumental in reducing the salience of political channels of need satisfaction' (1993, p. 178).

A connected point here is that the strength of the family has also helped knit together the transient population, obviating the need for government intervention (Lau and Kuan, 1991, pp. 22–3). What Lau (1981) calls 'utili-tarianistic familism' is both the adaptation of a traditional cultural pattern of family support and a response of immigrants to a new environment in which there is no alternative source of help to the family. It is an adaptation to the absence of public service provision which then becomes a justification for government inaction.

Finally there is the role of social values more generally. In 1976, Hodge spoke of Hong Kong as a society 'which stresses individualism, pursuit of self-interest, and competitiveness, and which has come to consider inequal-ity...as a "natural order of human existence"' (quoted in Chow, 1993, p. 12). Wong and Lui speak of 'utilitarian individualism' as 'the hallmark of the Hong Kong ethos' (Wong and Lui, 1994, p. 85). Given these values, Hong Kong people's support for free-market polices and the great stress on work are logical corollaries. However, because of their past experience, Hong Kong people lay great stress on consensus and stability, although past experience and an uncertain future has also contributed to an element of short-termism which, for example, militates against support for contributory social insurance which depends on confidence in the long term future.

The Future

To describe Hong Kong's welfare philosophy as residualist, though true in relation to social security, is to ignore the major role of the state in health, housing and education. The model of state welfare we see in Hong Kong is strongly economic growth-orientated and growth-dependent. Its aim is to facilitate economic growth because growth is seen as the main source of welfare, and as securing the full employment on which the model depends. The model depends heavily upon a young population with relatively few elderly people needing state support. It depends on the family playing a major role in service provision – particularly in relation to the care of elderly people. It depends, too, on limited expectations of politics and the state. It would be threatened by an extended politicisation of social needs and by the demands on the state which democratisation could generate. However, these patterns may come under pressure in the future from a number of quarters.

For a start, the East Asian financial crisis has sharply reduced the rate of economic growth in Hong Kong. The 5 per cent annual growth of the 1990s turned into a 5 per cent fall in GDP in 1997–98. The financing of future developments is problematic and increases in spending will no longer be painless.

Furthermore, demographic projections show that Hong Kong's population is set to rise quite dramatically and there are still important, unresolved issues about the right of abode of would-be immigrants from mainland China. The population is expected to reach 6.95 million by 2001 – a 10 per cent increase over 1996. By 2007 it is forecast to reach 7.47 million and 8.2 million by 2016 – almost a 25 per cent increase in 20 years. Such a rate of increase will put public and social services under great pressure. Hong Kong's population is also ageing rapidly. By 2006 the number over 65 will have risen to over 12 per cent of the population, and the number of very elderly people is also increasing. Families are finding it more difficult to provide the care they offered in the past – they are more geographically dispersed, they are smaller, more women are in paid employment, more parents are surviving into extreme old age and being very dependent for much longer.

More generally expectations have grown, with rising incomes, more education, and more public debate about social welfare issues all leading to rising aspirations for welfare. People want – and expect – better schools and better teachers and higher standards of health care, and expectations have broadened, too, to embrace increasing concern about the environment.

There is also mounting evidence about the extent and degree of poverty and inequality in Hong Kong in recent years. The rich have been taking an increasing share of national income – the top 10 per cent increasing their share from 35.5 per cent in 1986 to 41.8 per cent in 1996, while the share of the bottom 10 per cent fell from 1.6 per cent to 1.1 per cent. Between 1986 and 1996 the richest 20 per cent of households saw their incomes rise by 60 per cent while the bottom 20 per cent received average increases of only 20 per cent (*South China Morning Post*, 6 December 1997). There is also research showing significant numbers living in poverty. MacPherson and Chan (1997) showed 40 per cent of the population in one urban area living on incomes below the level of basic social security; and the Hong Kong

Social Security Society calculated that in 1996 14 per cent of the whole population were in poverty (Liu and Wu, 1998, table 9).

Finally, unemployment is increasing. In 1998 it reached 5 per cent, the highest level for many years; and experts point out that the official rate is a considerable underestimate. Hong Kong has been accustomed to full employment, however, and there is no specific form of income protection for the unemployed. In 1994–95 there were just over 5,000 unemployed cases on the CSSA (Comprehensive Social Security Assistance) roll. By September 1998 the figure was 26,215. If the rate of unemployment rises, and the length of unemployment increases, it will put more strain on the CSSA scheme and increase pressure for cuts in benefits.

Conclusion

The Hong Kong model has evolved shaped by particular economic, political and social circumstances. In many ways the model fitted well with Hong Kong society, and we need to remember that most public social services in Hong Kong are still less than 30 years old. The model developed and survived essentially for two reasons – high rates of economic growth eased or solved many problems, and people's expectations of government were both low and constrained by the absence of channels by which to express them. These key factors which helped to sustain and legitimate the model have weakened. The economic downturn has created and exposed new problems at the same time that people express higher expectations of government. Resolving this tension is one of the great challenges facing the new government.

References

Castells, M. *et al.* (1990) *The Shek Kip Mei Syndrome*, Pion.

Chan, R. K. H. (1996) *Welfare in Newly Industrialized Society*, Avebury.

Cheek Milby, K. (1995) *A Legislature Comes of Age*, Oxford University Press.

Chow, N. (1990) 'Social Welfare', in R. Y. C. Wong and J. Y. S. Cheng (eds), *The Other Hong Kong Report 1990*, Chinese University Press.

Chow, N. W. S. (1993) 'The Quest for Human Betterment', *Hong Kong Journal of Social Work*, XXVII(2).

Chow, N. (1994) 'Welfare and Development in Hong Kong – An Ideological Appraisal', in B. K. P. Leung and T. Y. C. Wong (eds), *25 Years of Social and Economic Development in Hong Kong*, Centre for East Asian Studies, University of Hong Kong.

Chow, N. W. S. (1995) 'Social Welfare: The Way Ahead', in J. Y. S. Cheng and S. S. H. Lo (eds), *From Colony to SAR*, Chinese University Press.

Chow, N. (1998) 'The Making of Social Policy in Hong Kong Before and After 1997', Paper delivered to the New Prospects for Social Welfare Systems in East Asia Conference, Taiwan.

Drakakis-Smith, D. (1979) *High Society*, Centre for Asian Studies, University of Hong Kong.

Esping-Andersen, G. (1990) *The Three Worlds of Welfare Capitalism*, Polity Press.

Gauld, R. (1997) 'Health', in P. Wilding *et al.* (eds), *Social Policy in Hong Kong*, Edward Elgar.

Goodman, R. *et al.* (1998) *The East Asian Welfare Model*, Routledge.

Haddon Cave, P. (1985) 'Introduction', in D. G Lethbridge, *The Business Environment in Hong Kong*, Oxford University Press.

Hong Kong Government (1995) 'Hong Kong: Our Work Together', Address by the Governor, The Right Honourable Christopher Pattern at the opening of the 1995–96 session of the Legislative Council, Government Printer.

Hong Kong Government (1996) 'Hong Kong: Transition', Address by the Governor, the Right Honourable Christopher Pattern at the opening of the 1996–97 session of the Legislative Council, Government Printer.

Hong Kong Government (1999) *Hong Kong in Figures*, Government Printer.

Jones, C. (1990) *Promoting Prosperity*, Chinese University Press.

King, A. Y. C. (1981) 'Administrative Absorption of Politics in Hong Kong: Emphasis on the Grass Roots Level', in A. Y. C. King and R. P. L. Lee (eds), *Social Life and Development in Hong Kong*, Chinese University Press.

Lau, P. K. (1997) 'Managing Public Finance', in J. Y. S. Cheng (ed.), *The Other Hong Kong Report 1997*, Chinese University Press.

Lau, S. K. (1981) 'Utilitarianism Familism; the Basis of Political Stability', in A.Y.C. King, and R. P. L. Lee (eds), *Social Life and Development in Hong Kong*, Chinese University Press.

Lau, S. K. (1992a) 'Social Irrelevance of Politics: Hong Kong Chinese Attitudes towards Political Leadership', *Pacific Affairs*, 65(2), pp. 225–46.

Lau, S. K. (1992b) 'Political Attitudes', in S. K. Lau *et al.* (eds), *Indicators of Social Development; Hong Kong 1990*, Chinese University Press.

Lau, S. K. (1993) *Society and Politics in Hong Kong* Chinese University Press.

Lau, S. K., *et al.* (1995) *Indicators of Social Development, Hong Kong 1993*, Institute of Asian Pacific Studies, Chinese University of Hong Kong.

Lau, S. K. (1997) 'The Fraying of the Socio-Economic Fabric of Hong Kong', *Pacific Review*, 10(3), pp. 426–41.

Lau, S. K. and Kuan, H. C. (1991) *The Ethos of the Hong Kong Chinese*, Chinese University Press.

Leung, J. C. B. (1995) 'Social Welfare', in S. Y. L. Cheung and S. M. H. Sze (eds), *The Other Hong Kong Report 1995*, Chinese University Press.

Liu, E. and Wu, J. (1998) *The Measurement of Poverty*, Research and Library Services Division, Provisional Legislative Council Secretariat, Hong Kong Special Administrative Region.

MacPherson, S. (1993) 'Social Security in Hong Kong', *Social Policy and Administration*, 27(1), pp. 50–7.

MacPherson, S. (1994) *A Measure of Dignity*, City Polytechnic of Hong Kong.

MacPherson, S. and Chan, C. K. (1997) *Housing and Poverty in Hong Kong*, Department of Public and Social Administration, City University of Hong Kong.

McLaughlin, E. (1993) 'Hong Kong: A Residual Welfare Regime', in A. Cochrane and J. Clarke (eds), *Comparing Welfare States*, Sage.

Miners, N. (1995) *The Government and Politics of Hong Kong*, Oxford University Press.

Mok, K. H. and Lau, M. K. W. (1998) 'Building Hong Kong for a New Era: New Directions for Social Development after 1997?', *Public Administration and Policy*, 7(1), pp. 47–56.

Scott, I. (1989) *Political Change and the Crisis of Legitimacy in Hong Kong*, Oxford University Press.

Sing, M. (1997) 'Economic Development, Public Support and the Endurance of Hong Kong's Political Institutions (1970s–1980s)', *China Information*, XII(1/2), pp. 215–39.

Sweeting, A. (1992) 'Education within Historical Processes', in G. A. Postigliore (ed.), *Education and Society in Hong Kong*, Hong Kong University Press.

Tang, K. L. (1997) 'Incremental Planning and Colonial State: The Style of Social Policy in Hong Kong 1966–1996', *Asian Profile*, 25(6), pp. 439–54.

Wilding, P. (1997) 'Social Policy and Social Development in Hong Kong', *Asian Journal of Public Administration*, 19(2), pp. 244–75.

Wong, T. and Lui, T. L. (1994) 'Morality and Class Inequality', in B. K. P. Leung and T. Y. C. Wong (eds), *25 Years of Social and Economic Development in Hong Kong*, Centre for East Asian Studies, University of Hong Kong.

Index

Note: The Index has been constructed to aid cross-referencing and comparison between individual country chapters. As each country chapter deals with most types of welfare provision (housing, income maintenance, pensions, health, education, etc.), and analyses provision in terms of a common framework (central government, local government, market, state, private, public, etc.), these themes are therefore not indexed separately here. Contemporary author references are given at the end of each chapter and individuals named here are therefore solely those whose historical impact on international welfare provision has been significant. General entries such as 'gender' draw together all discussion related to that topic whether specifically identified as 'gender' or not, within the different parts of the text.

257